100 YEARS OF ROUTE 66

A CELEBRATION OF AN AMERICAN ICON

MARK WILLIAMSON

AMBERLEY

Front cover: A Route 66 shield at Cadiz Summit looking west towards Chambless, CA.

Back cover: The author with Gary Turner at Gay Parita Station, Paris Springs Junction, MO.

First published 2026

Amberley Publishing
The Hill, Stroud
Gloucestershire, GL5 4EP

www.amberley-books.com

ISBN 978 1 3981 2879 8 (print)
ISBN 978 1 3981 2880 4 (ebook)

British Library Cataloguing in Publication Data.
A catalogue record for this book is available from the British Library.

Typesetting by SJmagic DESIGN SERVICES, India.
Printed in the UK.

Appointed GPSR EU Representative: Easy Access System Europe Oü, 16879218
Address: Mustamäe tee 50, 10621, Tallinn, Estonia
Contact Details: gpsr.requests@easproject.com, +358 40 500 3575

ACKNOWLEDGEMENTS AND IMAGE NOTES

I would like to thank my wife, Rita, for being my critical friend, red-penning the original manuscript and putting up with the self-centred nature of a writer and photographer; and my editor, Alison Flowers, for her guidance, useful suggestions and for being a fan of US travel!

All images in this book are copyright © Mark Williamson. Images on the pages listed below are available for licensing from the relevant stock agency; for others, please contact the author via the publisher.

Getty Images: 6, 10, 11 (road), 20 (dated sign), 23, 29 (cracked road), 31, 32, 39 (hose), 57 (El Vado), 78, 86, 92 (canyon), 95 (station), 115 (sign), 122 (signs), 123 (bench).

Science Photo Library: 15 (arrows), 29 (brick road), 33, 40, 41, 77 (giant), 85 (rocker), 87, 93, 94, 95 (arch), 112 (sign display).

Superstock: 21, 43 (logos), 92 (logs).

CONTENTS

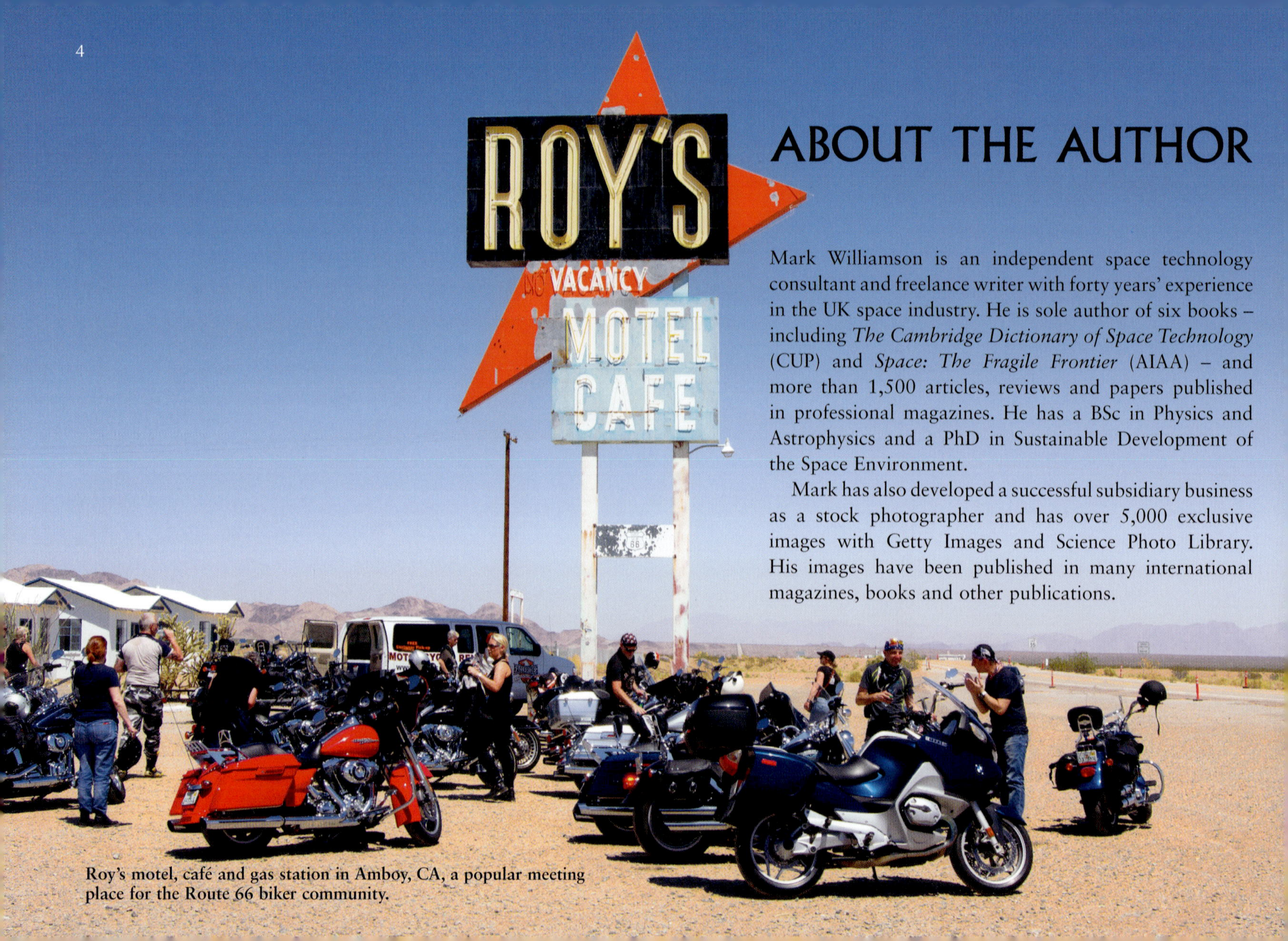

ABOUT THE AUTHOR

Mark Williamson is an independent space technology consultant and freelance writer with forty years' experience in the UK space industry. He is sole author of six books – including *The Cambridge Dictionary of Space Technology* (CUP) and *Space: The Fragile Frontier* (AIAA) – and more than 1,500 articles, reviews and papers published in professional magazines. He has a BSc in Physics and Astrophysics and a PhD in Sustainable Development of the Space Environment.

Mark has also developed a successful subsidiary business as a stock photographer and has over 5,000 exclusive images with Getty Images and Science Photo Library. His images have been published in many international magazines, books and other publications.

Roy's motel, café and gas station in Amboy, CA, a popular meeting place for the Route 66 biker community.

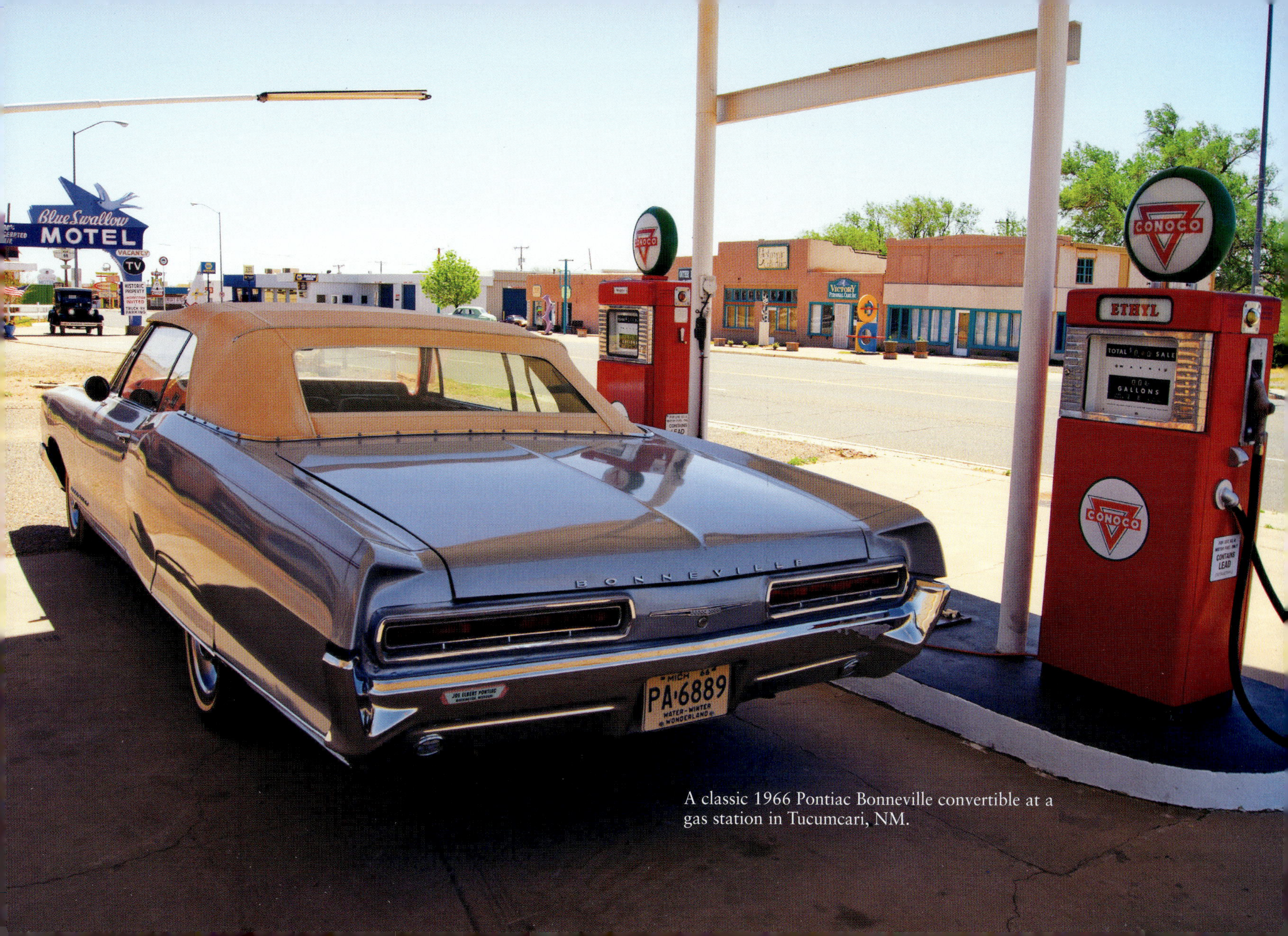

A classic 1966 Pontiac Bonneville convertible at a gas station in Tucumcari, NM.

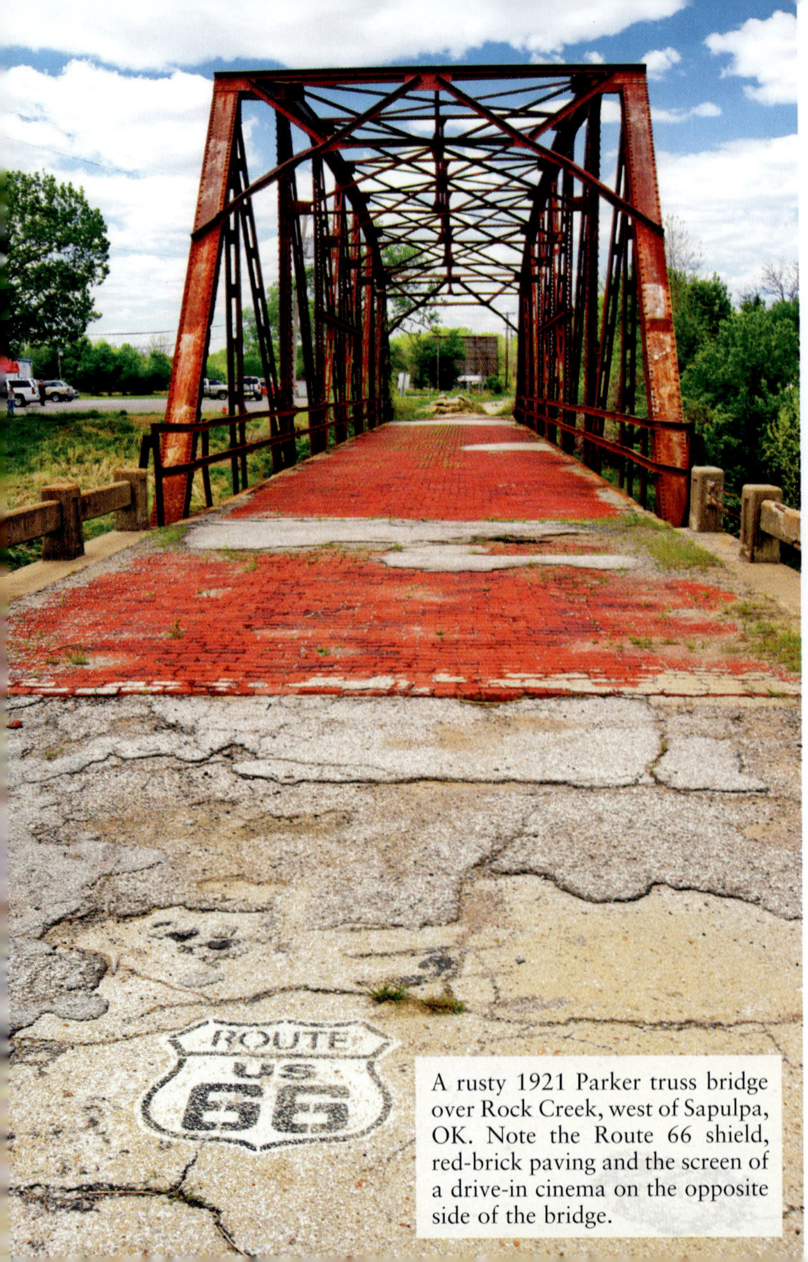

A rusty 1921 Parker truss bridge over Rock Creek, west of Sapulpa, OK. Note the Route 66 shield, red-brick paving and the screen of a drive-in cinema on the opposite side of the bridge.

PREFACE

Route 66 celebrates its hundredth birthday in 2026, so it seems appropriate to mark that centenary with a new book – one that not only celebrates the past but also looks forward to the future.

Whether you have visited Route 66 or not, you probably have a mental image of it. It might not be a fully formed image, simply a feeling about what the name involves, but you would probably recognise Route 66 as an American icon – a symbol of 'quintessential Americana'.

As a British writer and photographer, my own view of Route 66 was formed from the other side of the Atlantic and fuelled by a desire to document this mysterious phenomenon. However, as I explored the road itself, I experienced a gradual change that subtly and irreversibly affected my relationship with Route 66. I suppose you could say it got under my skin.

I've had a passion for photography since my early teens and have always been interested in travel, but that wasn't quite enough to get me 'on the road'. My impetus came from recognising the need for a professional challenge as I approached my fiftieth birthday. Although I was still enjoying my day job as a space technologist, I decided to develop a parallel business as a stock photographer (contributing science and technology images to online libraries). It eventually dawned on me that photographing Route 66 would make a nice project.

Unfortunately, the cost and time involved in driving from one end of Route 66 to the other in a gloriously indulgent road trip could not be justified, so I had to find another way. The solution was to extend conference trips to Chicago and Los Angeles, allocate a couple of days of a family holiday and, finally, organise what I called my 'Route 66 Completion trip' to fill in the gaps. That seven-day marathon brought the total to fourteen days, which saw me driving some 4,100 miles and capturing around 7,000 images.

This book is a distillation of that experience of driving, photographing and enjoying Route 66 and represents an opportunity to share my newfound affinity with others, who will hopefully be inspired to undertake their own road trips. It is not intended as a turn-by-turn route guide and is certainly not 'another Chicago-to-LA travelogue' – there are many excellent examples of these already.

Instead, the text is organised around iconic elements – such as gas stations, motels and diners – addressed as photo-projects in their own right. While the images have been chosen to capture the spirit and the mood of the Route, the text adds historical context and offers objective commentary on what Route 66 means now as a cultural icon and visitor attraction.

Although I use terms like 'gas stations' rather than 'petrol stations' to reflect the local vernacular, I write as an Englishman travelling abroad. Hopefully, this gives the story an additional perspective in highlighting elements that US nationals might overlook through familiarity.

The book is designed to celebrate the ethos, the history and the continued existence of Route 66, but is ultimately aimed at freeing armchair travellers captivated by Americana from their armchairs and getting them on the road. As a latter-day Route 66er, the author hopes to play a small part in 'keeping the dream alive' with this photographic celebration of an American highway.

Mark Williamson
Chester, UK

Photography Notes

All the images in this book were captured using Sony digital single lens reflex (DSLR) cameras: an Alpha 100 with a 10MP sensor, delivering images at 300dpi and 2592x3872 pixels; and an Alpha 580 (16MP/300dpi/3264x4912). I shoot RAW, as recommended by the photo libraries that represent some of my imagery, and process in Photoshop to tiff (a lossless format) or to jpeg when required.

The cameras embedded in high-end phones have improved significantly since I began shooting for stock, but DSLRs have several technical advantages and, for me, provide a feeling of comfortable familiarity that allows me to concentrate on capturing the image.

In cases where a specific image is used to illustrate a point, it is referenced in the text using square brackets, e.g. [p. 66]. The images themselves are captioned to locate the places of interest, but that does not necessarily mean they still exist – the heritage of Route 66 is as fragile as it is fascinating!

For non-Americans, the following US state abbreviations are used in the image captions: IL is Illinois; MO is Missouri; KS is Kansas; OK is Oklahoma; TX is Texas; NM is New Mexico; AZ is Arizona; and CA is California.

Chapter 1

DESTINATION

What is Route 66? In essence, it's just a road that used to run from Chicago, Illinois, to Los Angeles, California, crossing three time zones and the states of Missouri, Kansas, Oklahoma, Texas, New Mexico and Arizona.

Put like that, it's hard to see what all the fuss is about … but that's not all there is to Route 66, of course. Though it's no longer a navigable route from end to end, by some incalculable combination of innovation, perseverance and human spirit, it has become part of American culture, far more than any other major road across the USA.

As such, Route 66 still exists as 'a place to go', a destination and a tourist magnet for drivers, bikers and inveterate travellers of all types. For photographers, it offers artistic inspiration, a window to the past and a glimpse of the American need for history, culture and heritage.

That's quite a package for a worn-out stretch of concrete and tarmac, so what makes Route 66 so special? After all, there are many famous roads and highways around the world: the Great Ocean Road in South Australia; the Karakoram Highway linking Pakistan and China; and the world's longest driveable road, the Pan-American Highway from Alaska to Argentina. America, itself, also has its Oregon Trail (from the Missouri River to Oregon), Santa Fe Trail (from Missouri to New Mexico) and Old Spanish Trail, which once linked St Augustine, Florida, with San Diego, California.

These routes vary in their fame or popularity, in that some will appeal to drivers, tourists and adventurers, while others will be more of interest to historians. How does Route 66 compare? Well, it depends on your perspective and your interests … but it's hard to dispute that Route 66 has the better brand. Even the larger tour companies recognise its importance as a destination and continue to use the Route 66 brand as part of their advertising for holidays in the USA.

Now, let's assume you're keen to visit Route 66 and ready to drive, photograph and experience it as quintessential Americana. There is no particular template for this, but my single piece of advice to photographers wishing to capture the spirit and the mood of Route 66 would be to make planning your number one priority – not least to ensure that you don't miss the 'best bits'. In fact, I'd go as far as suggesting you think of Route 66 as a foreign country and plan as you would to visit Paris, Pisa or the Peloponnese, which means reading a little geography and history.

My own visits were business trips rather than holidays, so I wanted to go to as many sites of interest as possible in the short times available to me. That required a detailed daily plan and a careful check of the route using Google Maps and Street View to reduce the number of missed opportunities and, for me, often meant rising at dawn and driving to that night's motel in darkness.

Admittedly, those travelling with non-photographers or simply wishing to absorb the essence of Route 66 would be best advised to take a more relaxed attitude, but no one should embark on a road trip across the western deserts without some form of itinerary, including an idea of where you're going to sleep that night.

So, let's start with the route itself. The official starting point of Route 66 was Buckingham Fountain in Grant Park, Chicago, on the shore of Lake Michigan, but the practical start (and end) points have moved over the years. The modern-day 'Begin Route 66' sign is at the corner of Michigan Avenue and E Adam Street, while the 'End' sign is one block south on E Jackson Boulevard (largely due to changes in traffic priorities). Meanwhile, in tacit acceptance that Route 66 begins in Chicago, a bold sign on Santa Monica pier lays claim to the 'End of the Trail' (though officially it terminated a few blocks away at the intersection of Lincoln and Olympic Boulevards).

Tourists like to get their selfies with these signs – a bit like getting your passport stamped in the old days, I suppose – but the aficionados, the true '66ers', are far more interested in historical details and are sticklers for facts and figures.

For example, it's important to realise there is not just one Route 66, because the course of the highway evolved over the years. These different route segments are known as 'alignments' and reflect the fact that Route 66 was an amalgam of existing roads and newly-built sections that tied them together. Look out for signs with date ranges, which label specific sections [p. 20].

This variation in alignments makes it difficult to be definitive about the total length of Route 66. For example, an often-photographed sign in Adrian, Texas, which defines itself as 'Midpoint', is clear that it lies 1,139 miles from both Los Angeles and Chicago [p. 13], while an accompanying line painted across the road secures the impression that the midpoint of this 2,278-mile-long road has been accurately surveyed. In fact, the figures come from signs installed by the American automobile clubs on the National Old Trails Road in 1914 and do not reflect the actual length.

Moreover, while a display board on Santa Monica pier states categorically 'The End 2448 miles', this was the predicted length when originally commissioned and fails to reflect the elimination of a diversion through Santa Fe in 1937, which cut more than 100 miles from the Route. Perhaps the greatest exaggeration of the Route's length, however, is that of an old mural in Amarillo, Texas, which tagged it as '2,727 miles'. By way of modern comparison, the Google Maps 'directions' feature, tweaked to reflect the true course of Route 66, gives its length from Chicago to LA as a touch under 2,200 miles (along with a hugely optimistic thirty-three-hour travel time!).

This common definition of Route 66 as running from east to west is interesting in itself; roads run in both directions, so why this directional bias? There are a number of practical reasons, which include the earlier development of the eastern sections and its designation as a 'strategic defence highway' during the Second World War, because of the link it provided between the ordnance factories outside Chicago and the aerospace industries further west.

However, it seems likely that the bias is as much to do with the historical movement of populations from east to west which formed a key part of America's development and the cultural expectations personified by the 1850s phrase 'Go west, young man', usually credited to the American newspaper editor Horace Greeley. One twenty-first-century brochure described the concept as 'connecting the bustle of the industrial heartland to the promise of the golden southwest', and if there's one word in this definition that seems to define Route 66 as a destination, it is 'promise'.

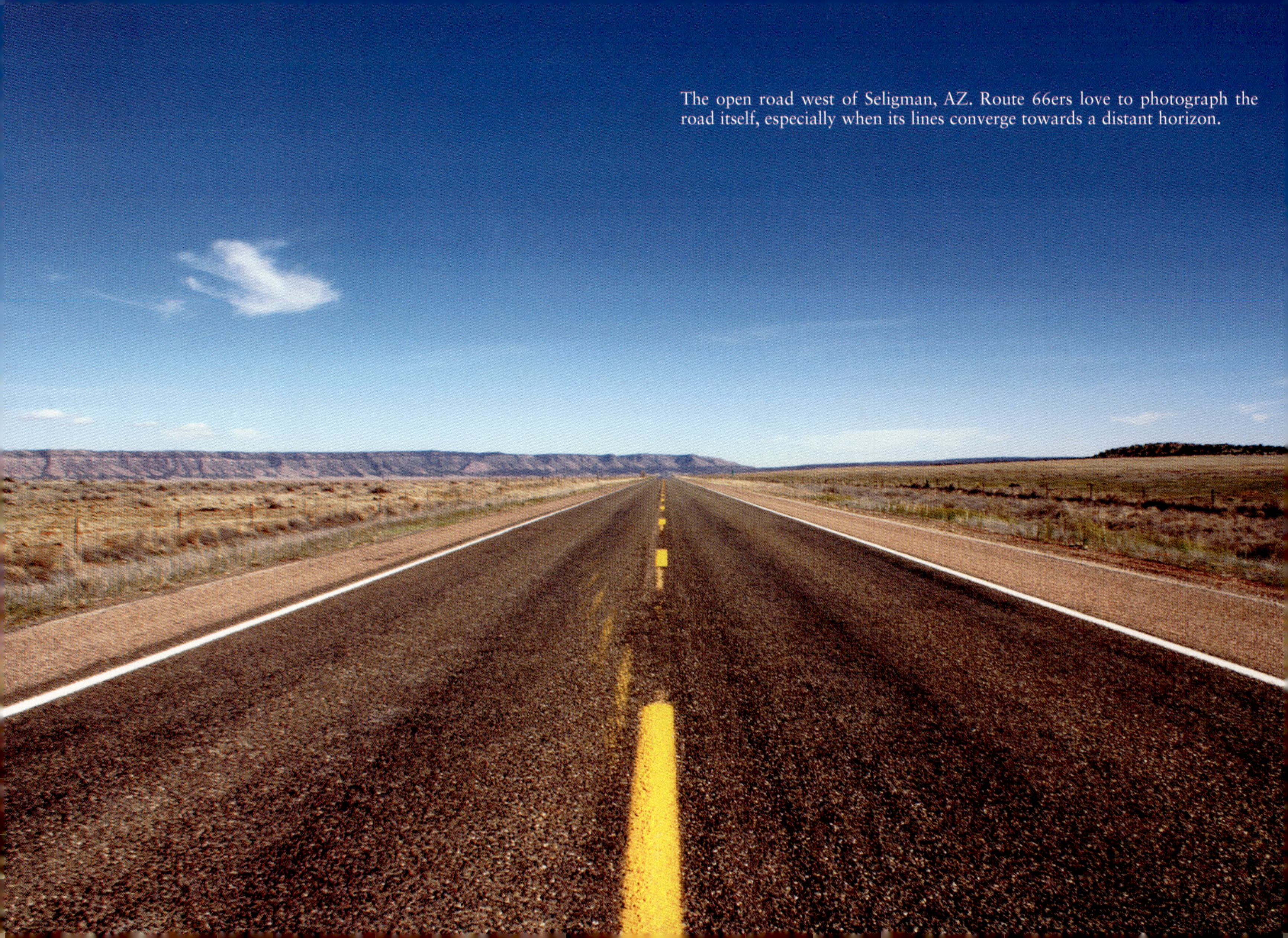

The open road west of Seligman, AZ. Route 66ers love to photograph the road itself, especially when its lines converge towards a distant horizon.

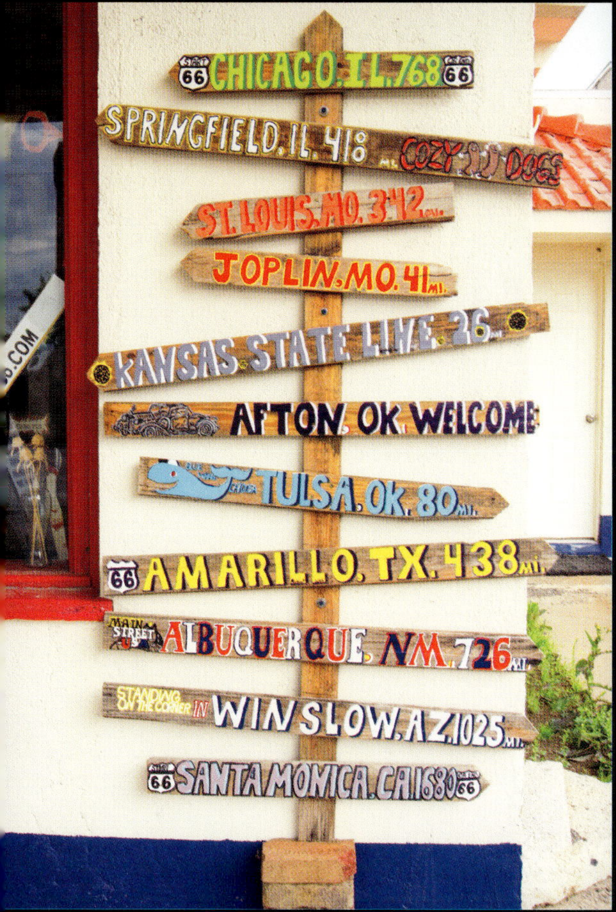

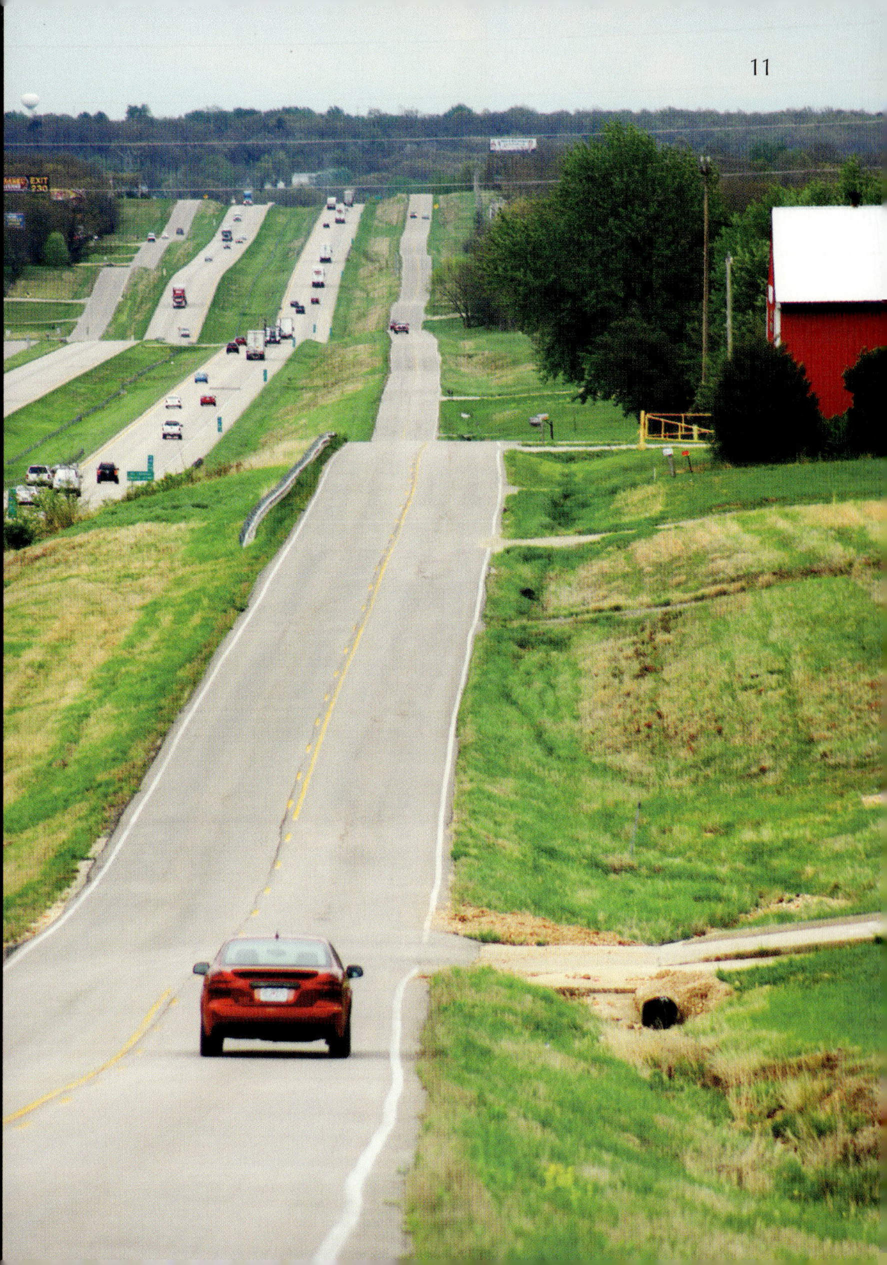

Above: Destination signs at Afton Station in Afton, OK. Note the references to attractions such as the Cozy Dog Drive-In in Springfield, IL, Blue Whale in Catoosa, OK, and the Eagles' tribute in Winslow, AZ.

Right: The undulating landscape east of Rolla, MO, where old Route 66 is now a frontage road north of I-44.

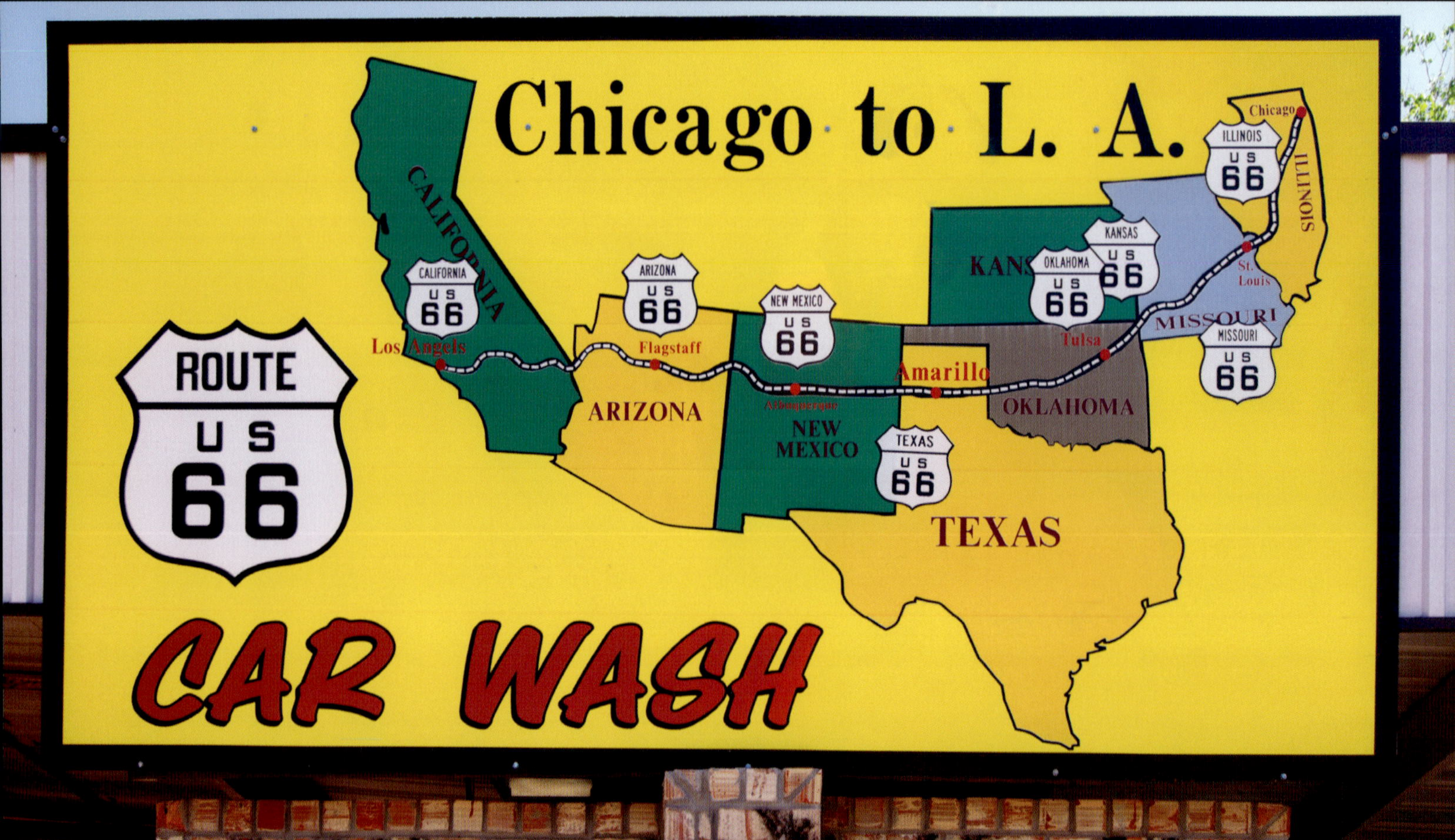

Above: A sign above a car wash in Sayre, OK, showing how Route 66 crosses eight states between Chicago and Los Angeles.

Opposite: The much-photographed welcome sign in Adrian, TX, the self-styled 'Midpoint' of Route 66.

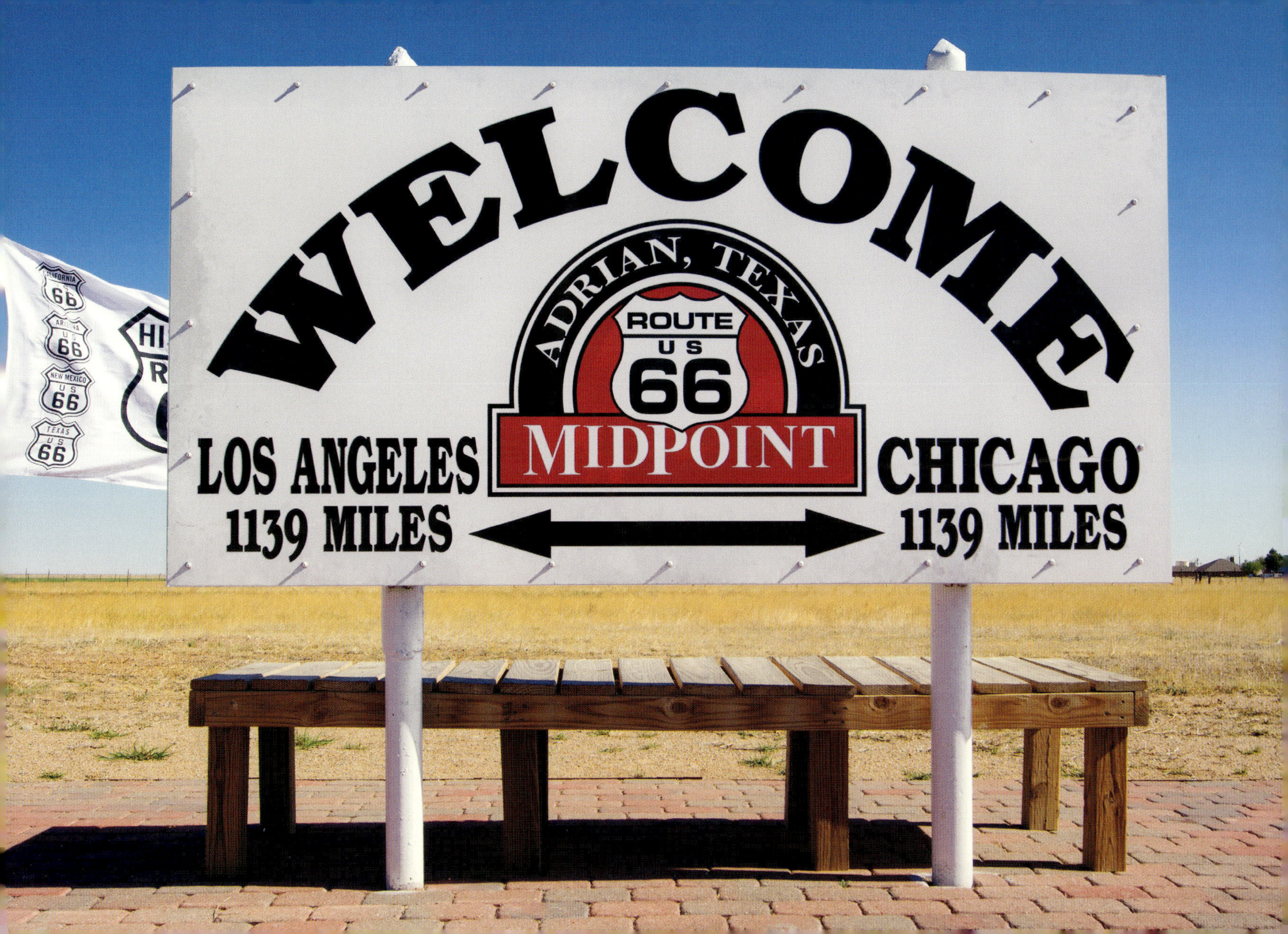
WELCOME
ADRIAN, TEXAS
ROUTE
US
66
MIDPOINT
LOS ANGELES
1139 MILES
CHICAGO
1139 MILES

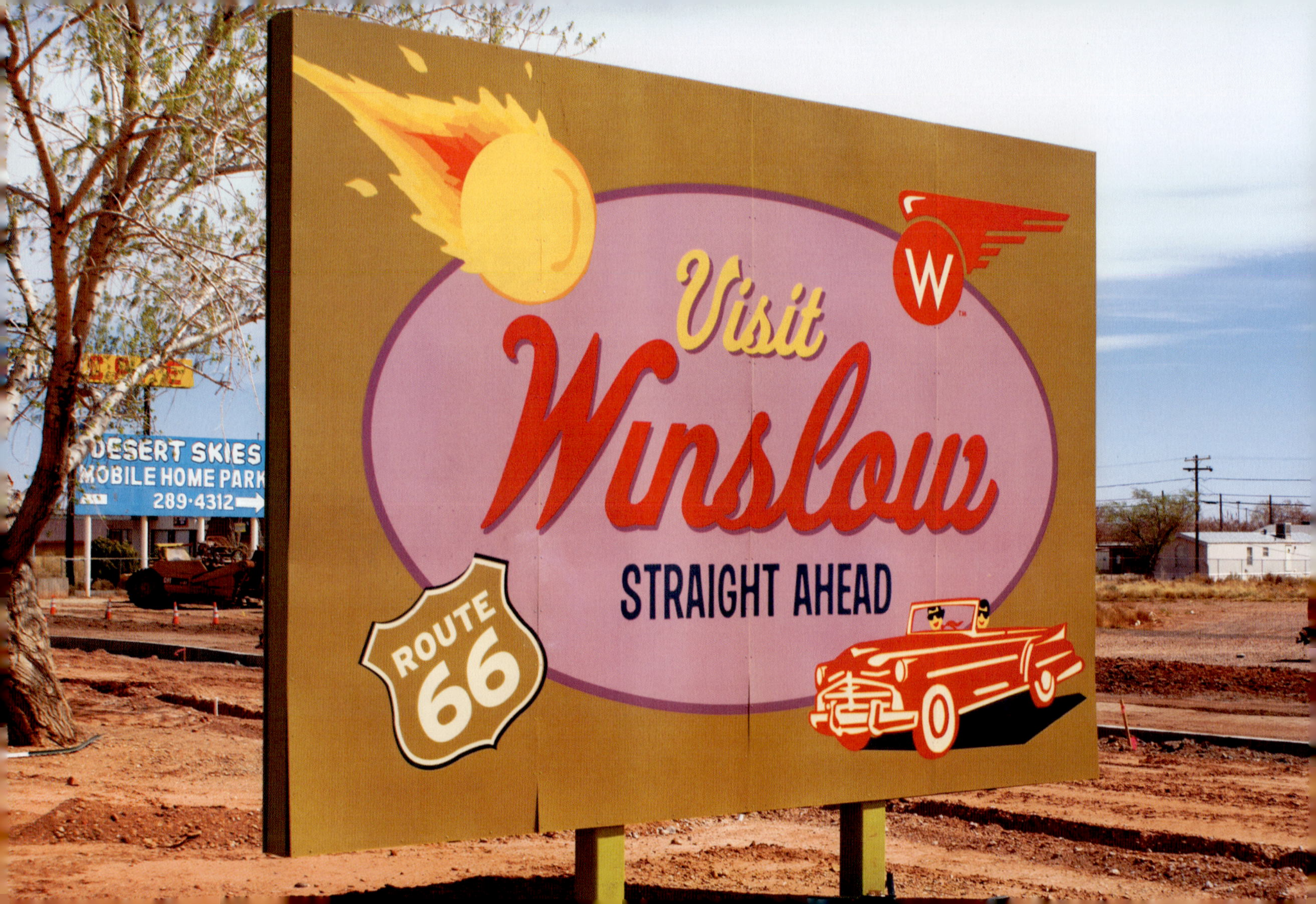
Visit
Winslow
STRAIGHT AHEAD
W
ROUTE 66
DESERT SKIES
MOBILE HOME PARK
289-4312

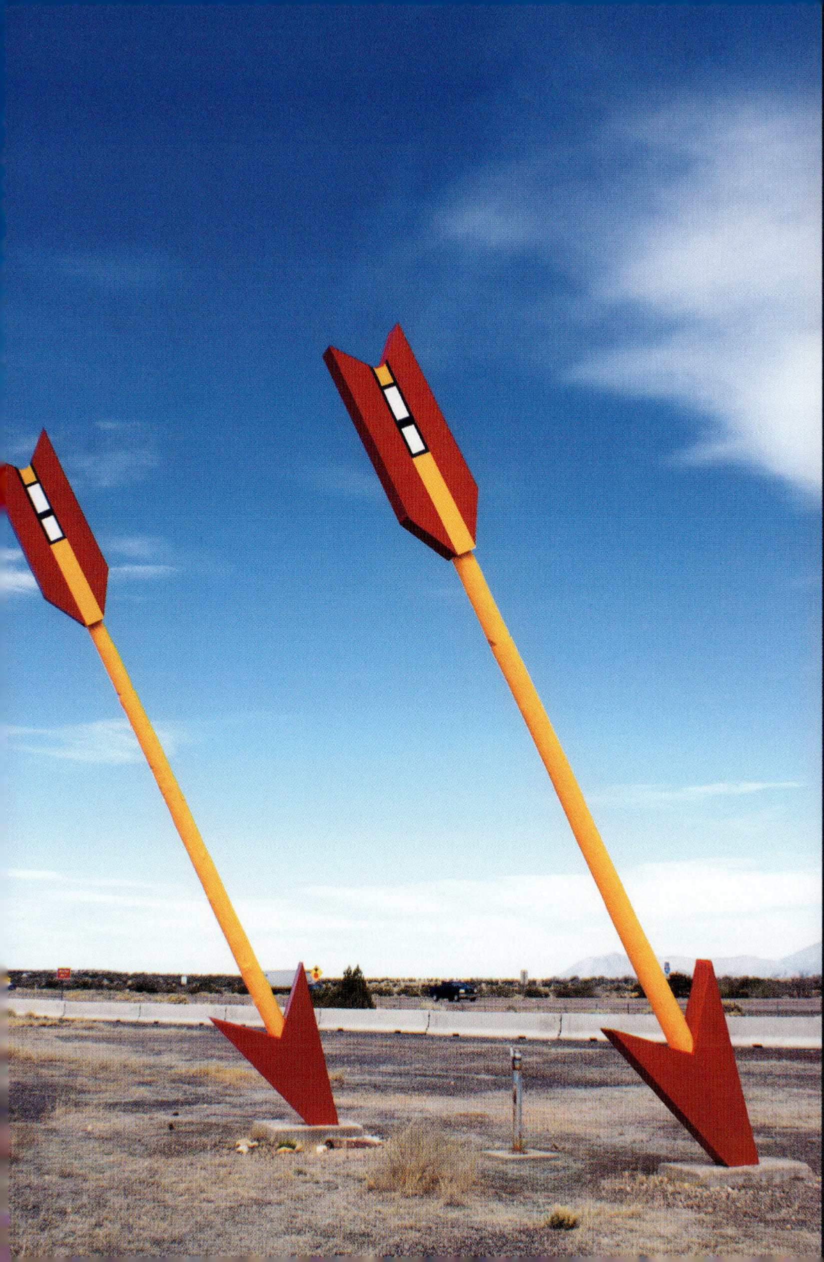

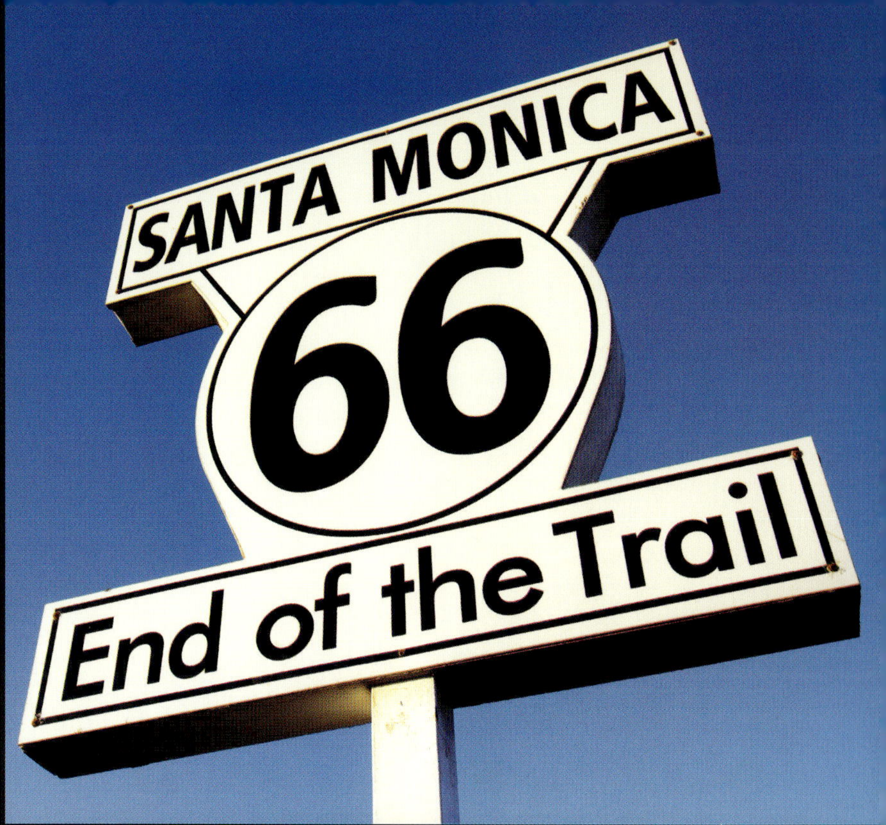

Above: The End of the Trail sign on Santa Monica pier in southern Los Angeles, CA. The sign was resurrected in 2009, having been 'lost' for nearly fifty years.

Left: The renovated Twin Arrows sign, practically all that remained of this Arizonan tourist destination in 2011; a decade later, only one graffitied arrow was still standing.

Opposite: A modern tourist sign evoking the artwork of yesteryear on the approach to Winslow, AZ, which advertised itself as the staging post for visits to Meteor Crater.

Chapter 2
ORIGINS

Route 66 is a tourist destination and an undeniable American brand that invokes travel, freedom and the 'open road', but to limit its cultural influence to such frivolity would be a disservice to a nation. Compared with its sibling nations across the pond, the USA is still a young country, striving to identify its own sense of history. For this reason, Route 66ers hang on to their potted histories of the road as tenaciously as the encroaching weeds and rotting timbers will allow. In many ways, the history of the road is the history of American transport.

When the first cars powered by internal combustion engines were introduced to the USA in the 1890s, the existing roads were intended for horse-drawn carts and wagons, so it was no coincidence that the early 'horseless carriages' were designed with similarly 'ruggedised' suspension systems. The need for improved roads was initially recognised by the US Congress in its Federal-Aid Road Act of 1916, which sought to fund a state highway programme. Progress was interrupted by the First World War, but a system of paved, two-lane interstate highways was eventually authorised by the Federal Highway Act of 1921 and, following a comprehensive construction plan published in 1925, Route 66 was conceived.

A key figure in the development of Route 66 was Cyrus Avery, a businessman and highways commissioner from Tulsa, Oklahoma, who lobbied for the creation of the highway. Although, by necessity, Route 66 was formed by patching together existing state and local roads, and parts of the 1912 National Old Trails Road, Avery realised the need to unify the Route as a marketable concept, which began with the numerical designation itself. The story goes that Avery resisted the allocation of 'US 62' because he didn't like the number, but when he discovered that US 66 was also up for grabs, the numerical symmetry was a 'no-brainer'.

The numerical designation was assigned on 30 April 1926, at a meeting in Springfield, Missouri, and the road was officially established as a US highway on 11 November of that year. As a result, Springfield is known as the 'birthplace of Route 66' and Avery as its 'Father'. In 1927, he was instrumental in forming the US Highway 66 Association, which promoted the paving of the highway from end to end; he is also credited with coining one of the road's leading epithets – 'The Main Street of America'.

However, it would be a mistake to think that Avery was acting purely altruistically; as a businessman with interests in oil and real estate, he understood the power of branding and recognised the benefits of creating the road as an enduring entity, as opposed to an anonymous piece of infrastructure. Arguably, it was the naming and the branding that tied Route 66 together from the very beginning, a unification effort exemplified by the signage and the famous route-marking shield.

The shield itself was developed in 1925 as a route marker for numbered highways crossing more than one state, but for Route 66 it has become emblematic. As a nod to the original graphic design, the shield is usually divided by a horizontal line with the state name in the top part and 'US 66' in the lower section [p. 20]. Today, the word 'Historic' is often added in recognition of its tourism potential and, in key locations, visitors will find a shield painted on the road surface. In fact, the shield has become a key part of Route 66 iconography, attracting photographers like moths to a lantern, sometimes oblivious to the possibility of becoming roadkill!

It is hard to overemphasise the importance of signage to the Route 66 photographer, not just the shields and other route markers but signs that advertise everything from tourist attractions to commercial products. Perhaps the best-known example of roadside advertising was produced by the shaving cream manufacturer Burma-Shave. It featured a sequence of signs bearing marketing prose or simple doggerel, such as: 'Pa likes the cream / Ma likes the jar / Both like the price / so there you are!'. Some were more amusing, and educational at the same time: 'Big Mistake / Many Make / Rely on Horn / Instead of / Brake' [p. 22]. Like Chevrolet and Shell, the Burma-Shave brand was not unique to Route 66, but it has become part of the sub-branding of the road.

By the time Route 66 was completely paved in 1938, the road had become more than America's Main Street, thanks in part to the Great Depression of the 1930s and the extended period of drought and dust storms suffered by the central prairies. The hardships of the period and the development of Route 66 as a key migration route from the 'Dust Bowl' to California are documented in John Steinbeck's 1939 novel *The Grapes of Wrath*, from which 66ers have appropriated the Route's most enduring nickname – 'The Mother Road'. Apparently, Steinbeck coined the term after seeing Dorothea Lange's famous photo, *Migrant Mother*, channelling the protection of her arms in his description of the road as a refuge from hard times. However, Steinbeck doesn't make as much of the term as Route 66 devotees have. His book includes just one instance of the phrase: '66 is the mother road, the road of flight'; it's on the first page of Chapter 12, which introduces 'Highway 66', and doesn't even rate initial capitals! Nevertheless, Route 66ers have made it their own.

Also dating back to the 1930s is a now less prolific epithet for Route 66, 'Will Rogers Highway', which recognised the American actor and humourist, an early advocate of the Route and a man who, himself, travelled west from his roots in Oklahoma to Hollywood. Today, it seems that, not content with 'Route 66' as a brand for what was officially just 'Highway 66', supporters were keen for more. Perhaps it was a reaction against the unofficial Route 66 monikers, such as 'killer highway' and 'bloody 66', which arose as a result of driver inexperience and a lack of speed limits in the face of the oft-mentioned 'treacherous curves' and soft shoulders.

Having entered its terminal phase as a US highway, Route 66 was officially decertified on 27 June 1985, which puts its official lifetime at just less than fifty-nine years. However, more than forty years later, it's clear that Route 66 has refused to die. It inhabits a different phase, born of nostalgia and a need to preserve and celebrate what history America has as a young nation, but it remains a living entity. As 66ers prepare to celebrate the hundredth anniversary of the formation of Route 66, it is a happy coincidence that 2026 is also the two-hundred-and-fiftieth birthday of the USA.

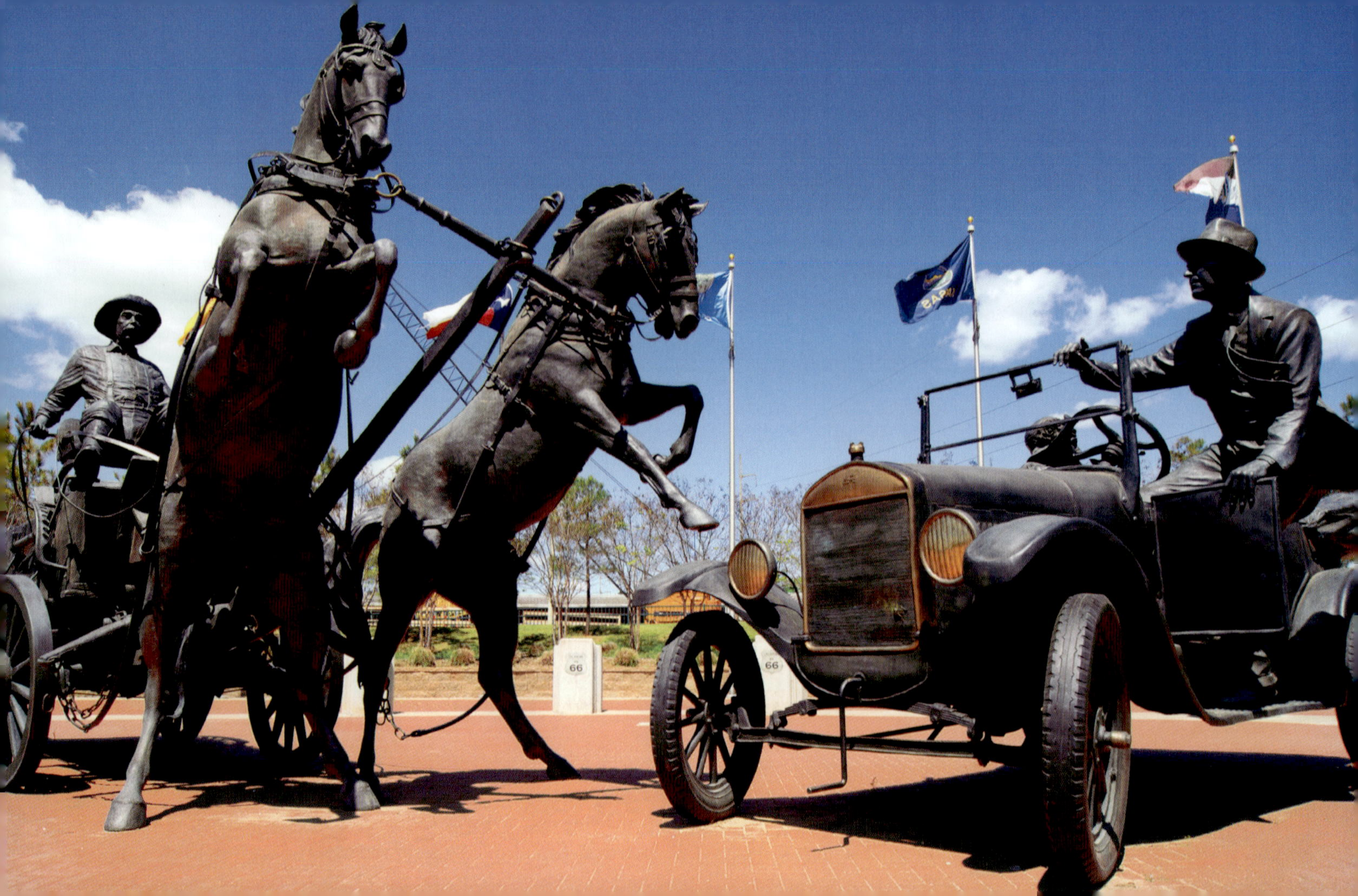
66
66

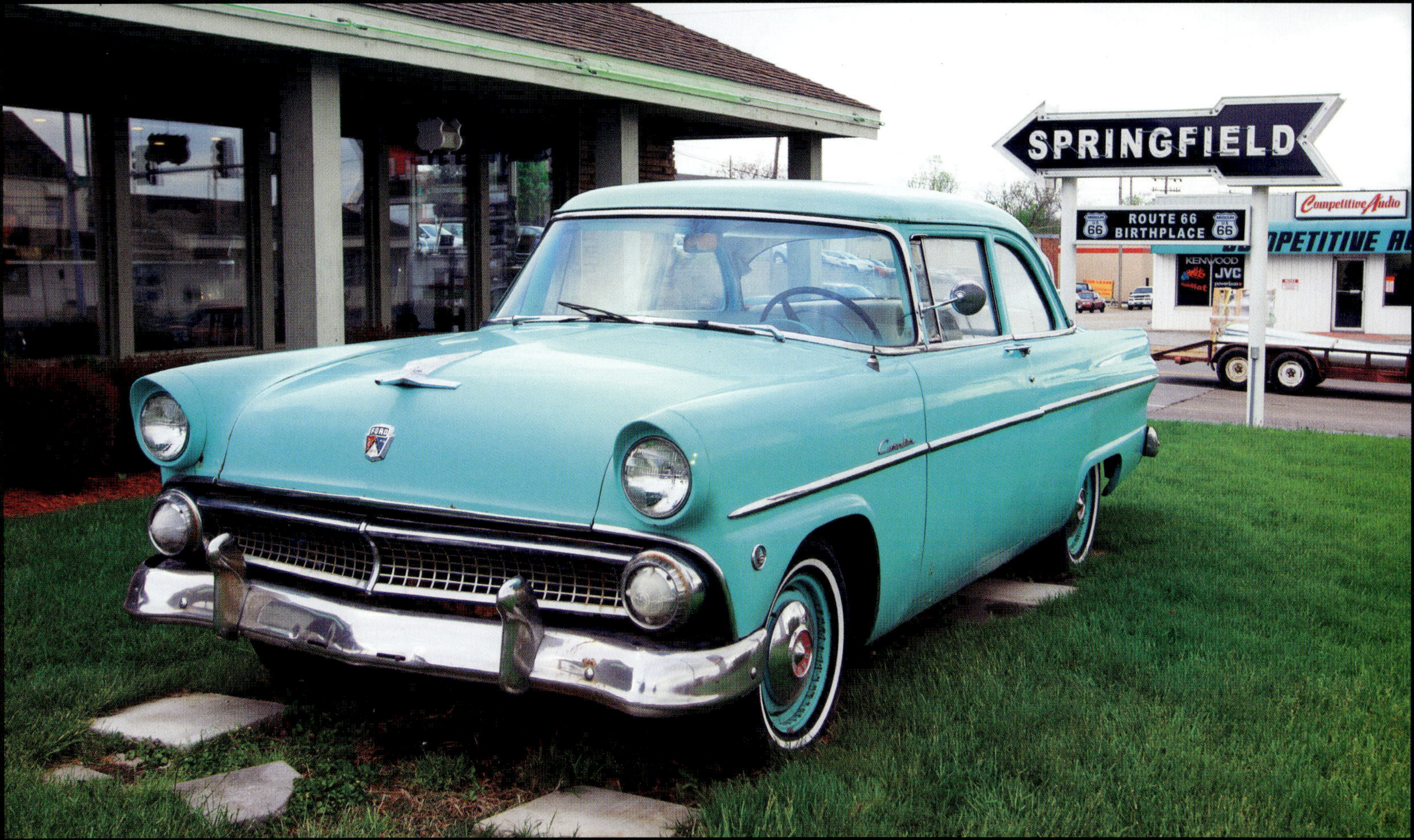

Above: A 1955 Ford Customline outside Rail Haven Motel in Springfield, MO, the 'birthplace of the Mother Road'.

Opposite: A sculpture by Robert Summers at Cyrus Avery Centennial Plaza in Tulsa, OK, which depicts a conflict between the Avery family's Model-T Ford and a pair of horses.

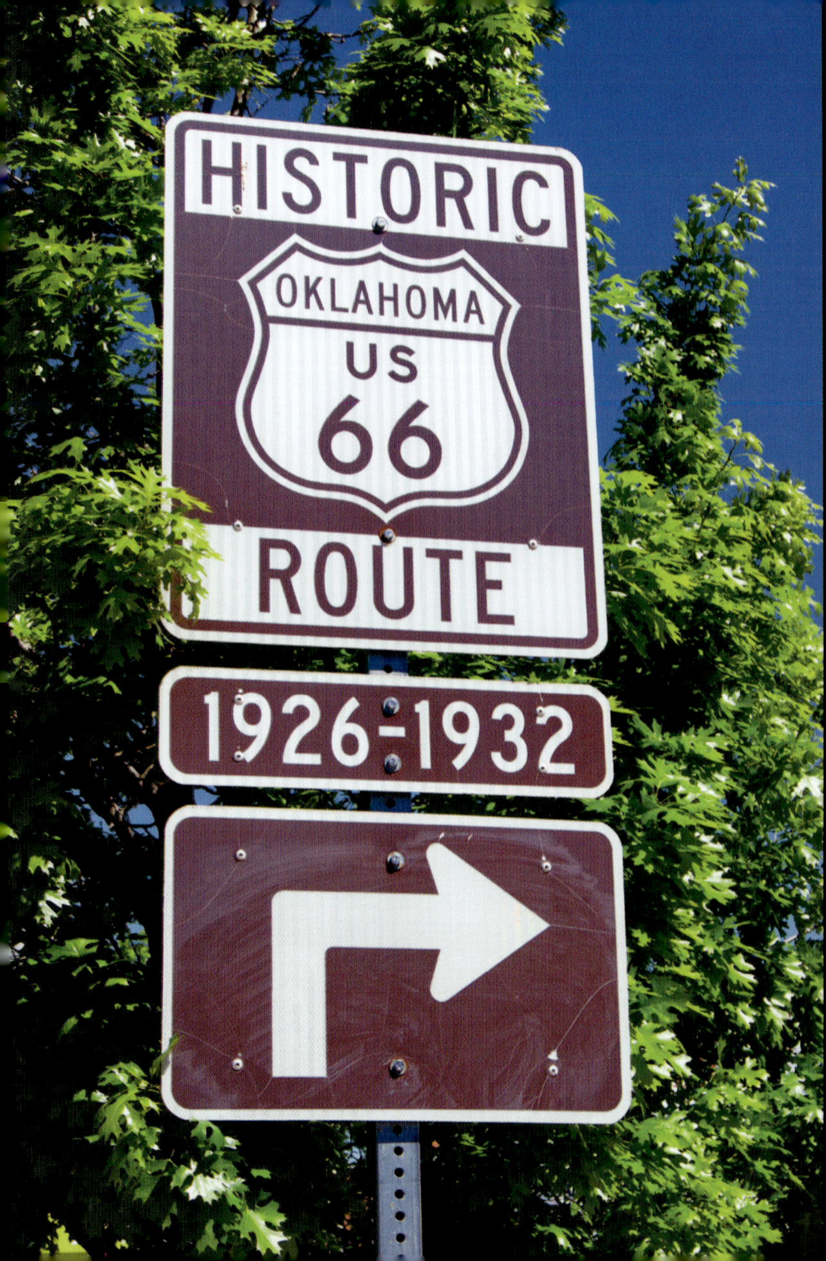

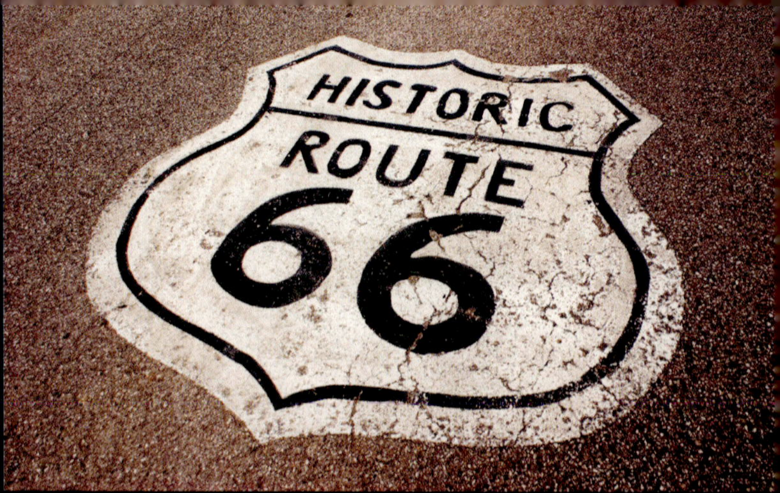

Above: Historic Route 66 shield on a road in Illinois.

Left: A route marker in Tulsa, OK, provides an example of a modern-day 'Historic Route' sign with dates specifying when the alignment was operational.

Below left and below right: Signs reflecting two of the nicknames for Route 66: 'America's Main Street' in Galena, KS, and 'The Mother Road' in Carthage, MO. (Perhaps 'Route 66: the Mother of all Roads' would make a good book title – if you use it, remember you heard it here first!)

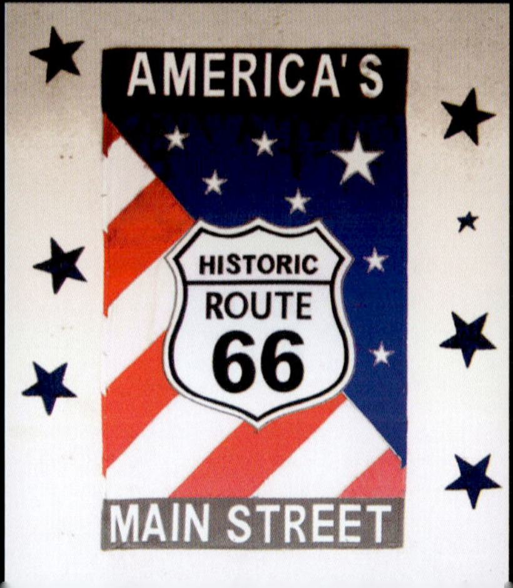

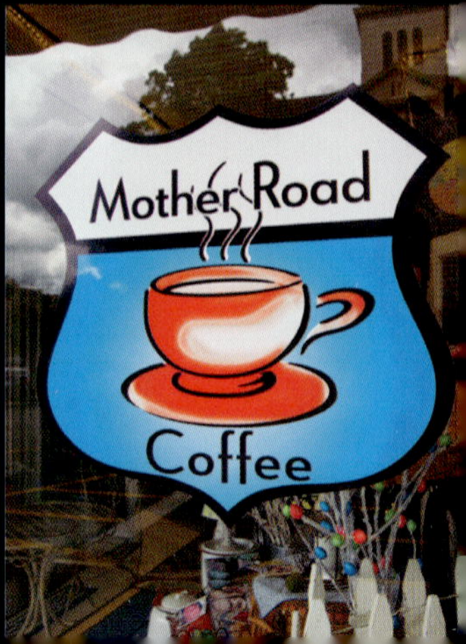

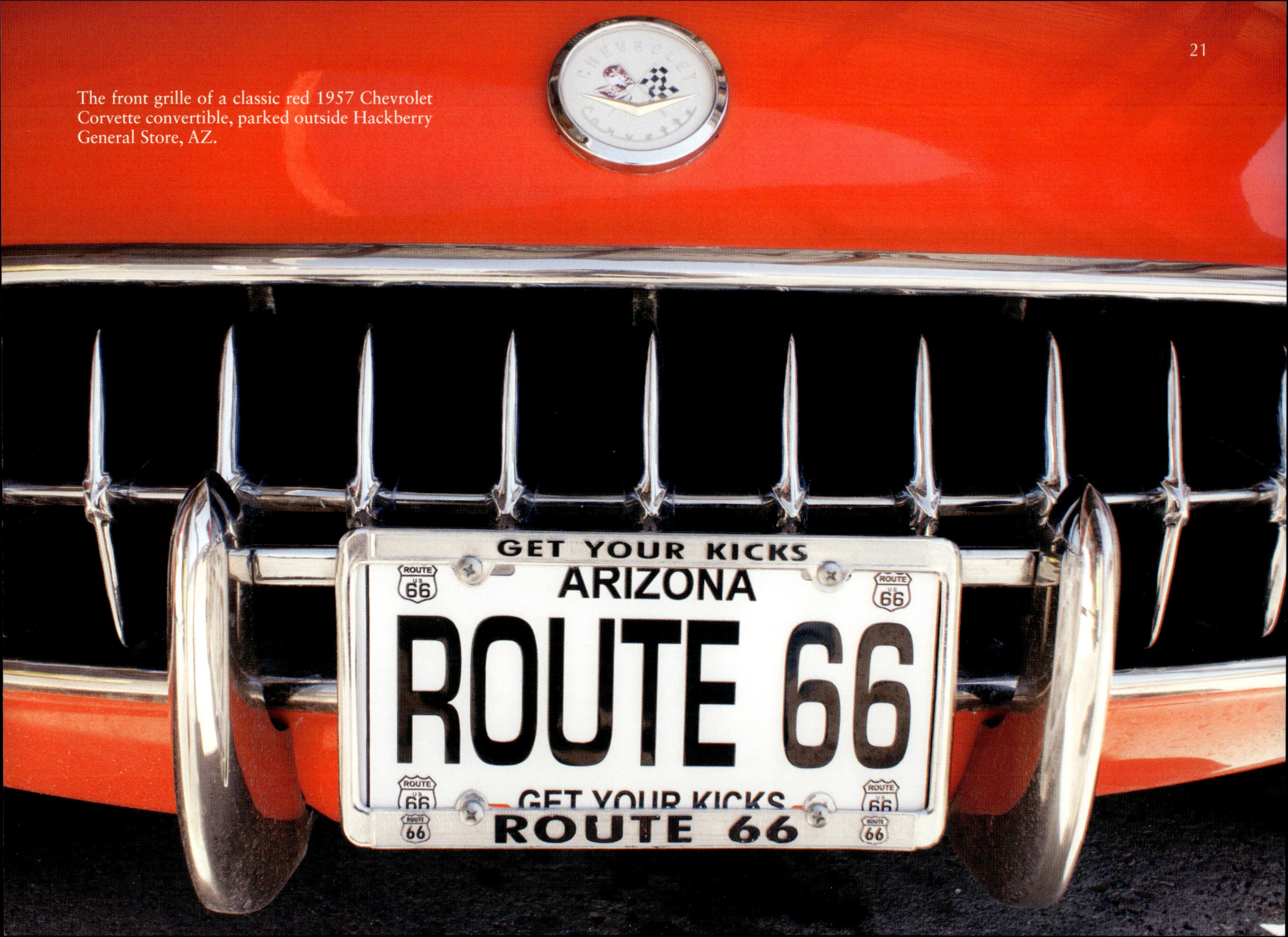

The front grille of a classic red 1957 Chevrolet Corvette convertible, parked outside Hackberry General Store, AZ.

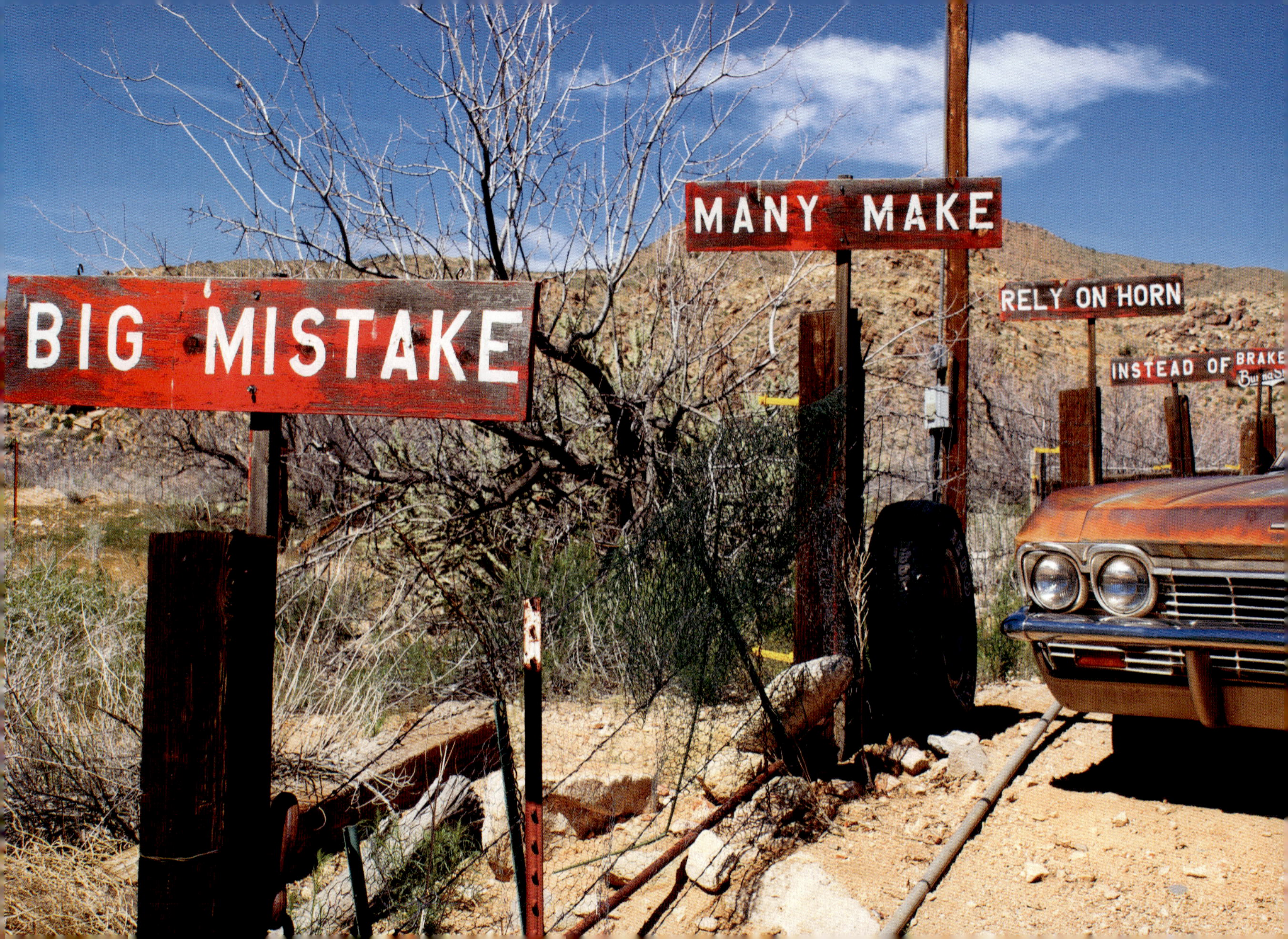
BIG MISTAKE
MANY MAKE
RELY ON HORN
INSTEAD OF BRAKE

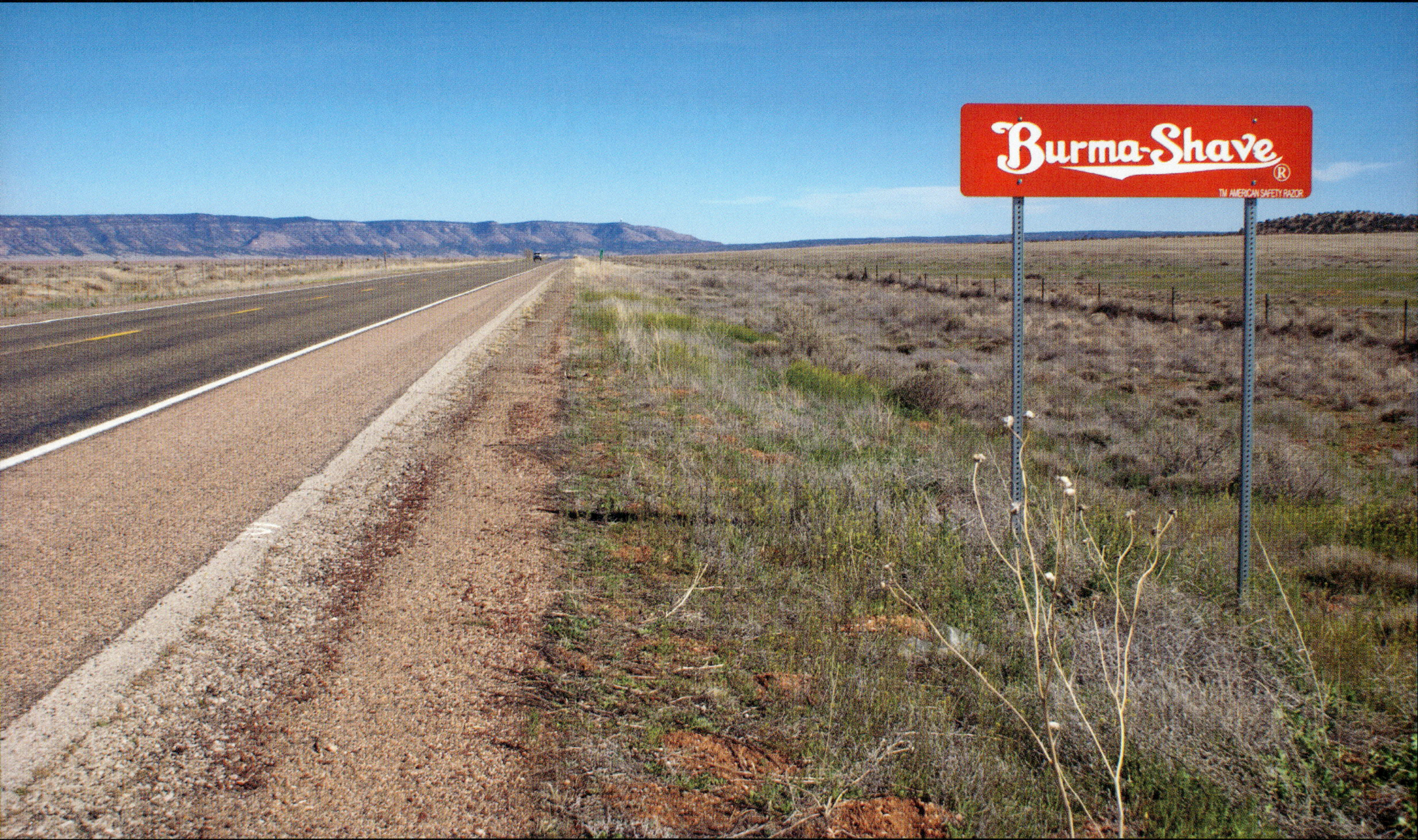

Above: A resurrected Burma-Shave sign on Route 66 west of Seligman, AZ.

Opposite: A set of Burma-Shave roadside advertising signs at Hackberry General Store, AZ. When installed at the roadside, the signs would typically be placed a hundred paces apart.

Chapter 3

ENGINEERING

Route 66 is such a rich source of imagery that it's easy to ignore the photo-project staring you in the face – the road itself! For the photographer, there is something about those converging lines that seem to meet a visible horizon that evokes a sense of wanderlust in the soul of the would-be explorer and adventurer. But look a little deeper into the engineering of the road and you realise that its surface, layout and topography not only vary significantly, but offer a wider scope for photography.

Given the received wisdom of the Wild West movie genre, it is tempting to characterise all American roads of the nineteenth century as little more than dirt tracks and cart ruts, but this would be unfair. In the more developed east, with its higher population density, road users demanded better technology and, rather than 'reinvent the wheel', looked back across the Atlantic where a degree of expertise had been developed.

One of the best-known names in road building is Scottish engineer John McAdam, who began his experiments with road construction in the 1780s. By 1816, having been appointed surveyor to the Bristol Turnpike Trust, he had developed what later became known as the Macadamised System. In essence, it comprised a 'graded' mix of crushed stone bound with gravel set on a base of larger stones; importantly, its profile exhibited a slight camber, sloping down towards the edges, so that rainwater would run off rather than penetrate the foundations. The first such surface in the US was laid in 1823, on the Boonsboro Turnpike Road, a toll road between Hagerstown and Boonsboro, Maryland.

When Henry Ford introduced his popular Model T in 1908, he flagged the start of America's love affair with the automobile. Better roads were required, not only to protect the cars' pneumatic tyres, which were becoming more common, but also to protect the road surface itself. The problem was that lowered air pressure under moving vehicles caused dust to be drawn out of the mix, which gradually degraded the road. Initially, this was addressed by spraying tar onto the surface, creating 'tar-bound macadam', but by the 1920s the paving method of choice was to mix asphalt with the aggregates before they were laid, creating what was known in the USA as blacktop and elsewhere as tarmac.

Despite efforts to upgrade Route 66, the quality of the surface varied significantly throughout its first decade, being especially poor 'out west' where parts were indeed little more than a dirt track. For example, a section in Texas known as the Jericho Gap appears to have been left deliberately muddy for the benefit of local tow-truck businesses. By contrast, the existence of the Pontiac Trail, built in 1918 to provide a good surface between Chicago and St Louis, allowed Illinois to boast of 'slab all the way'.

Today, it's clear that different sections of Route 66 have different surface types, in that some are tarmacked, some concreted and some paved with engineering bricks, such as the 1.4-mile stretch of red brick road north of Auburn, Illinois [p. 29]. Some lengths even have integral concrete curbs, including the so-called 'curbed highway' from west of Hinton Junction to Weatherford, Oklahoma.

While the majority of Route 66 has one lane in each direction, some parts of the road differ significantly in width: for example, near Devil's Elbow, Missouri, and in Glenrio, Texas, it becomes a dual carriageway ('divided highway' in the USA) [p. 31]. In contrast, a 15-mile stretch between Miami and Afton, Oklahoma, is single track, a strip of tarmacked 'pavement' just 9-ft wide, bordered by unpaved overruns [p. 30]. This Ribbon Road or Sidewalk Highway was completed in 1922 and taken out of service in 1937, another example of how the alignment evolved over the years.

Driving along Route 66, one is struck by the differing character of the road as it progresses from east to west. Consider the change in elevation alone: from around 200 m in Chicago, it rises to over 2,200 m (7,275 ft) at the Continental Divide (midway between Grants and Gallup, New Mexico), then falls to near sea level in Santa Monica.

While Illinois is relatively flat and offers few challenges to road builders, when it came to crossing the Mississippi and forging a highway through the high desert of Arizona, the engineering challenge was far greater. The Mississippi was spanned by the Old Chain of Rocks Bridge, a 1,600-m-long truss structure that carried Route 66 across the river just north of St Louis; it also reminds photographers that bridges are as much a part of the infrastructure as the road itself [pp. 32–33]. The challenge of crossing the higher elevations is typified by the Oatman Highway, which punches its way through the mountains west of Kingman, Arizona [p. 30]; this is fun to drive in a modern car but was far more stressful in an underpowered 1930s jalopy (again, the towing businesses prospered).

The car is clearly an important part of American culture and the road system developed to accommodate it continues to make an indelible impact on the landscape. A key element of this is the Interstate Highway System, famously championed by President Eisenhower and authorised in 1956. As history records, the interstates bypassed the old highways and the older infrastructure went into decline. Almost overnight, the so-called 'superslab' took business away from the small towns that lined the old routes, and the gas stations, motels and diners along those routes began to die, eventually turning some communities into 'ghost towns'.

Navigating an American interstate today, on one of the system's estimated 47,000 miles of roadway, it is hard to imagine the old days, but the evidence is often just a few metres away in the form of a parallel 'frontage road', which preceded the interstate in many places. Explore a little further and you may come across a smaller, more meandering thoroughfare, now downgraded to a local road or, in towns, a 'business loop'. Some of these frontage roads and business loops are remnants of 'Historic Route 66'.

In the context of terminology, the nomenclature of American roads is complex and not always consistent: whereas turnpikes were, at least originally, toll roads, freeways are not de facto 'free'. The term freeway was coined by US lawyer Edward Bassett, who distinguished between highways, parkways and freeways. Essentially, highways were roads that property owners could build next to and gain access to; parkways were roads meant for recreation; and freeways were designed to shift traffic, being free of encroaching properties and access roads. To add complexity to the definitions, divided highways can also be termed expressways.

Of course, building a transport infrastructure is not just about roadbeds and routings. It also includes the support infrastructure of gas stations and service garages for the vehicles, motels and restaurants for their occupants and roadside attractions for the tourists. These aspects are covered in the following chapters.

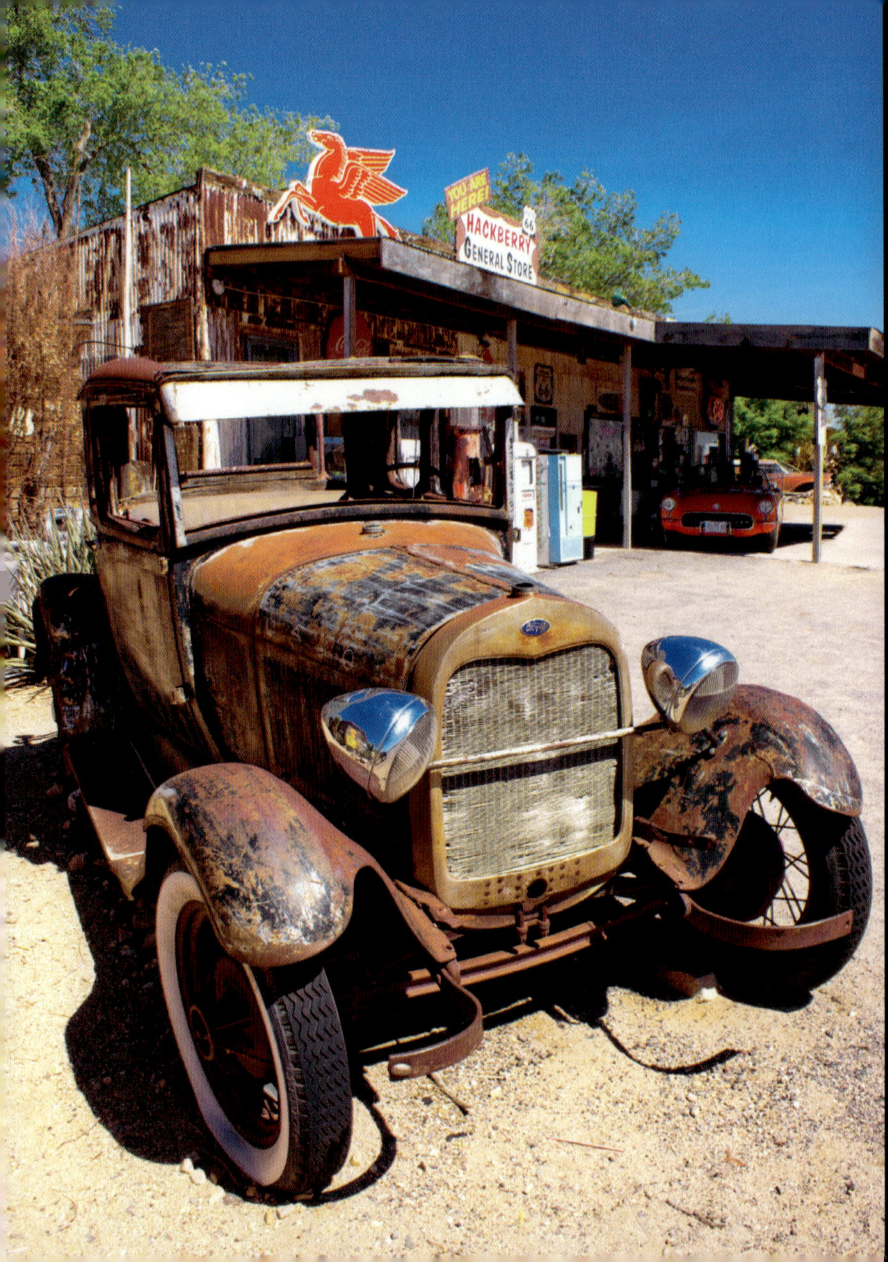

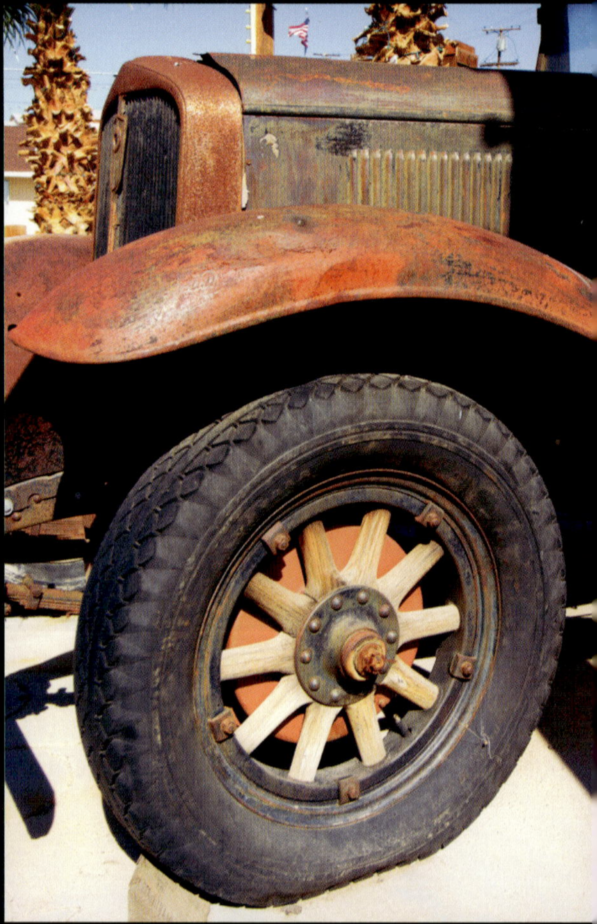

Above: A rusty old jalopy with wooden spoked wheels displayed outside the Route 66 Motel in Barstow, CA.

Left: A Model-T Ford at Hackberry General Store, AZ. The store was built in 1934, abandoned in the 1980s and redeveloped by Route 66 artist Bob Waldmire in the 1990s. It remains a great place for a photoshoot.

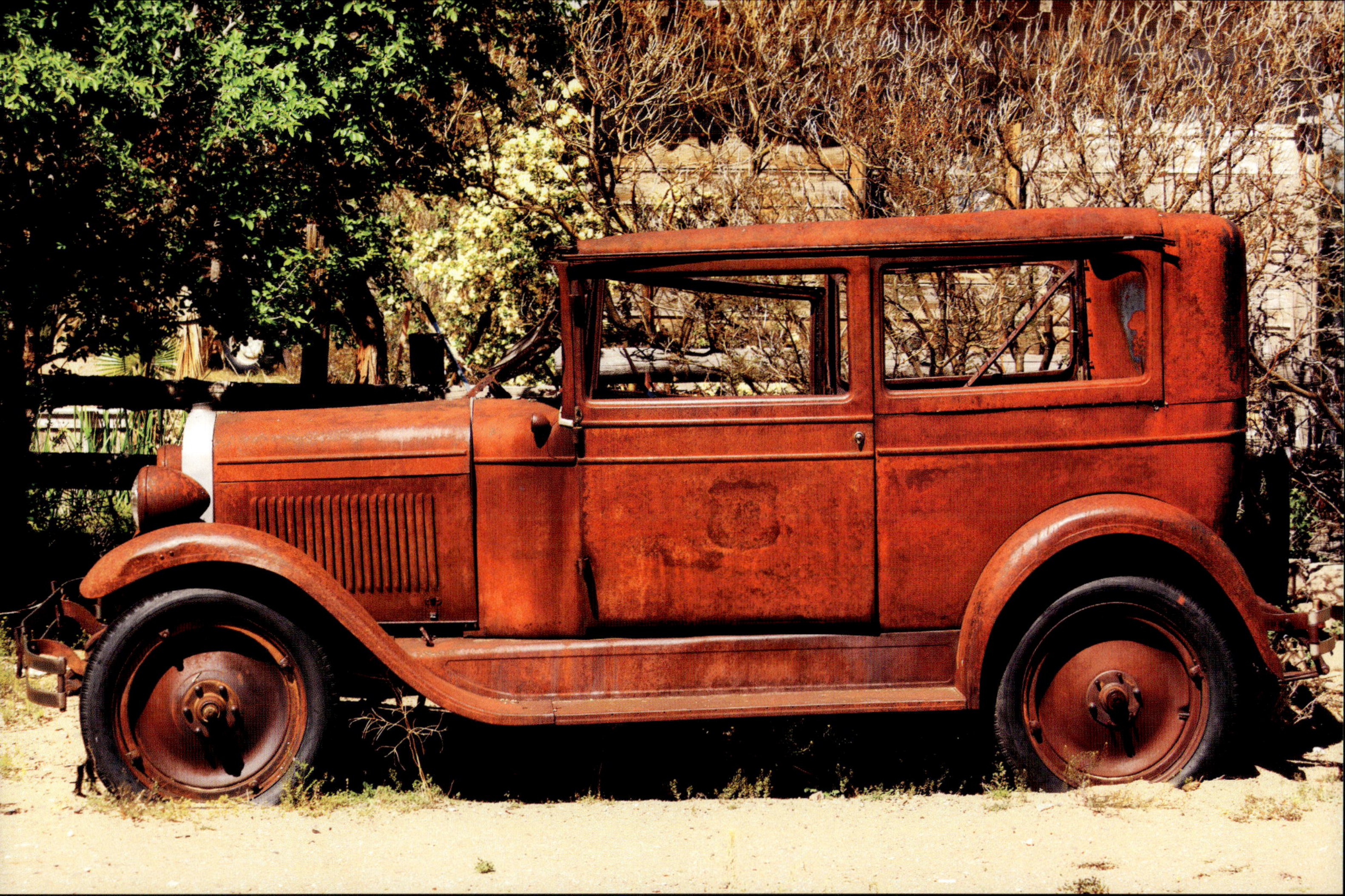

An abandoned 'chariot of the road' at Hackberry General Store, AZ. Whatever Henry Ford said about the colour of his cars, the predominant shade on Route 66 is rusty red; photographers should not be afraid of a little post-production enhancement!

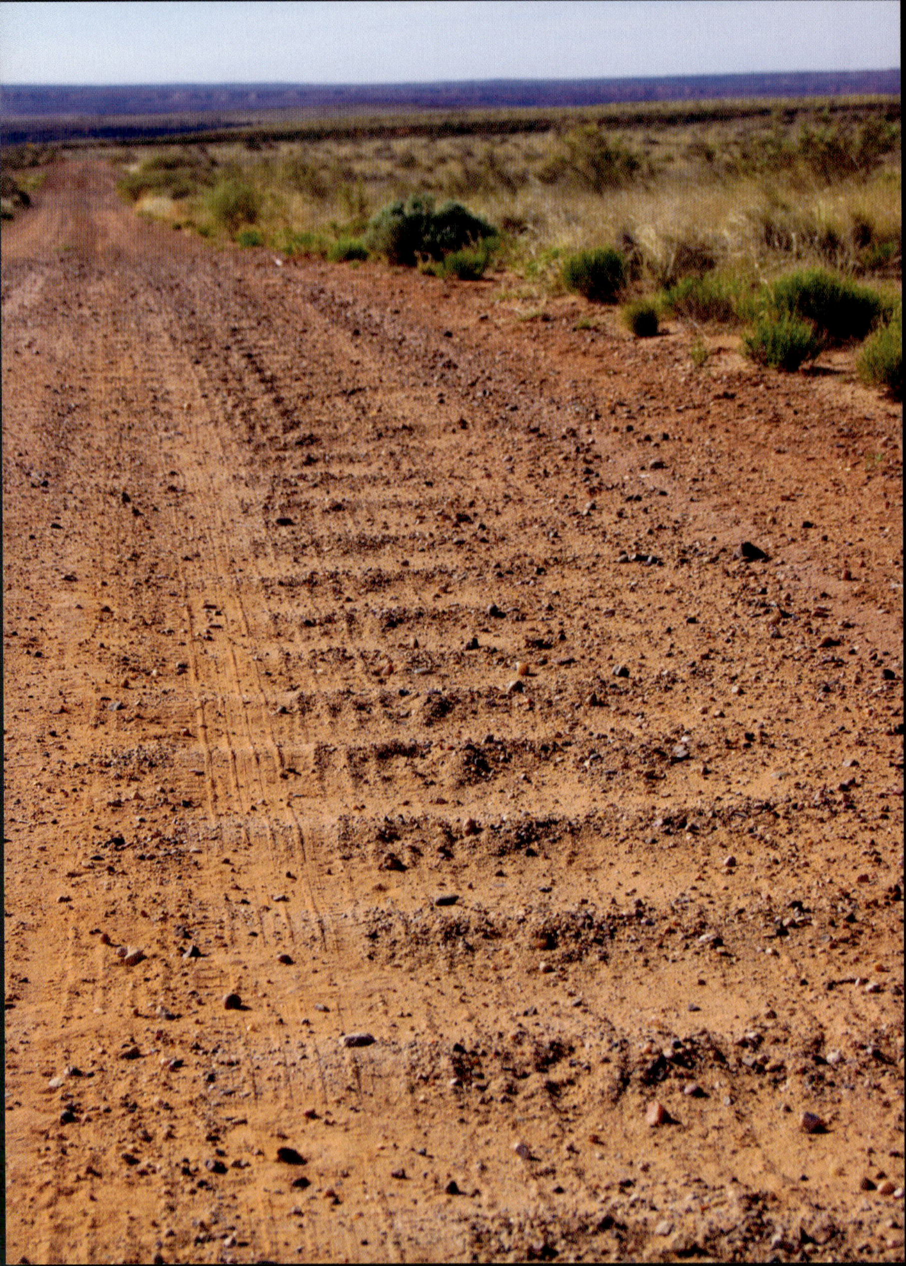
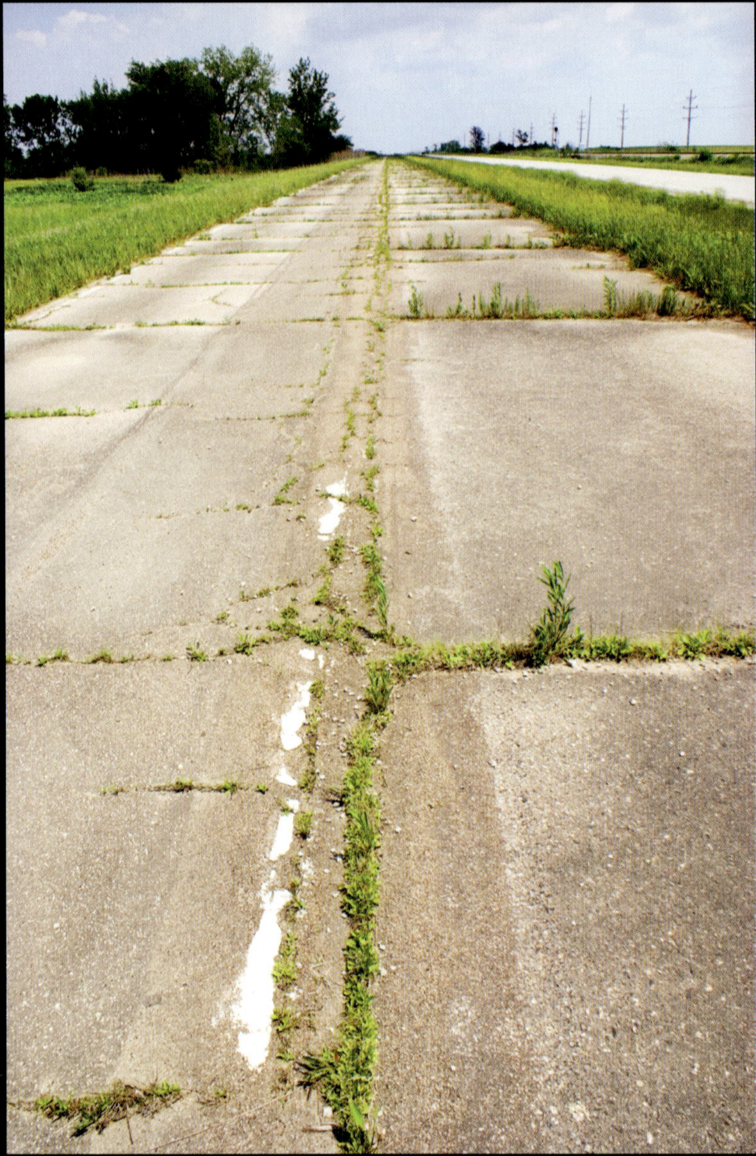

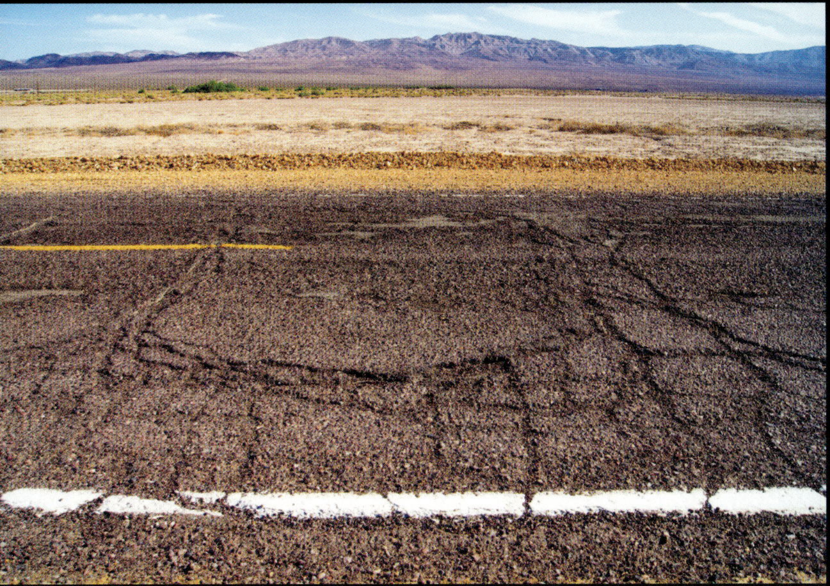

Above: The traffic-worn surface of Route 66 west of Ludlow, CA.

Right: Part of the 1.4-mile stretch of Snell Road/Curran Road, north of Auburn, IL, which was paved with bricks over a concrete road-bed in 1931 (rumour has it that a local dignitary owned a brick factory).

Opposite left: A washboard road east of the Painted Desert trading post, AZ, which leads to an unpaved section of the original Route 66 alignment (both named Pinta Road and accessed from I-40 exit 320). Well worth exploring, but uncomfortable to drive on!

Opposite right: A section of the original Route 66 alignment between Dwight and Odell, IL, running parallel to the modern road.

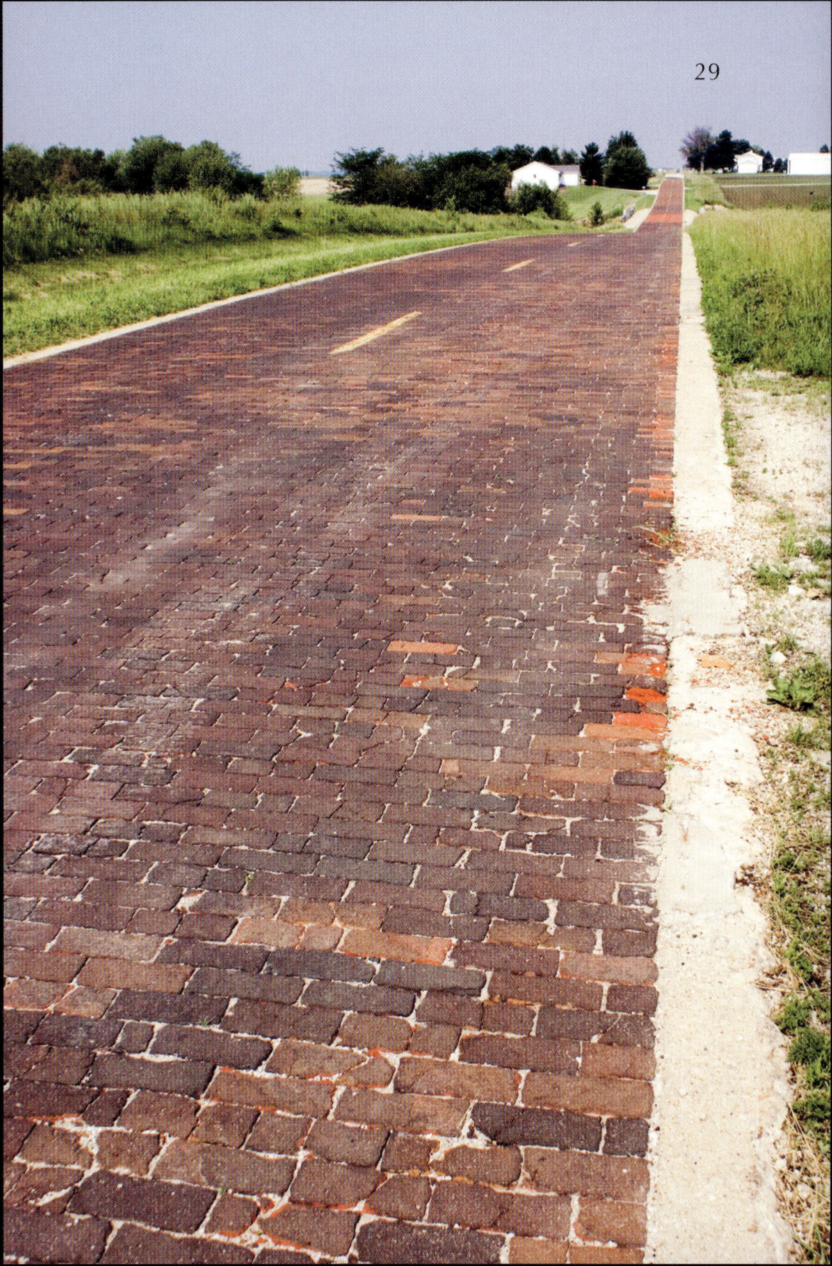

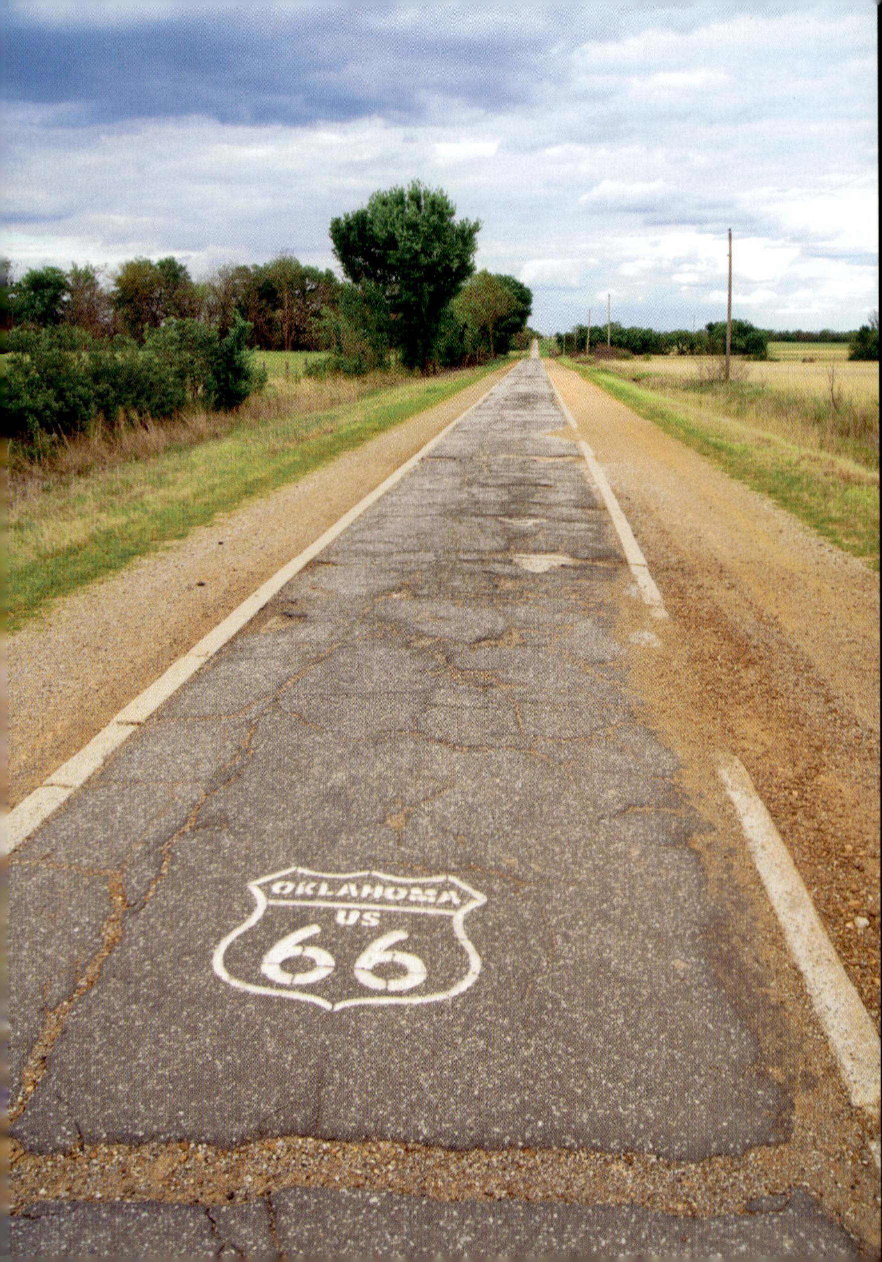
OKLAHOMA
US
66
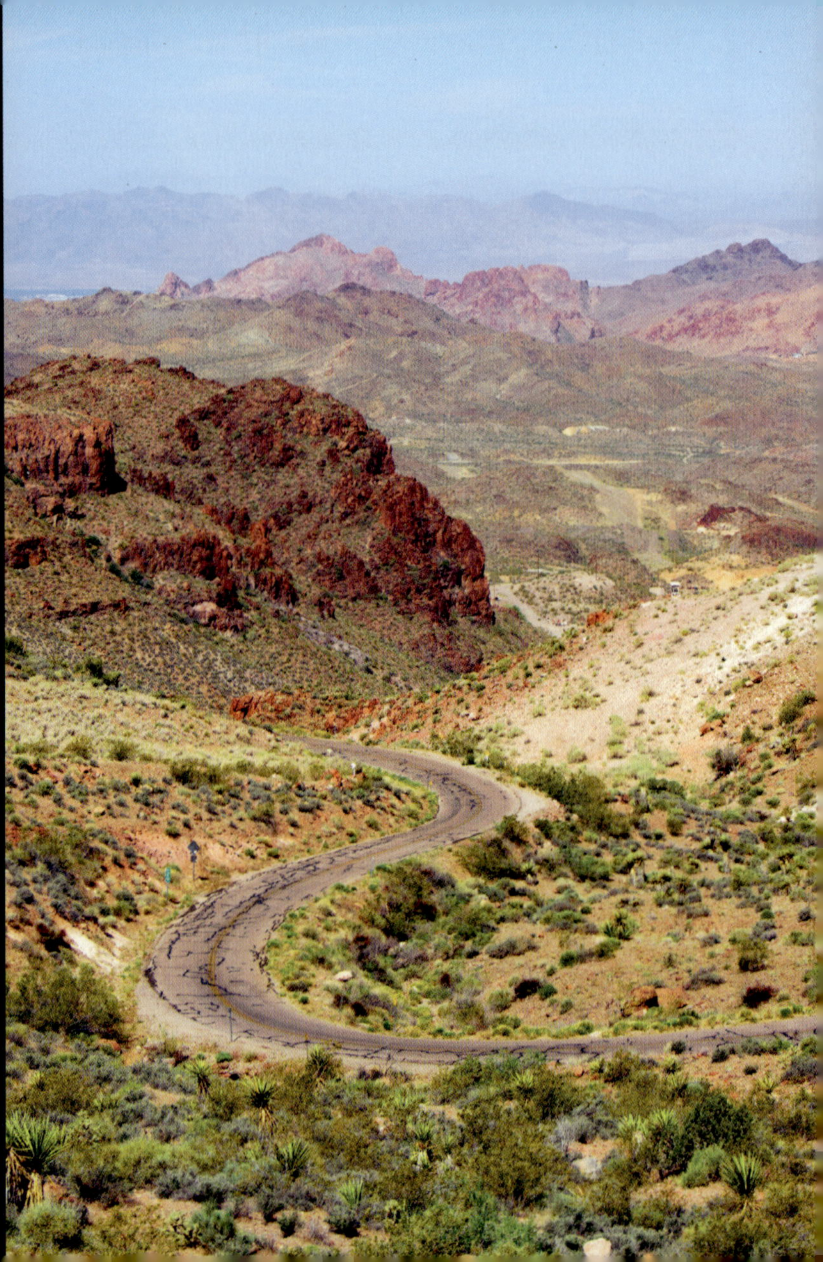

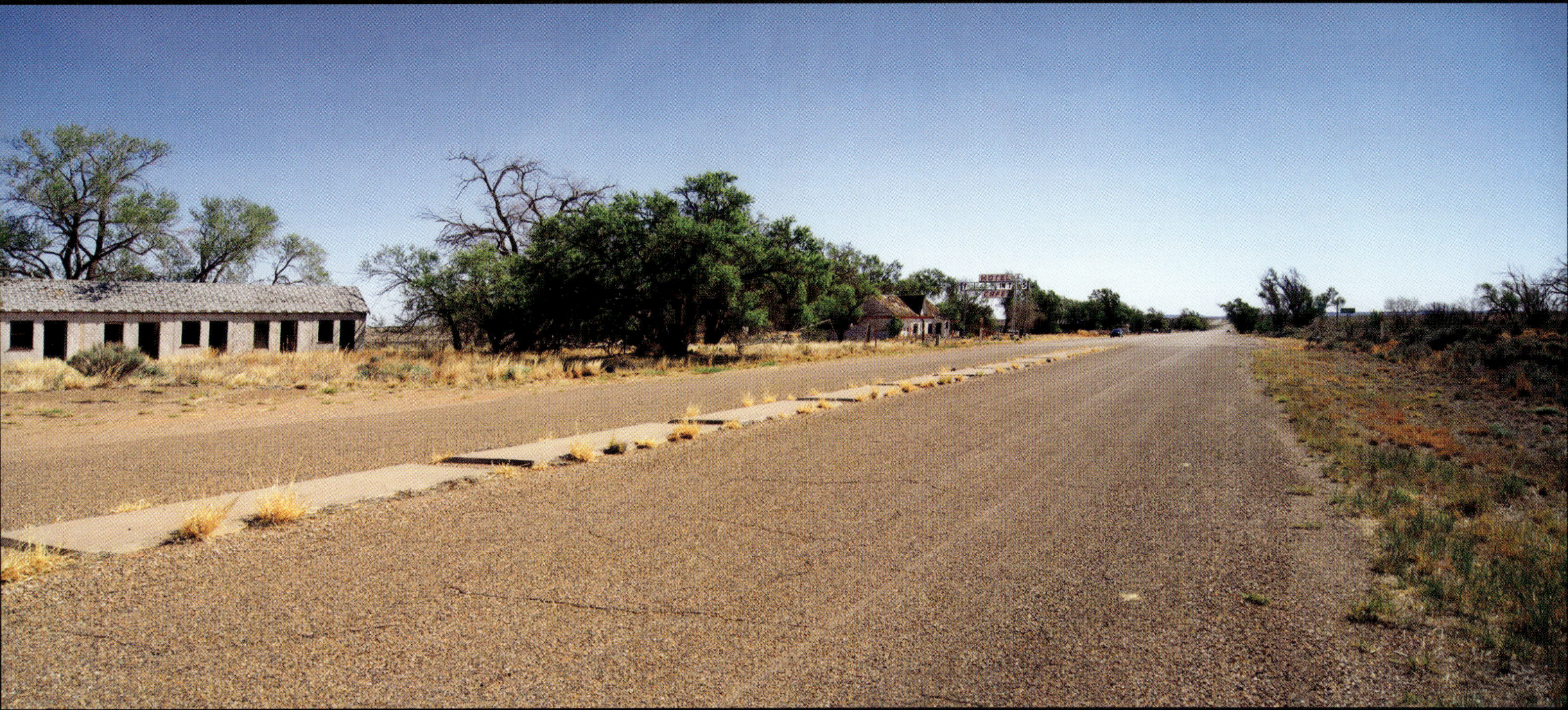

Above: Glenrio, TX – once a *Grapes of Wrath* film location, now a ghost town – viewed across the border with New Mexico. The former Longhorn Motel and Stateline bar, at right-centre, included the sign 'First in Texas'/'Last in Texas' on alternate sides. Note the unusual concrete median which makes the road a dual carriageway at this point.

Opposite left: The Sidewalk Highway, a 15-mile segment between Miami and Afton, OK, comprising a strip of tarmacked 'pavement' just 9 ft wide, bordered by unpaved overruns; it was completed in 1922 and taken out of service in 1937.

Opposite right: Sitgreaves Pass on the Oatman Highway (max. elevation 3,550 ft) is one of the most scenic sections of Route 66.

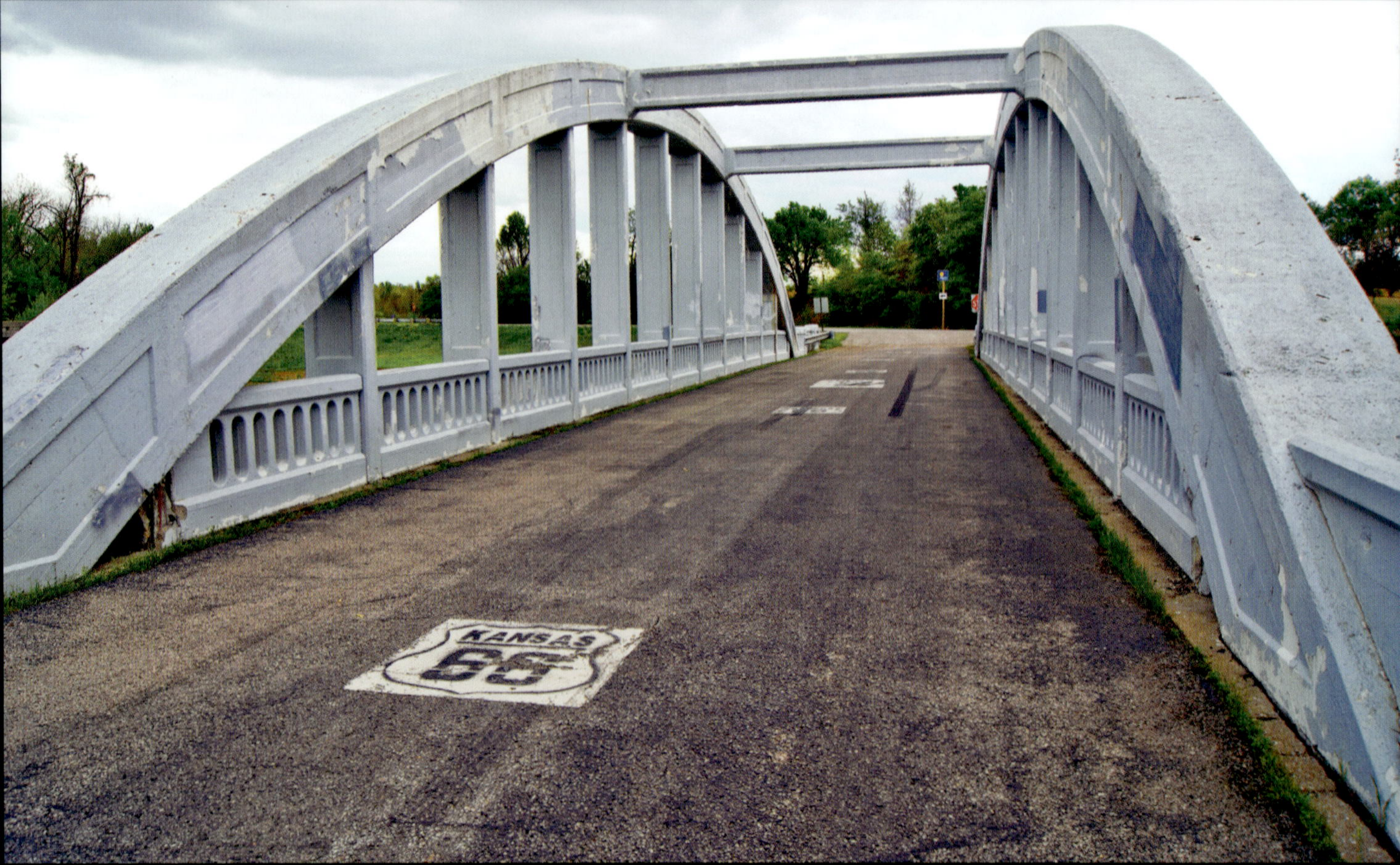

Above: Rainbow Curve Bridge over Brush Creek, north of Baxter Springs and west of Riverton, KS. Designed by James Barney Marsh and built in 1923, this is the only remaining 'Marsh Arch' bridge on Route 66.

Opposite: Chain of Rocks Bridge at St Louis, MO, which carried Route 66 across the Mississippi between 1929 and 1968. Named after a series of rapids, the 1,630-m-long Warren truss bridge was built with a 22-degree bend in the middle due to the proximity of a water intake tower and bedrock issues.

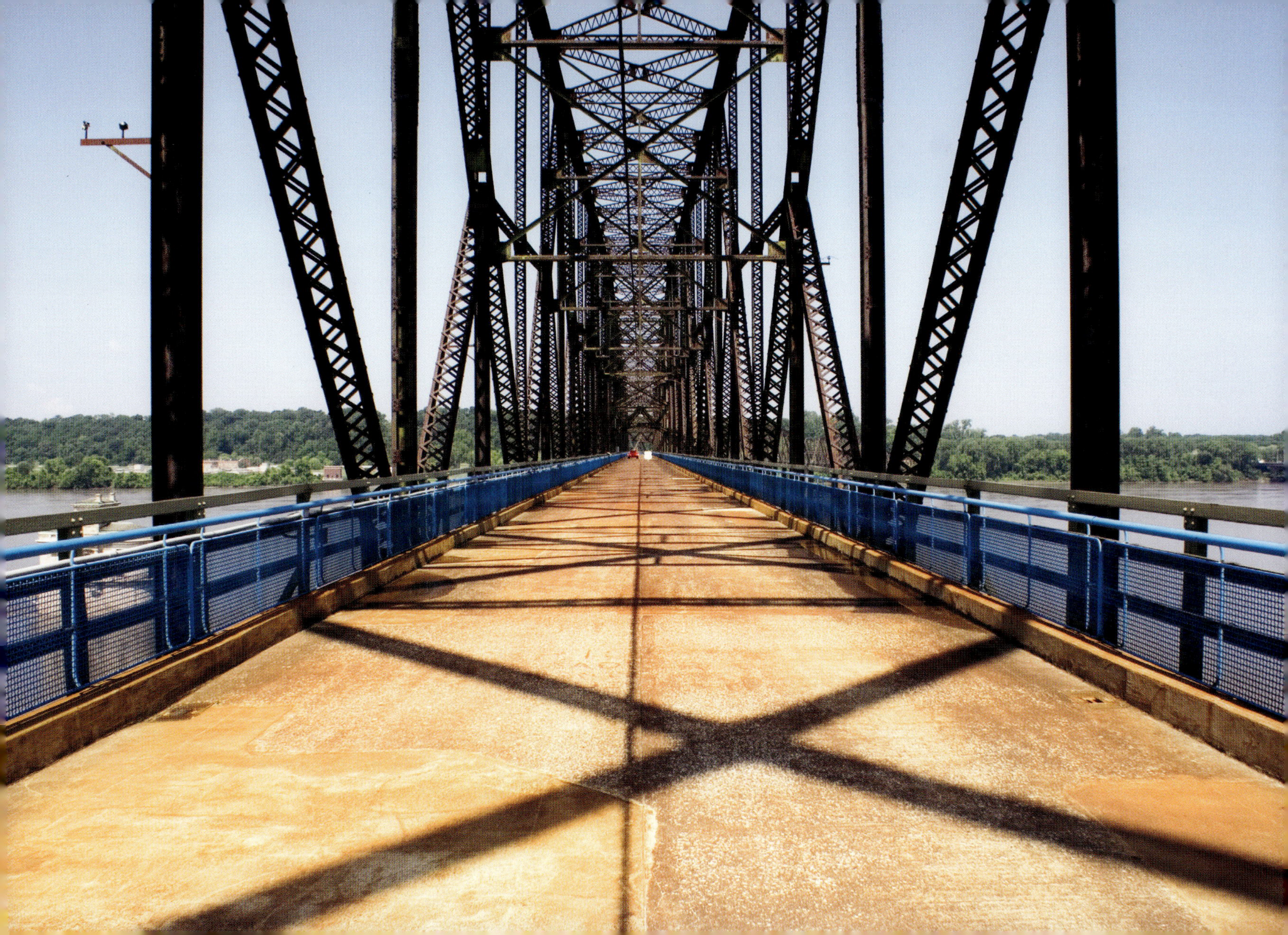

Chapter 4

GAS STATIONS

Any vehicle travelling along Route 66 needed fuel, so it was inevitable that gas station businesses would grow in number as the traffic increased. Although cars were far simpler mechanically than they are today and drivers expected to do their own basic maintenance, there was also an increased need for mechanics to deal with breakdowns along the Route. As a result, a service garage was often incorporated with the filling station.

The first gasoline pump was invented in 1885 by Sylvanus Bowser of Fort Wayne, Indiana. It comprised a wooden barrel and plunger and, of all things, marble valves! Its main advantage was the reduction of dangerous spills, especially in enclosed spaces, and it sold well to grocery stores where it was used to dispense kerosene for domestic lamps and stoves. Bowser patented his pump in 1887 and, just as 'hoover' became the common word for a vacuum cleaner, the term bowser became synonymous with the fuel pump (and, by extension, any tanker vehicle with a pump).

By the mid-1890s, Bowser was pitching an improved 'filling station design' of his pump to the first kerbside gas dispensers, thus launching an industry dedicated to the manufacture of gas pumps. And though he could never have guessed it, he also created a photographic icon to captivate Route 66ers for decades to come!

The observant photographer will find a plethora of different gas pump designs on Route 66, carefully renovated and repainted to evoke the era of their construction (though rusty discarded pumps can be equally photogenic). To modern eyes, the most interesting are the narrow columnar pumps topped by a tall sight-glass used to measure the amount dispensed. The fuel would first be pumped into the sight-glass from an underground tank and then dispensed into the vehicle's fuel tank. Later pumps were squarer in cross-section and of a bulkier design – much like modern-day pumps – but retained the sight-glass as a much smaller window (often with a rotating vane), not least to assure the buyer that fuel was actually being dispensed [p. 38].

Of course, it was important for the many competing oil companies to brand their pumps, so the majority were crowned with a circular sign emblazoned with their logo and usually illuminated. These logos and other branded memorabilia have become part of the language of Route 66, in that gas stations will often be referred to as the 'Standard Oil station' or the 'Conoco station', for example. Another oil brand that populates the Route is Sinclair, founded by an oilman of the same name in 1916; its logo features a silhouette of a green brontosaurus, which was apparently based on a belief that oil deposits were the liquified remains of dinosaurs.

Another oil company familiar to Route 66 fans is Phillips, founded in 1917 and identified by the Phillips 66 brand, which dates back to 1927 (the year after the Route was inaugurated). Although some of the historical details are disputed, legend has it that the rebrand resulted from a fuel test on Route 66 using a car that achieved 66 mph on fuel with a specific gravity of 66. Too many coincidences perhaps, but it all adds to the wonderful mix of myths and legends that is Route 66.

The architecture of the gas stations themselves is also of interest to Route 66 aficionados, who identify a number of 'standard pattern' and 'entirely unique' designs. Arguably, the design that typifies the image of the historic gas station is the 'House with Canopy' style developed by Standard Oil of Ohio in 1916 [p. 37]. The drive-through canopy offered some weather-protection to the pumps, their attendants and the vehicle being filled, but it also served to push the building's structure out towards the road, allowing three faces for names and logos along with mounting positions for signs [p. 46]. Combined with the elevated pole-mounted signage, this ensured that prospective customers were in no doubt about which station brand they were approaching. Today, the pumps and signage offer a snapshot in time, not least in terms of fuel pricing [p. 42]!

One of the most distinctive non-canopy designs is the 'Cottage Style' station adopted by Phillips 66, among others, in an attempt to better integrate what could be rather ugly facilities into local neighbourhoods. It featured a steeply pitched roof (often brightly coloured), a cross-gable porch over the entrance door and a chimney. In some cases, a right-angled extension was added to house a service garage, typically featuring a large vehicle access door facing the street [p. 40].

Equally interesting are the 'unique' designs, unique today because similar examples have been demolished but also because they were built to reflect a wider architectural style. A prime example is the Shamrock Conoco station with its art deco styling: a pair of ribbed canopies extend from a hub-like tower styled to resemble a large cog, no doubt referencing the mechanical nature of the automobile [p. 44]. The design is so distinctive that it was adapted for use in the animated movie *Cars*, along with other iconographic aspects of Route 66.

Gas stations also differ in their basic construction materials, with an observed prominence for wood in the east and stone in the west. This is by no means a definitive division, but the preference for stone in the western deserts of New Mexico and Arizona is understandable given the relative lack of trees. It is interesting to note, however, that the standard canopy design wins through, whether the supporting pillars are made from wood, brick or stone [pp. 48–49].

As with much of 'restored Route 66', it is important to recognise that what we see today is not necessarily either the original structure or a correct facsimile of the past. Many stations underwent several design iterations throughout their lifetimes and some were even burned to the ground before being reinstated as tourist attractions. That said, one has to celebrate the hard work and commitment of the groups and individuals along the Route who have painstakingly restored the stations and other structures to offer a window into the glory days of Route 66.

Sadly, the one thing missing from most Route 66 gas stations today is the car. For obvious reasons, most of the presentable machines have found homes in museums or private collections, which means that Cadillacs posed under canopies are a rarity. But keep your eyes peeled: although even the rusting, abandoned hulks are gradually disappearing from the roadside, you never know what you might find.

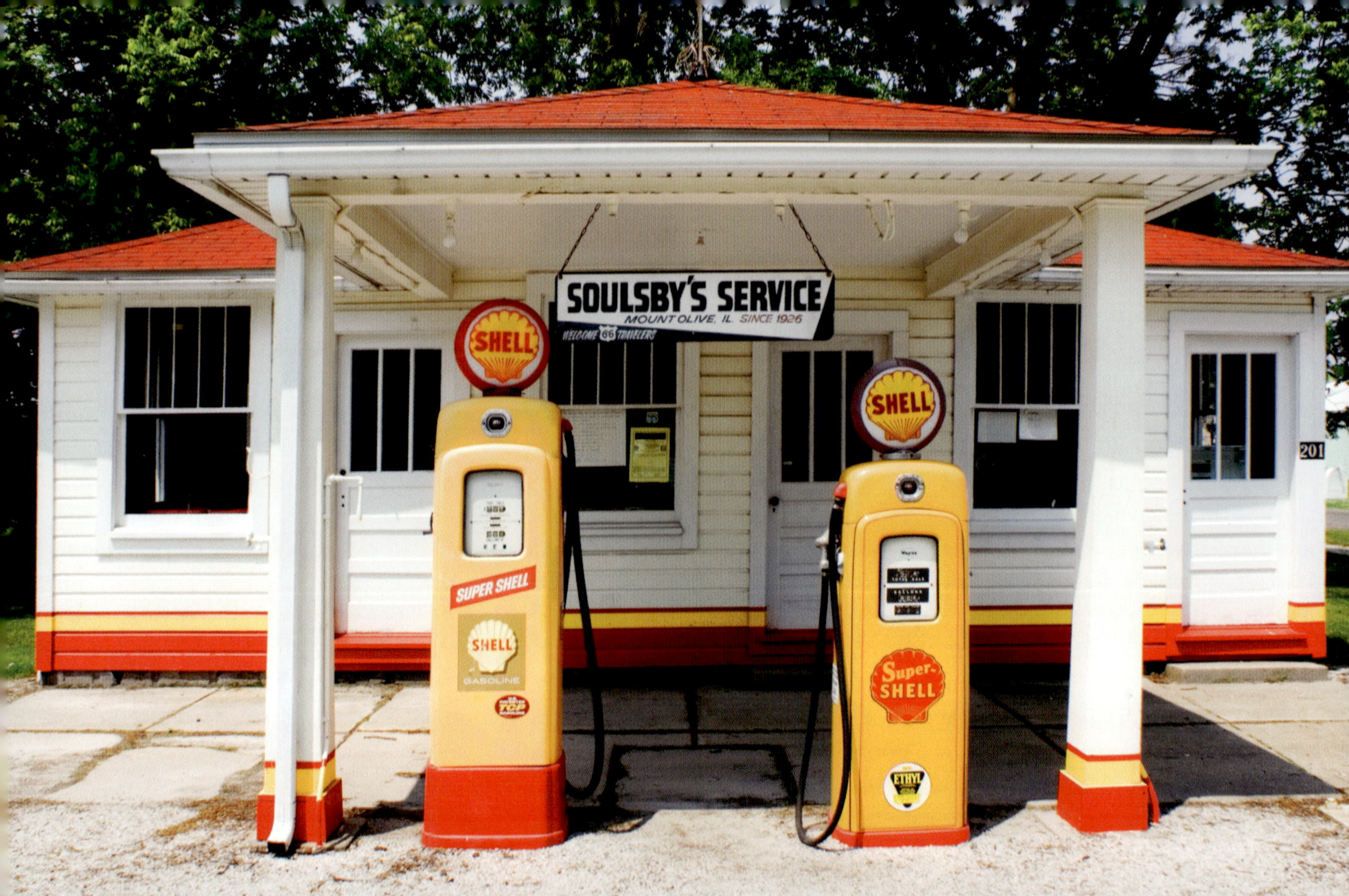

bove: The 1926 Soulsby Service Sation, Mount Olive, IL, is said to be one of the oldest filling stations still standing on Route 66. It remainec perational into the 1990s.

Ɔpposite: The 1932 Standard Oil station in Odell, IL, represents the 'House with Canopy' style developed by Standard Oil. This example vas operational until 1975, renovated in the 1990s and listed in the US National Register of Historic Places.

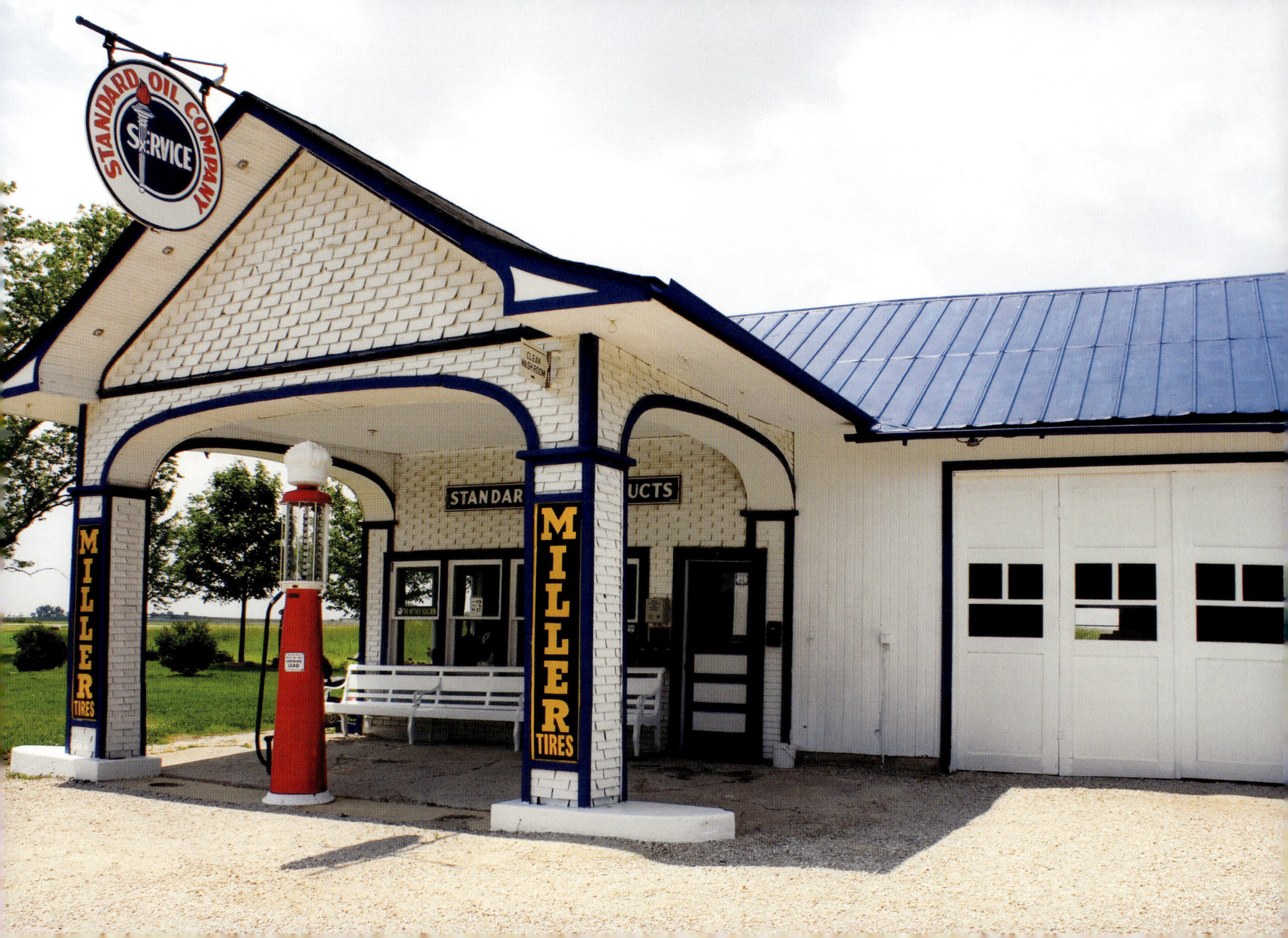
STANDARD OIL COMPANY
SERVICE
CLEAN WASH ROOM
MILLER TIRES
MILLER TIRES

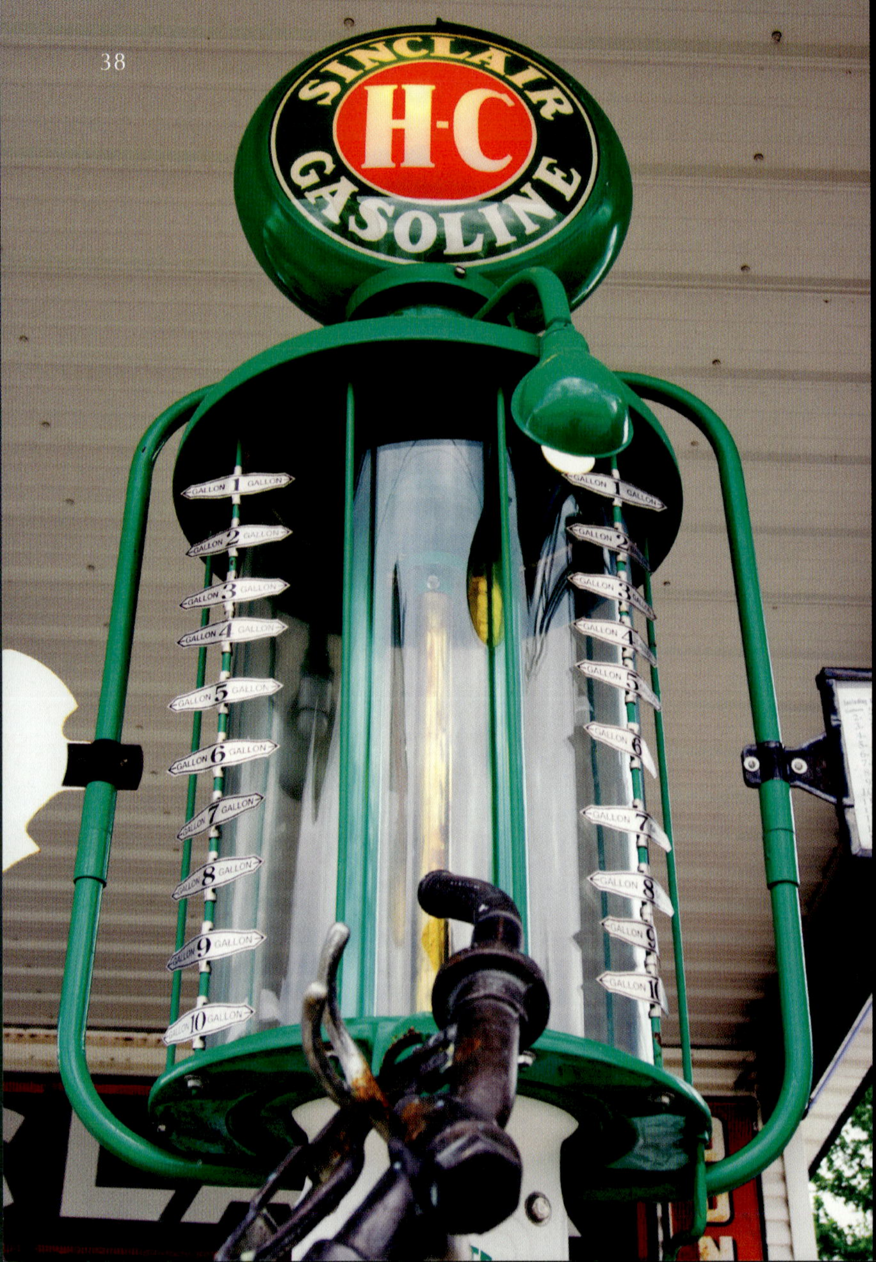

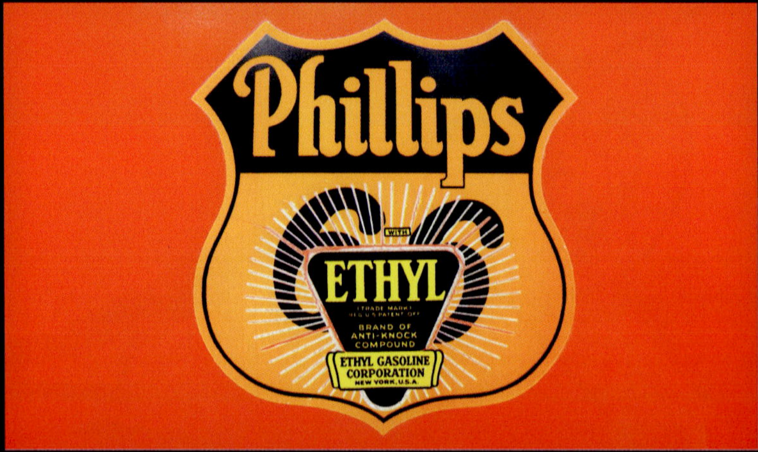

Above: A Phillips 66 sign advertising its ethyl brand of anti-knocking compound on a pump outside Rail Haven Motel in Springfield, MO.

Left: A gas pump with fuel-level indicators at Gay Parita garage, Paris Springs Junction, MO.

Below: A view glass with rotating vane on a pump at Soulsby Service Station, Mount Olive, IL.

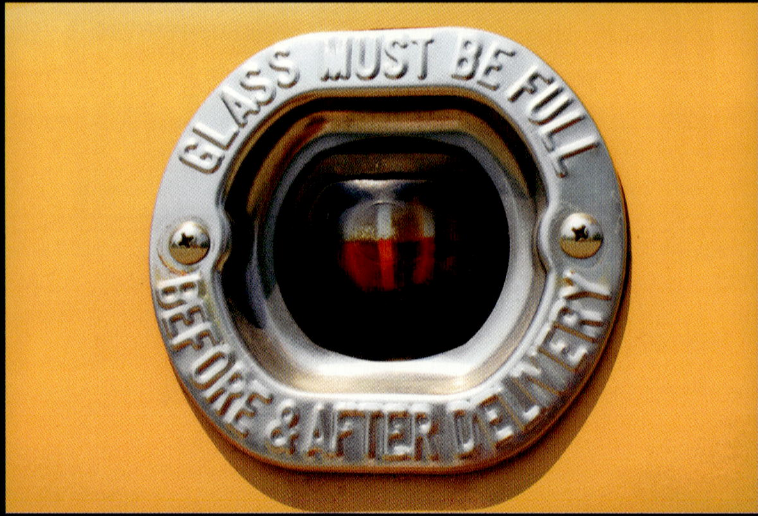

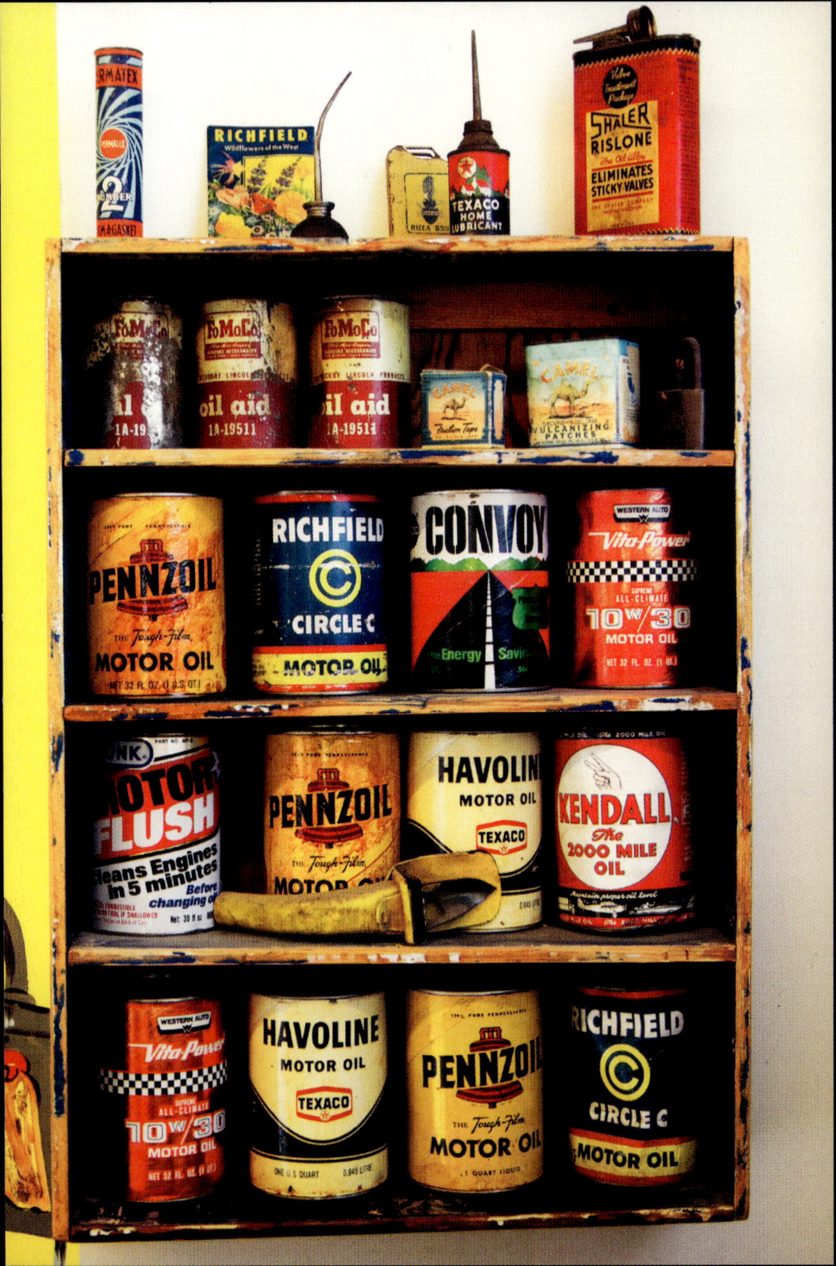

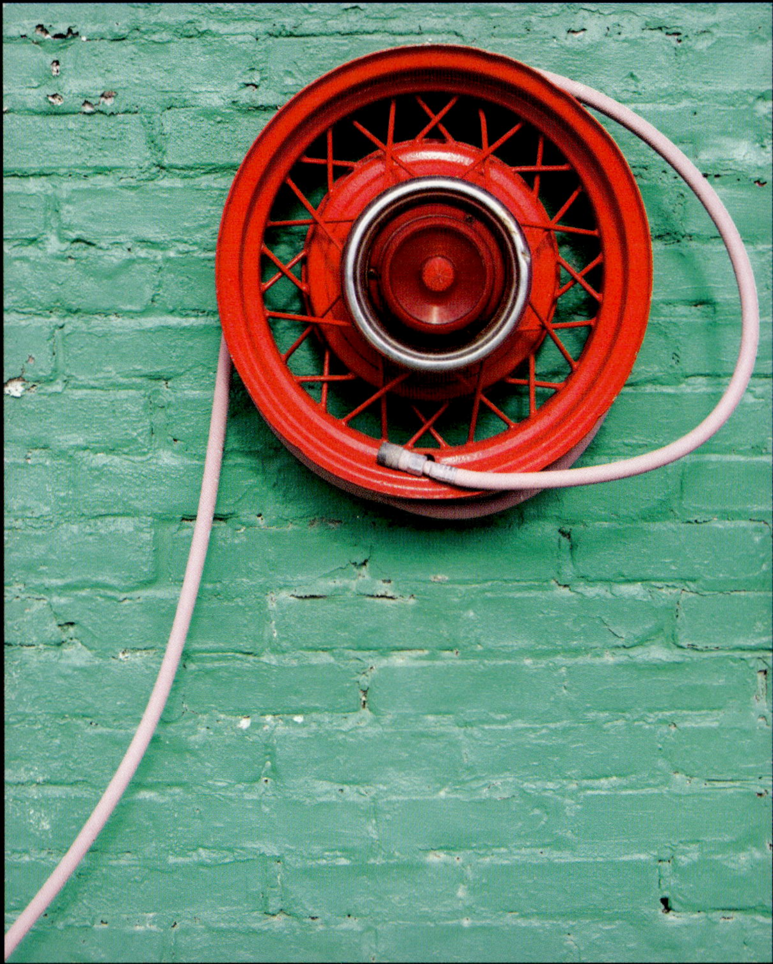

Above: Hose reel on the wall of Allen's Filling Station, a Conoco gas station in Commerce, OK.

Left: Oil can display at the Arizona Route 66 (Powerhouse) Museum in Kingman, AZ.

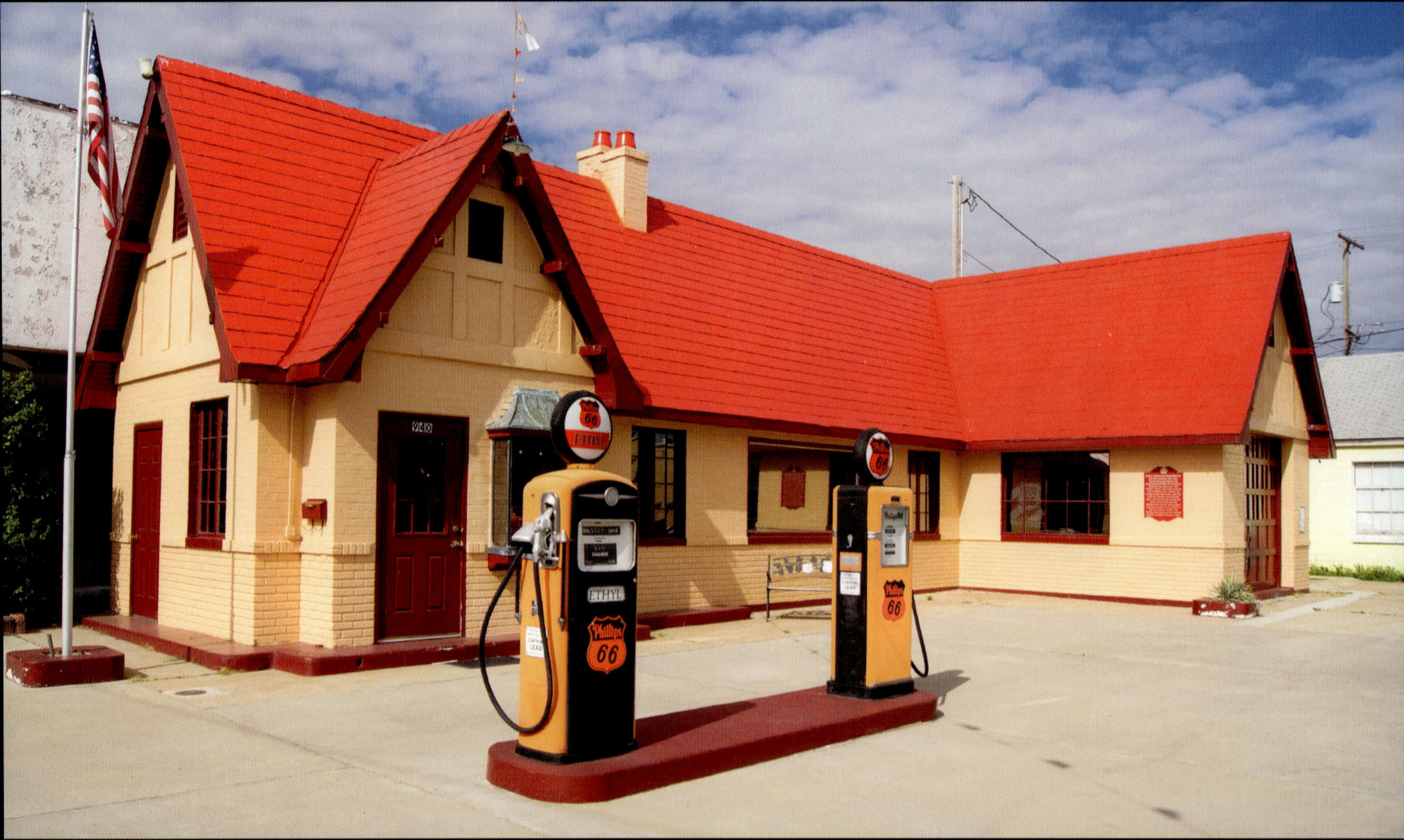

Above: A restored 1930s Phillips 66 station in Baxter Springs, KS, an example of the 'Cottage Style' station with a service garage in the return section.

Opposite: Gay Parita garage and Sinclair station at Paris Springs Junction, MO. Gary Turner built this recreation of a 1930s gas station in 2006 as a tourist

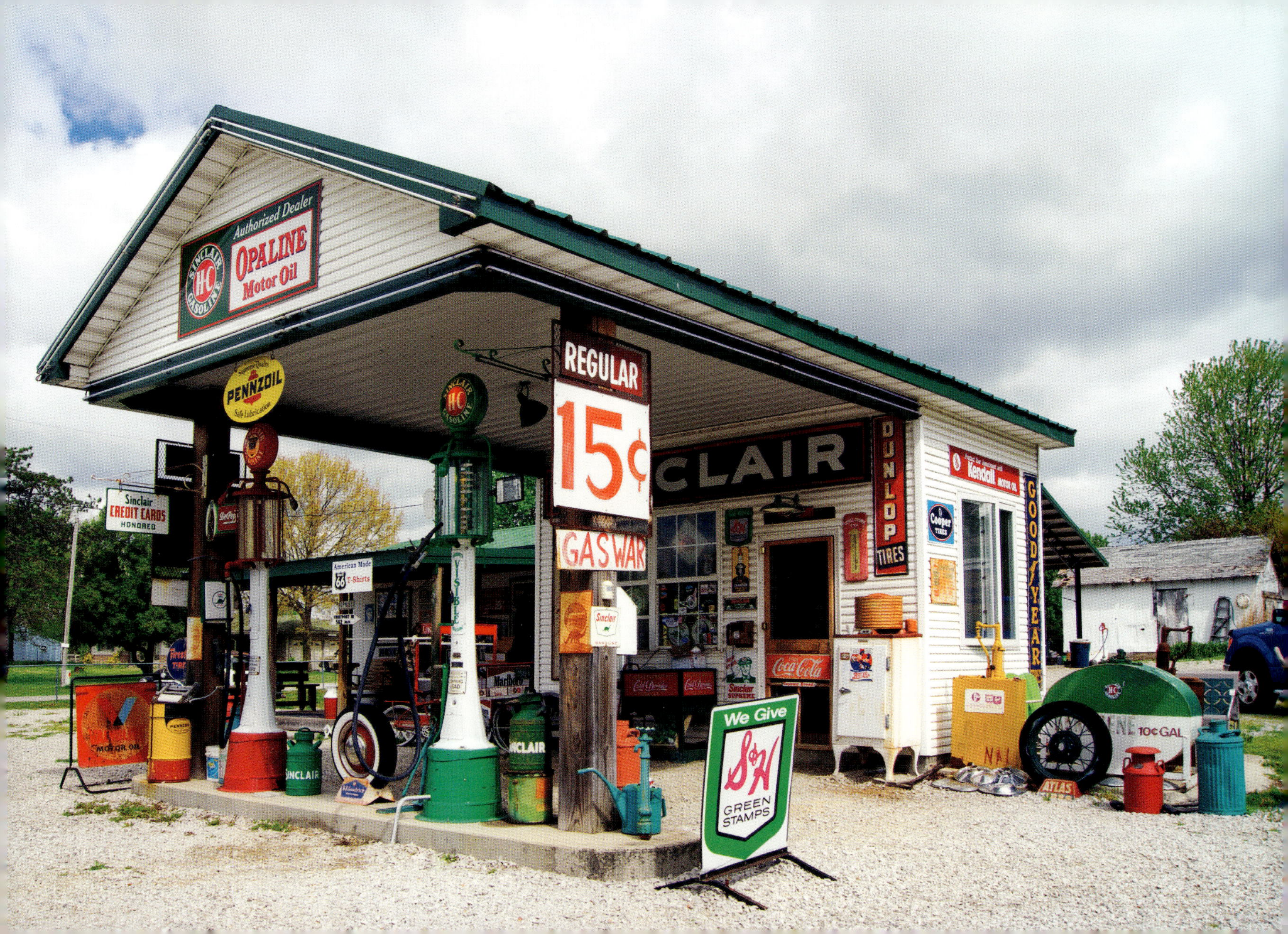
SINCLAIR H-C GASOLINE
Authorized Dealer
OPALINE
Motor Oil
PENNZOIL
Safe Lubrication
REGULAR
15¢
GAS WAR
CLAIR
DUNLOP TIRES
GOODYEAR
Kendall MOTOR OIL
Cooper TIRES
Sinclair
CREDIT CARDS
HONORED
American Made
66
T-Shirts
Coca-Cola
VISIBLE
SINCLAIR
We Give
S&H
GREEN STAMPS
10¢ GAL
ATLAS

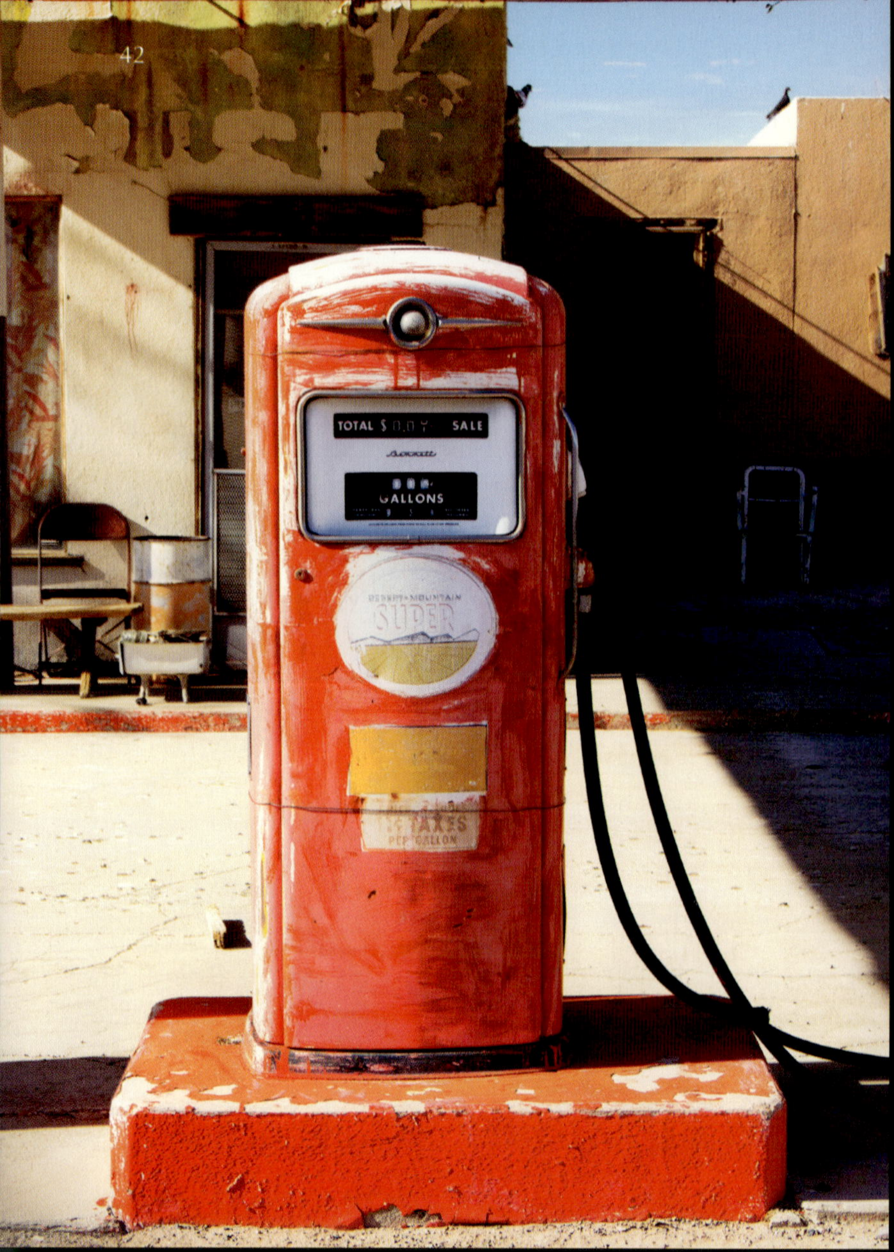
TOTAL $ SALE
GALLONS
SUPER

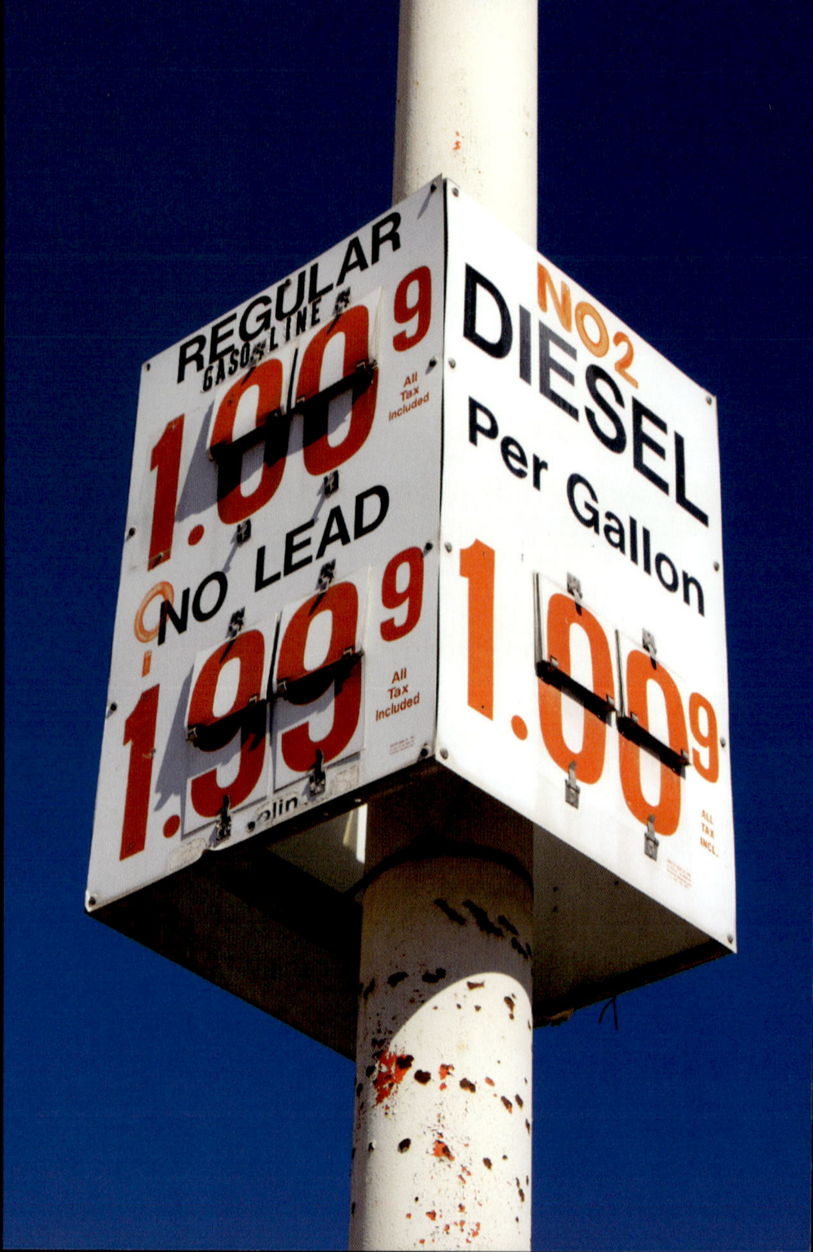
REGULAR
GASOLINE
1.00 9
All Tax Included
NO LEAD
1.99 9
All Tax Included
NO2
DIESEL
Per Gallon
1.00 9
ALL TAX INCL.

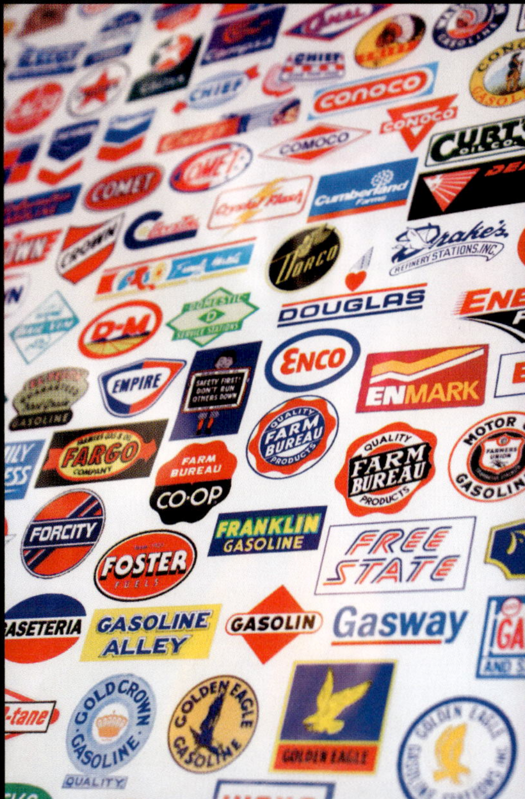

Above: Display of petroleum company logos at Bill Shea's gas station, Springfield, IL.

Opposite left: Gas pump at Whiting Brothers gas station east of Newberry Springs, CA.

Opposite right: Gas price sign at Mohawk gas station and Mini-Mart, Oro Grande, CA.

Right: Gas pumps at Cool Springs on the Oatman Highway in Arizona, one of the most scenic locations for a gas station.

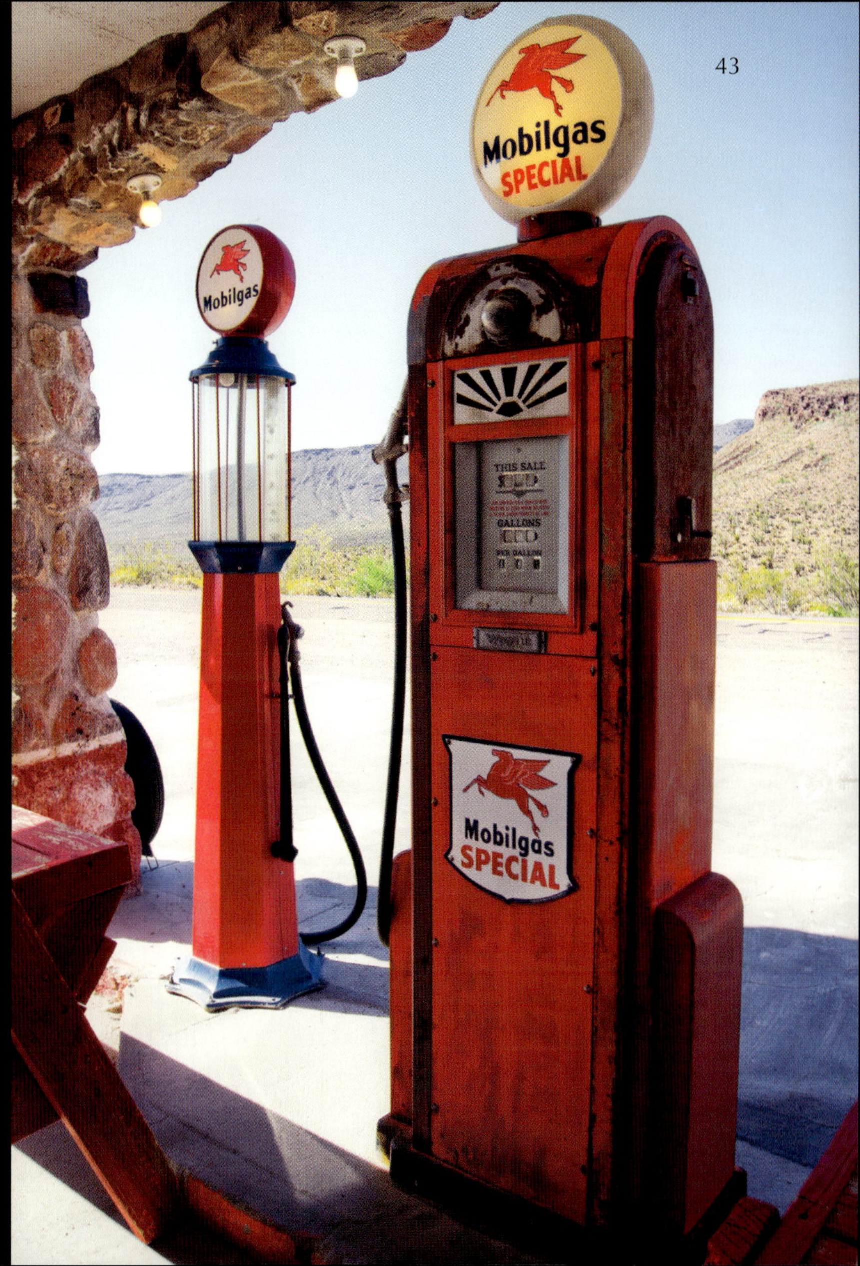

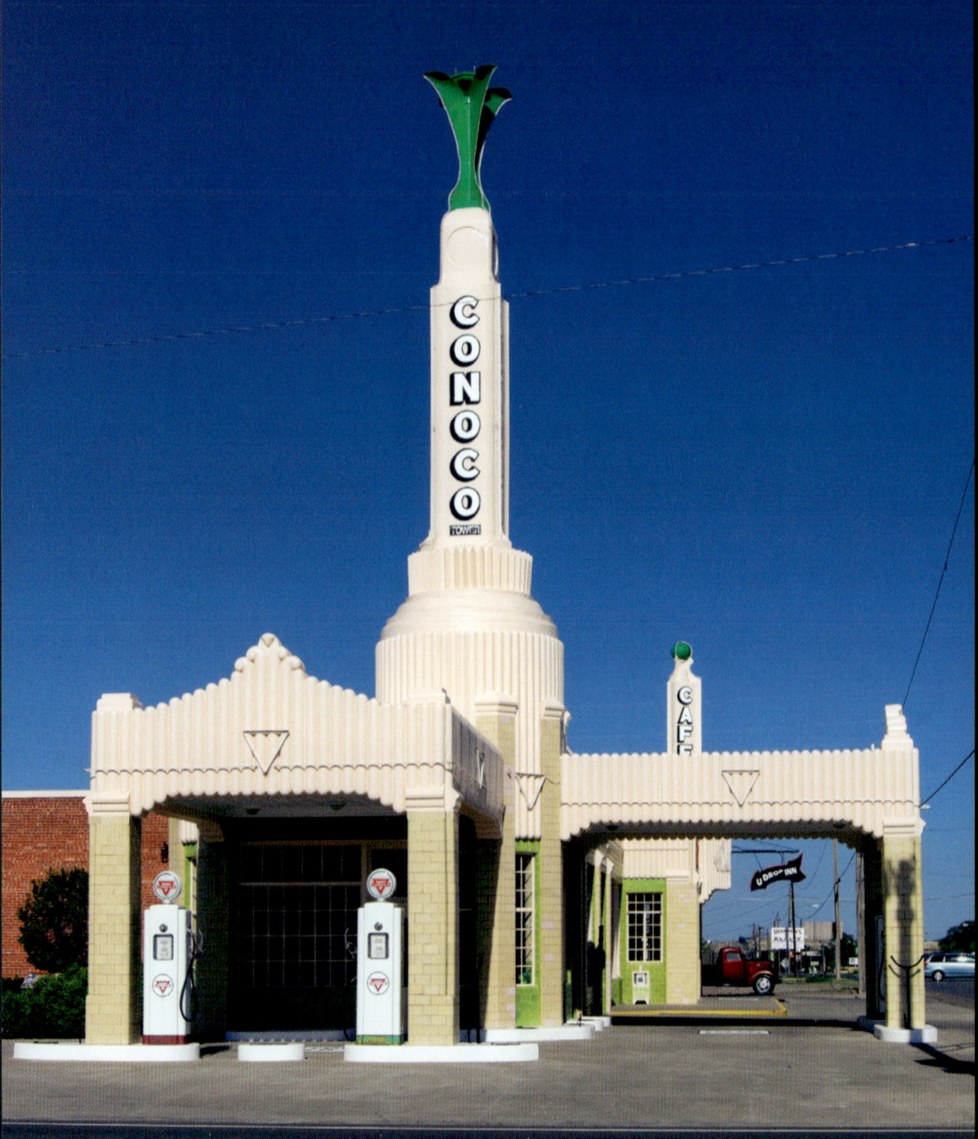

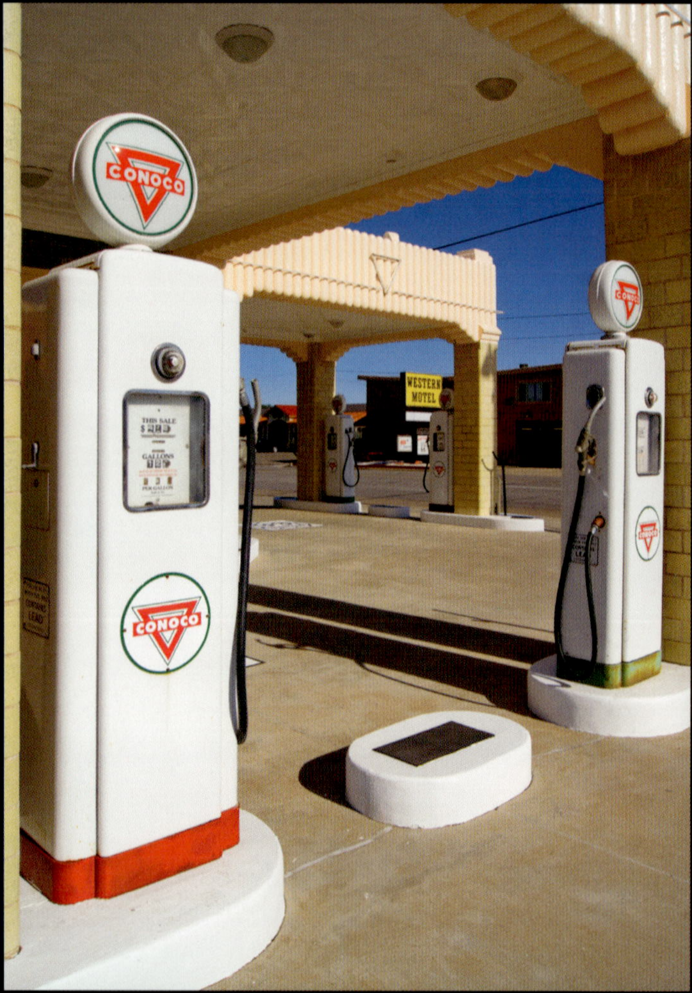

Left and above: The 1936 art deco-style Conoco gas station in Shamrock, TX, known as the U-Drop Inn and Tower; the gas pumps have simplified art deco styling to match the station.

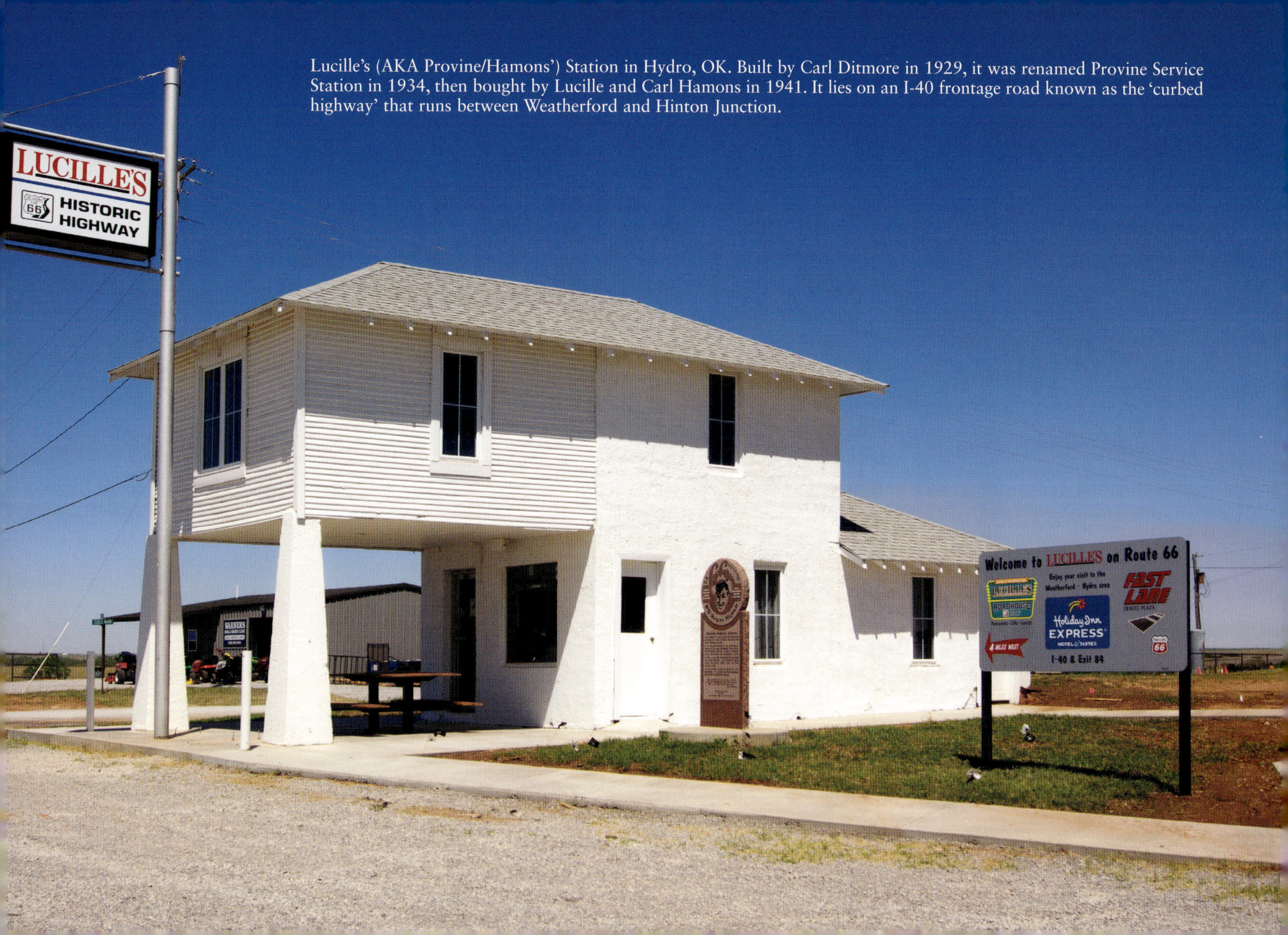

Lucille's (AKA Provine/Hamons') Station in Hydro, OK. Built by Carl Ditmore in 1929, it was renamed Provine Service Station in 1934, then bought by Lucille and Carl Hamons in 1941. It lies on an I-40 frontage road known as the 'curbed highway' that runs between Weatherford and Hinton Junction.

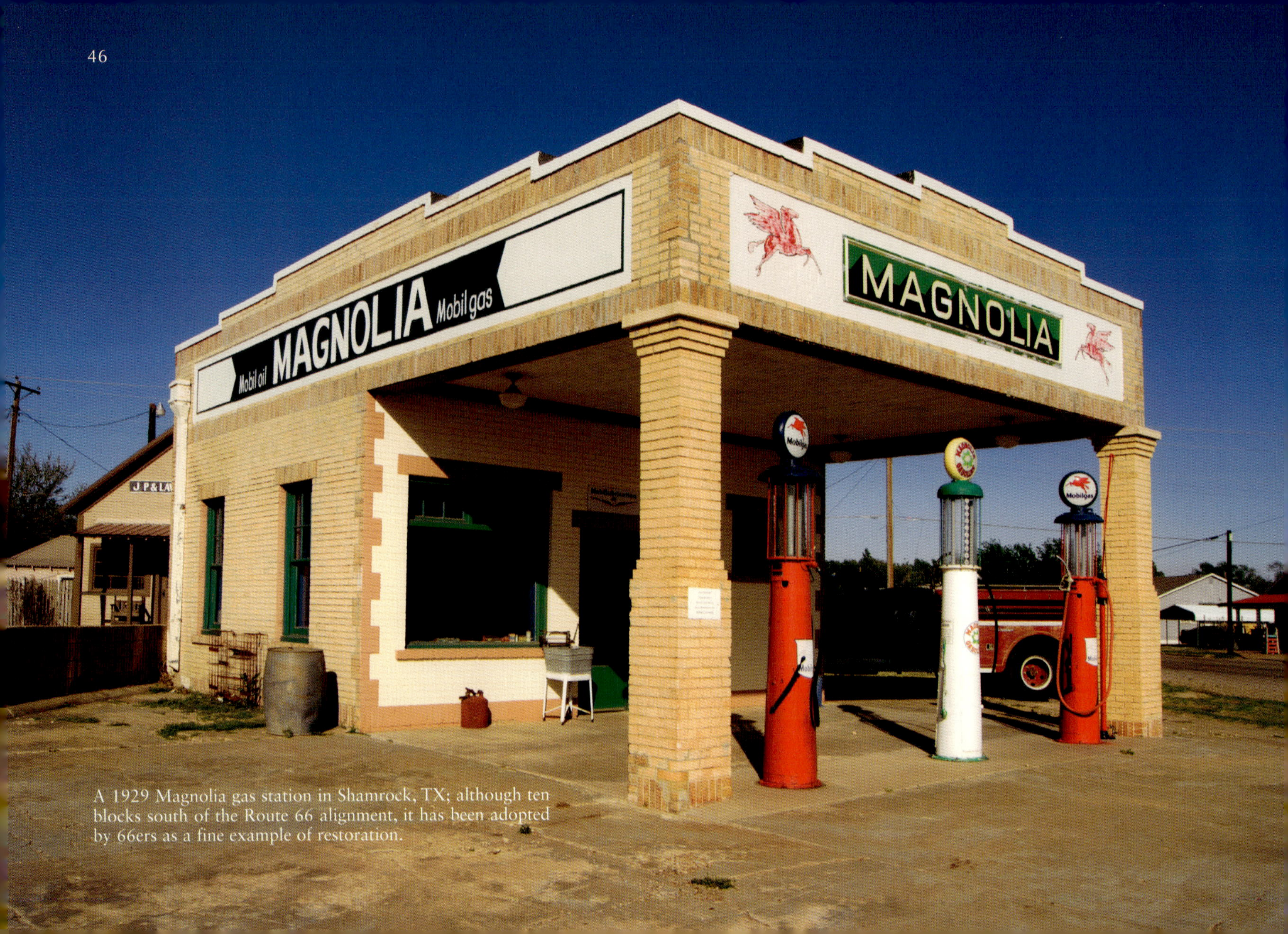

A 1929 Magnolia gas station in Shamrock, TX; although ten blocks south of the Route 66 alignment, it has been adopted by 66ers as a fine example of restoration.

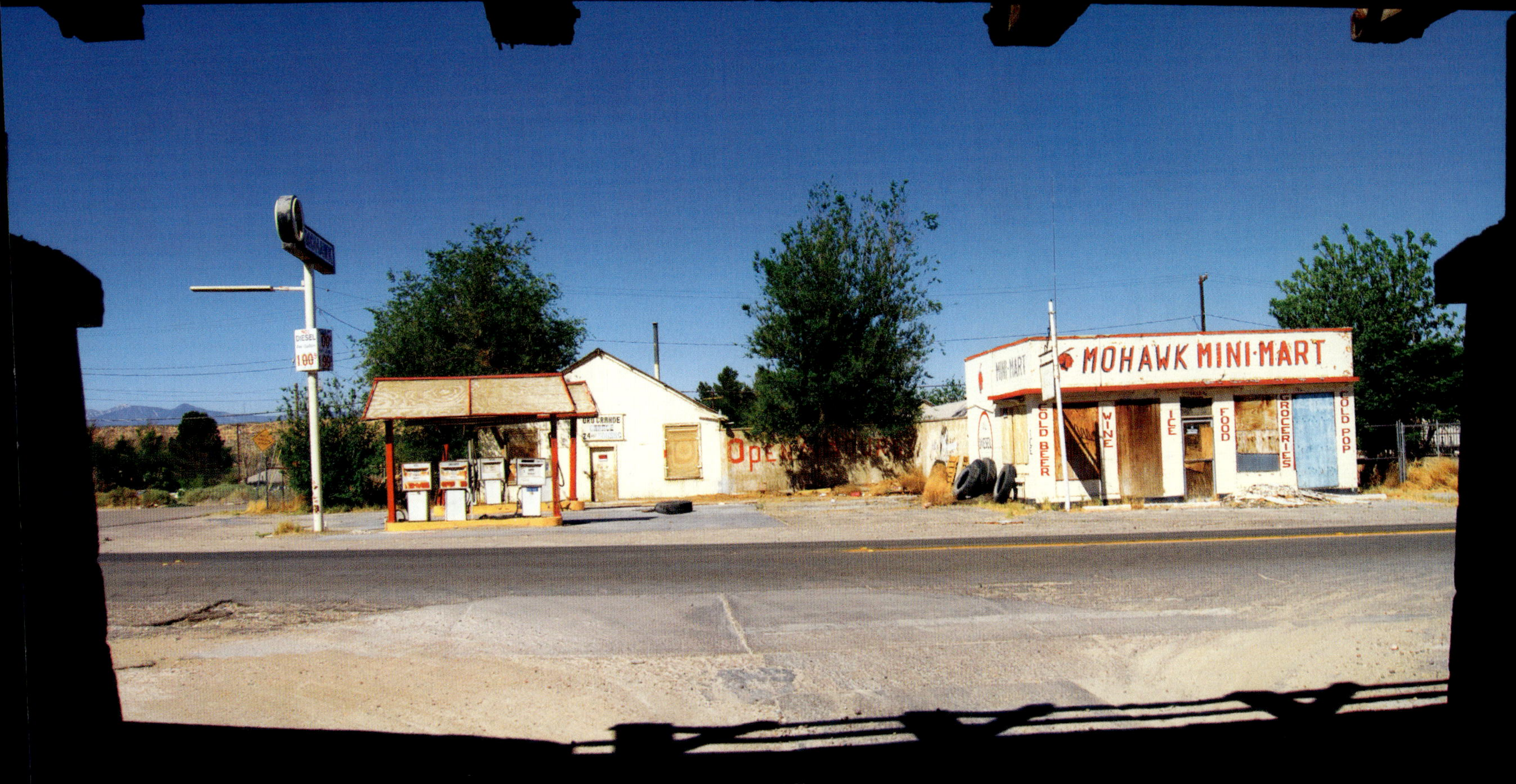

Mohawk gas station and Mini-Mart, Oro Grande, CA (partly demolished by 2023).

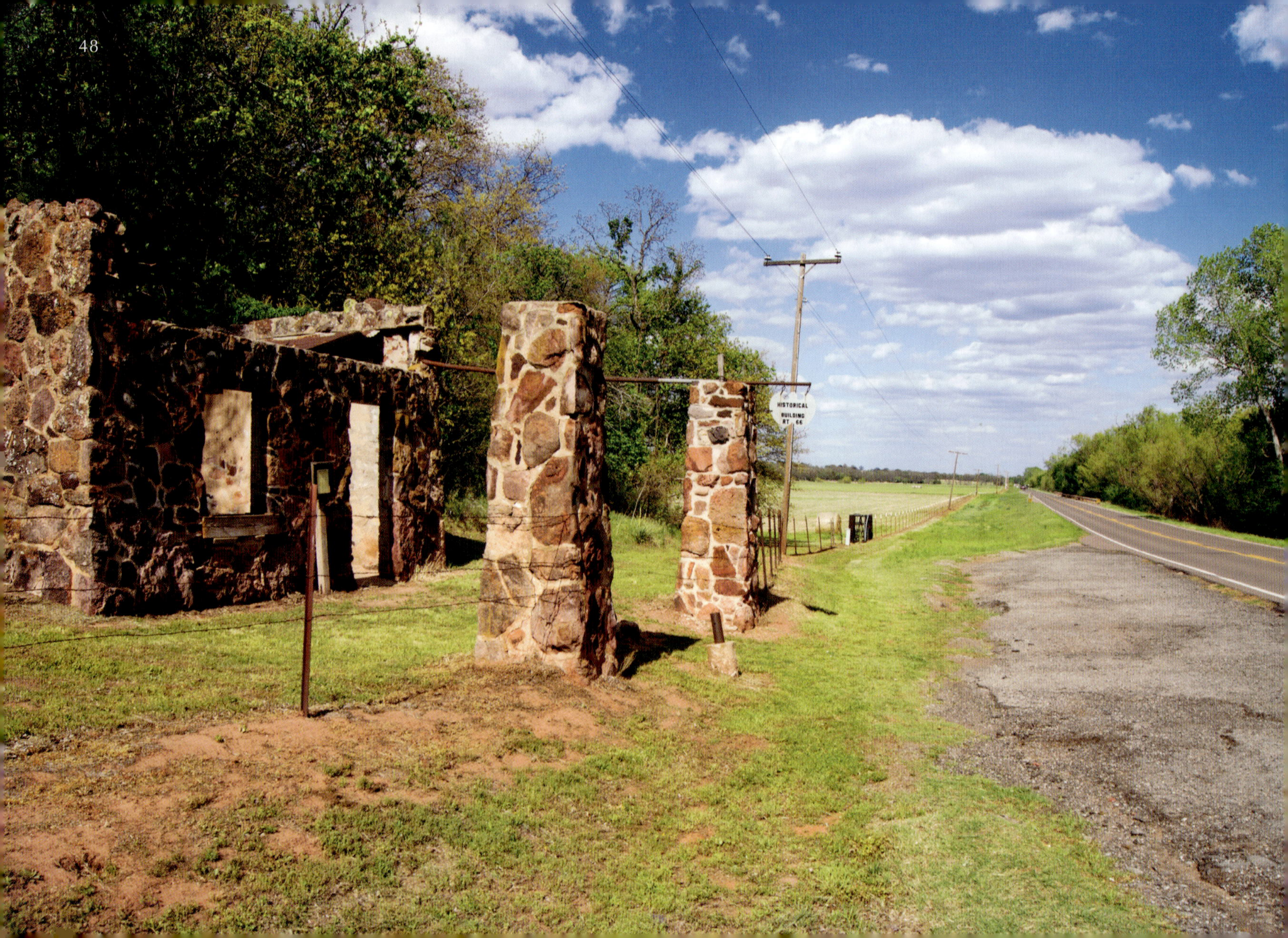
HISTORICAL
BUILDING
RT 66

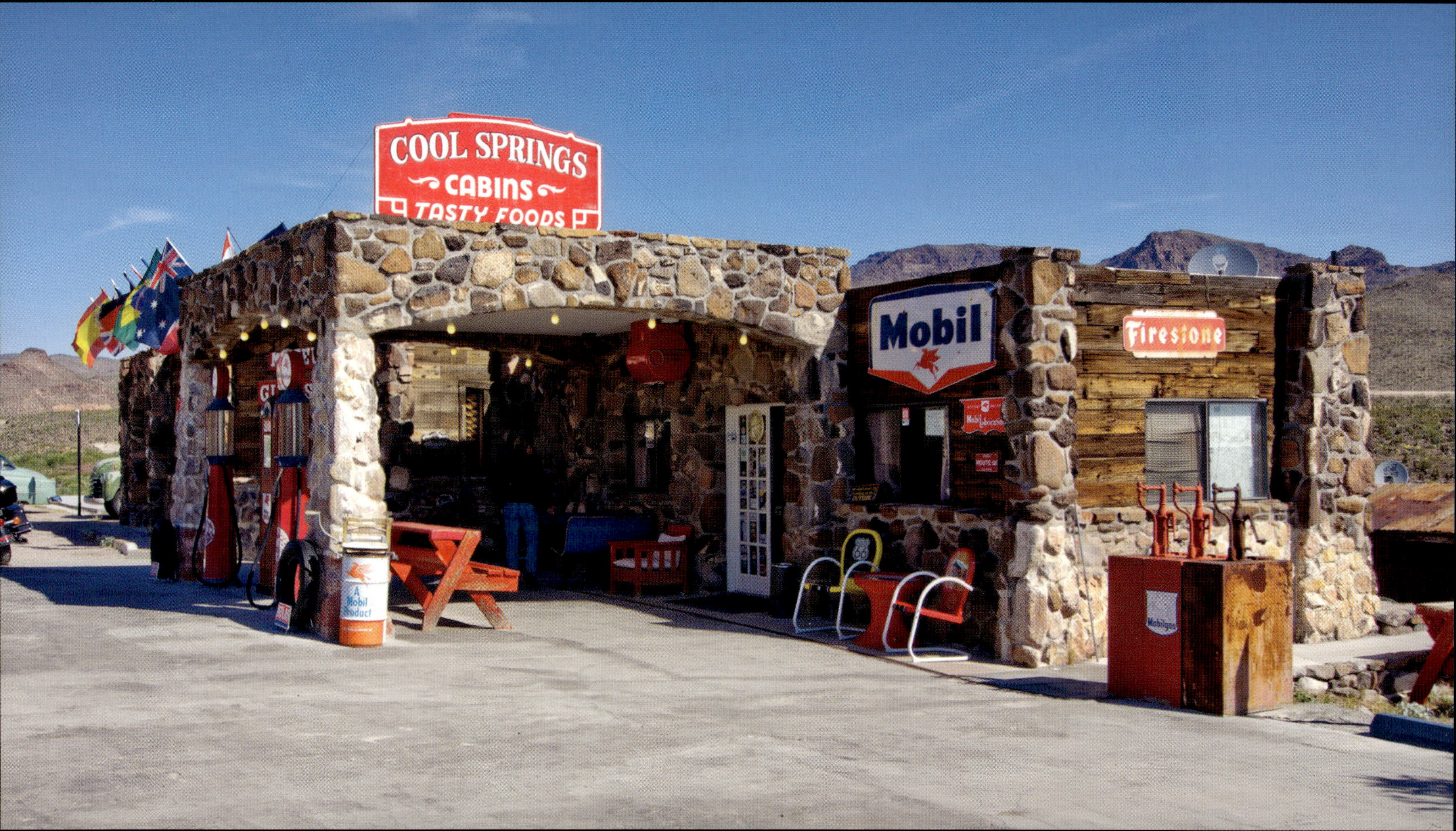

Above: A reconstructed gas station and cabins at Cool Springs on the Oatman Highway in Arizona. Originating from 1926–27, it was extended in stone in the late 1930s and operated successfully until the 1960s. It burnt down in 1966, leaving only the pillars and a few low walls, but was rebuilt in 2007.

Opposite: An ex-Conoco gas station, east of Arcadia, OK, known as the 'Arcadia rock station'. Built *c.* 1915–20, it is one of the earliest gas stations on Route 66. Allegedly, a tiny backroom was used to counterfeit dollar bills in the 1920s, leading to jail for the owner and closure of the station.

Chapter 5

MOTELS

As the realm of long-distance motoring developed, with both trucks and tourists taking to the road, the need for overnight accommodation increased. In contrast with the early hotels, which had no need to cater for motorists, vehicle accommodation was a fundamental part of motel design. The word 'motel' – short for motor-hotel – is attributed to real estate speculator Arthur Heineman, who built the Milestone Mo-Tel in California in 1925. So, although motels are obviously not unique to Route 66, the concept predates the birth of the Route by only a year or so.

In common with other structures, a 'standard pattern' emerged; it featured a row of identical rooms, each with direct access from a dedicated parking space, and a check-in office at one end. Smaller motels had a single row, while larger ones were extended into an L-shape. Most common, however, was the classic U-shaped plan – the motel court – built with the opening on the road and the office, sometimes with a canopy, at one end of the inverted U. Larger properties would eventually be graced with a reception area, sometimes enhanced by a small diner and, often, a swimming pool within a widened court.

In built-up areas, where land prices were higher, motels were built with two storeys, but out on the open road they tended to be single storey. Although chains were eventually developed, the majority of the early motels were independently owned and operated, which led to some quirky designs and branding. No surprise, then, that they have become part of the attraction and culture of Route 66.

The architecture, too, often depended on where the motel was built: those in the eastern states generally expressed a more urban vibe, while western out-of-town motels adopted a less formal ranch style, sometimes with wooden verandas [p. 54]. In Albuquerque, for example, the number of adobe or pueblo-style buildings is notable [p. 57], while elsewhere one can find art deco or railroad-inspired architecture.

Some motels on Route 66 were built in a non-standard pattern, comprising a number of separate cabins, which harked back to the pre-motel era of campsites and 'auto camps'. Examples pictured here include the three rendered-blockwork cabins of the Avon Motel in Afton, Oklahoma [p. 58], and the dilapidated wood cabins of John's Modern Cabins near Arlington, Missouri [pp. 64–65]. However, perhaps the quirkiest examples on Route 66 are the Wigwam Motels in Holbrook, Arizona, and San Bernadino, California, which are based on a number of self-contained, air-conditioned concrete wigwams [pp. 56, 62].

In some cases, motel designers went the extra mile in pandering to the car owner by providing integrated garages. This innovation is depicted in a mural on the side of the Blue Swallow Motel in Tucumcari and, in glorious art deco reality, by the Boots Court Motel in Carthage, Missouri [pp. 60–61].

Another key element of the motel is its signage, which is a big draw for photographers because it typifies the artistry and iconography of Route 66. Of course, most feature the word 'motel', often in large capital letters, along with its name and sometimes a motif or logo. A good majority also include a graphical item such as an arrow, which both confirms the entrance point and adds a sense of motion. Basically, they shout 'Motel! Here! Come on in!' [pp. 52–53].

This attitude was taken to the extreme for the otherwise unknown settlement of Tucumcari, New Mexico, which became famous on the Route for its slogan 'Tucumcari Tonite', boldly advertising it as a place to stay. Indeed, in its heyday, the diminutive settlement boasted of more than 2,000 motel rooms!

Signs were, of course, important for any business – be it gas station, motel or diner – but there were differences in motivation. While brand awareness was of prime importance for gas stations, motels were more concerned with garish originality. On the outskirts of a town, for example, travellers would often be confronted with a 'motel row' of independents all competing for their attention – and the way to distinguish themselves from the competition was to have the tallest, brightest sign.

Moreover, while gas stations were not overly concerned with night-time trade, that was exactly the premise of the motel, which is why so many were emblazoned with colourful, often flashing, neon signs. In fact, the term 'neon' is a bit loose in a technical sense, because neon gas produces only the colours at the red end of the spectrum, while blue, yellow and green colours are generated by another inert gas, argon, with the addition of mercury. But popular culture has adopted the term neon, so neon signs they remain.

More importantly, the modern fluorescent tube was demonstrated as early as 1910, but it became particularly popular in the USA in the 1920s and was a technology development ideally timed to benefit Route 66. For the 66er not completely exhausted by the day's photography, they offer a bright and easy subject from dusk onwards.

One significant aspect of Route 66 may only come into focus when, lying in a motel bed before succumbing to sleep, you hear the characteristic tones of the freight-train air horn. Suddenly, you realise the intimate proximity of the railroad lines along many parts of the Route. This apparent coincidence has a simple explanation: the motor vehicles of the 1920s and 1930s were generally underpowered and found steep inclines difficult; so, like the railroads, they were consigned to routes that tended to follow the topography around high points rather than over them. This led to the 'transport corridors' we find today along many alignments of the highway.

For many, visiting Route 66 evokes mixed feelings, which can swing from excitement at opening a window on a glorious past to despair at the destructive nature of time. For most photographers, both ends of the spectrum – from the wonderfully restored art deco motel to the dilapidated wood cabin – are grist for the mill, often because they feel no personal attachment to the material. However, for me, the 'mixed feelings' were typified by staying at the homely El Rancho Motel in Barstow, California, in 1990 ... then learning, as I wrote this book, that it was destroyed by fire in 2022. I offer here the photo I took in 2012 [p. 54] as a celebration of that archetypal Route 66 motel ... and in recognition of the fact that you know you're a 66er when you mourn the passing of another motel!

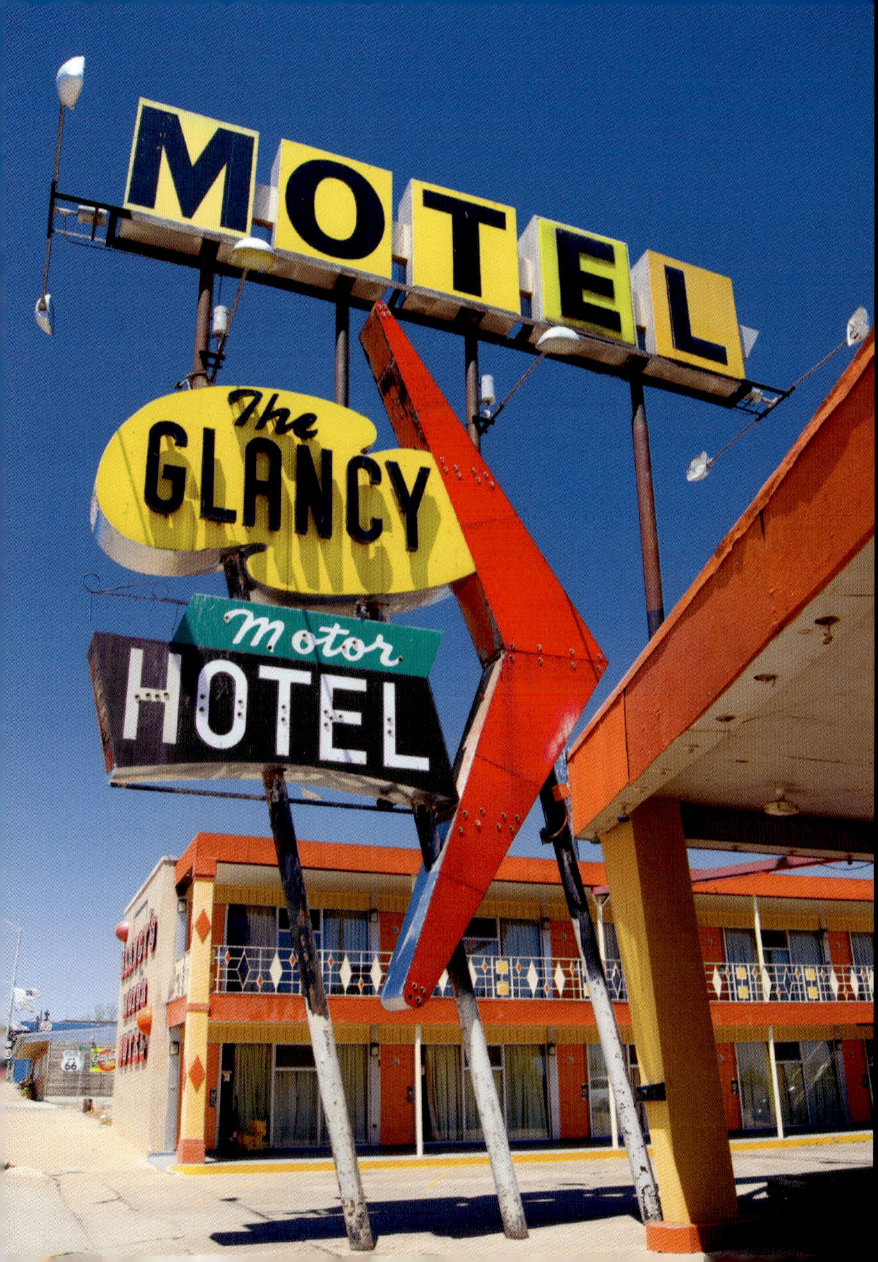

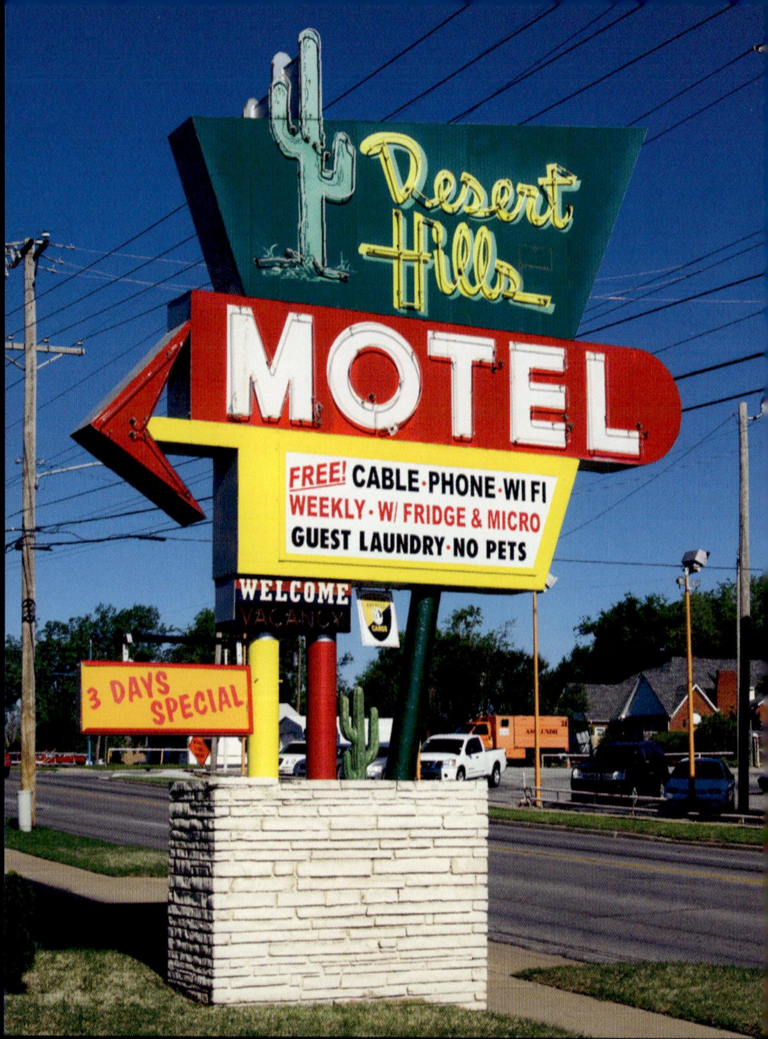

This spread: Welcoming motel signs on Route 66 (left to right): Glancy Motor Hotel, Clinton, OK (demolished except for the sign); Desert Hills Motel, Tulsa, OK; Route 66 Motel, Kingman, AZ; 1946 Munger Moss Motel, Lebanon, MO.

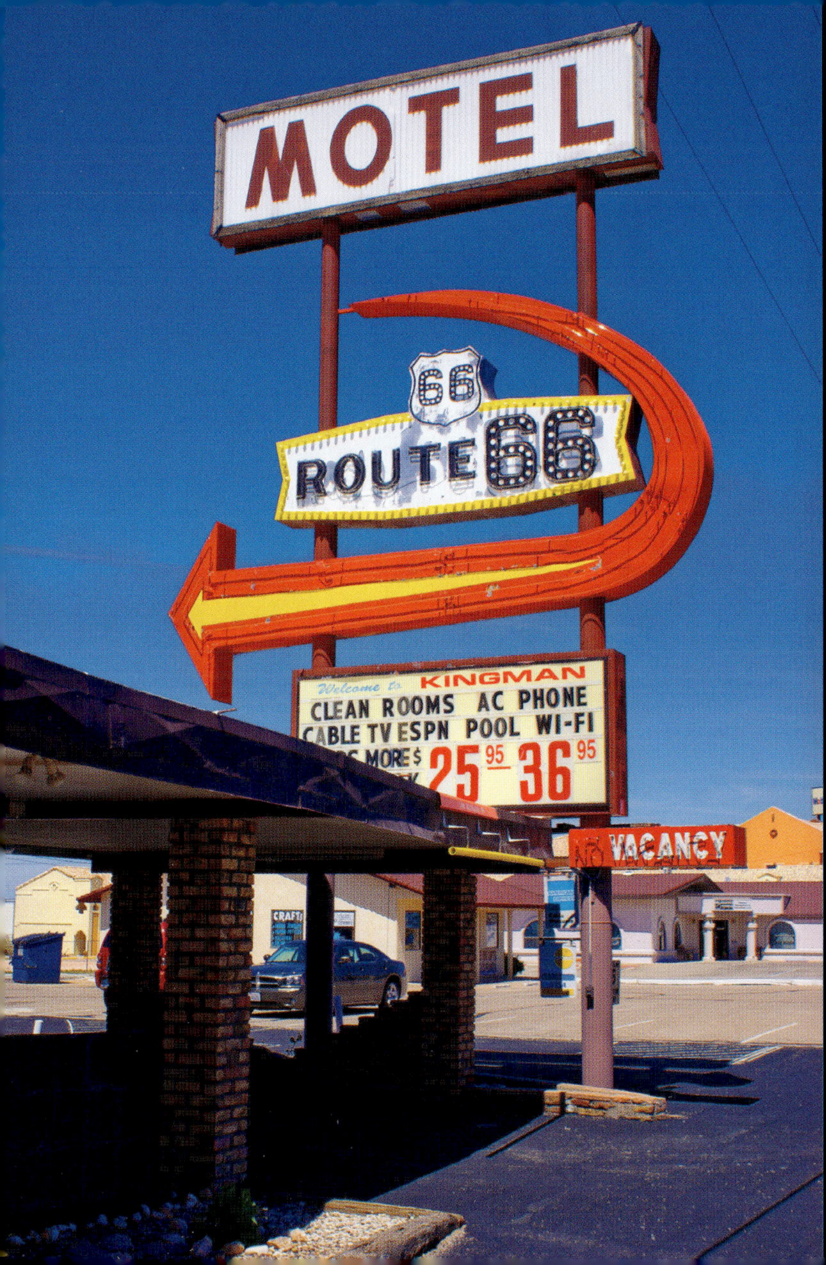
MOTEL
66
ROUTE 66
Welcome to KINGMAN
CLEAN ROOMS AC PHONE
CABLE TV ESPN POOL WI-FI
MORE $ 25 95 36 95
VACANCY

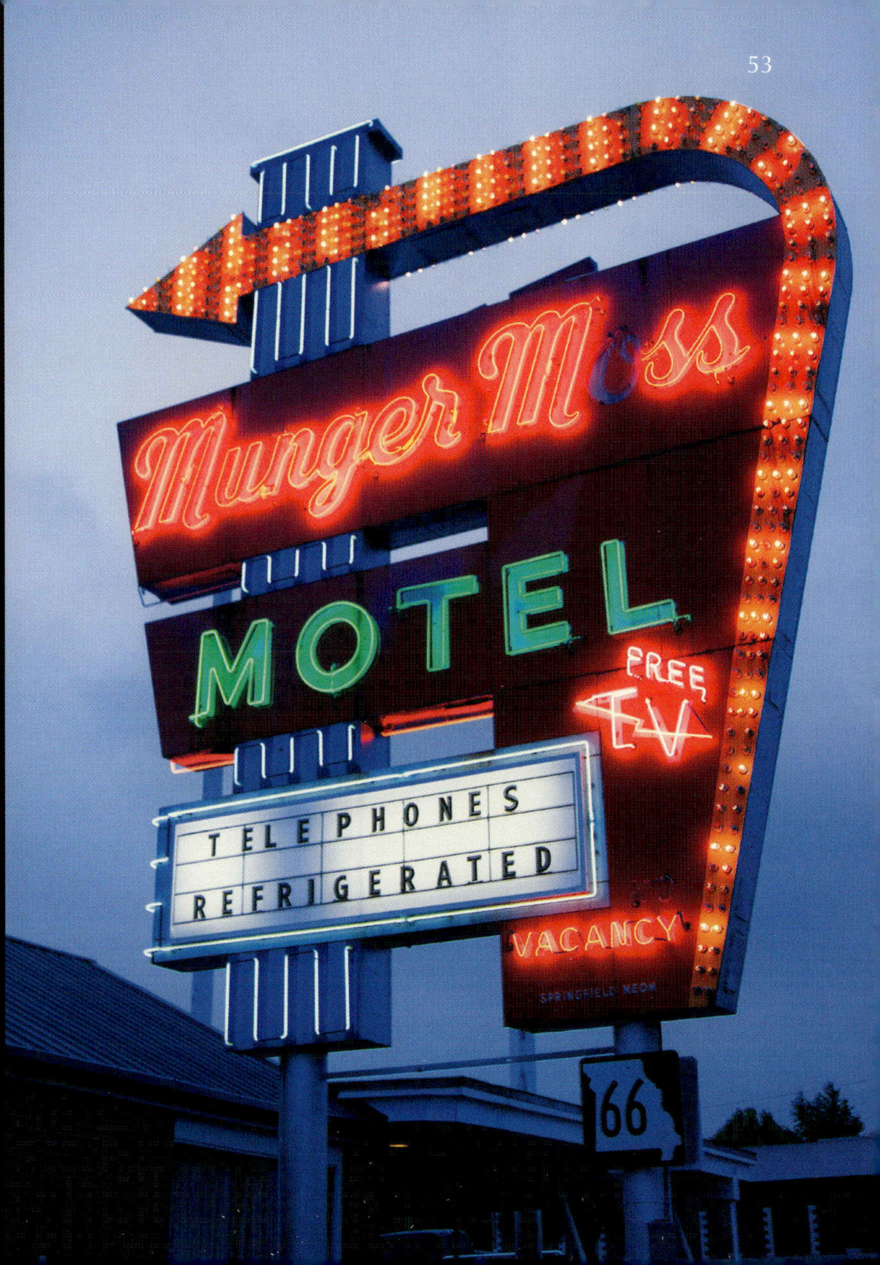
Munger Moss
MOTEL
FREE TV
TELEPHONES
REFRIGERATED
VACANCY
66

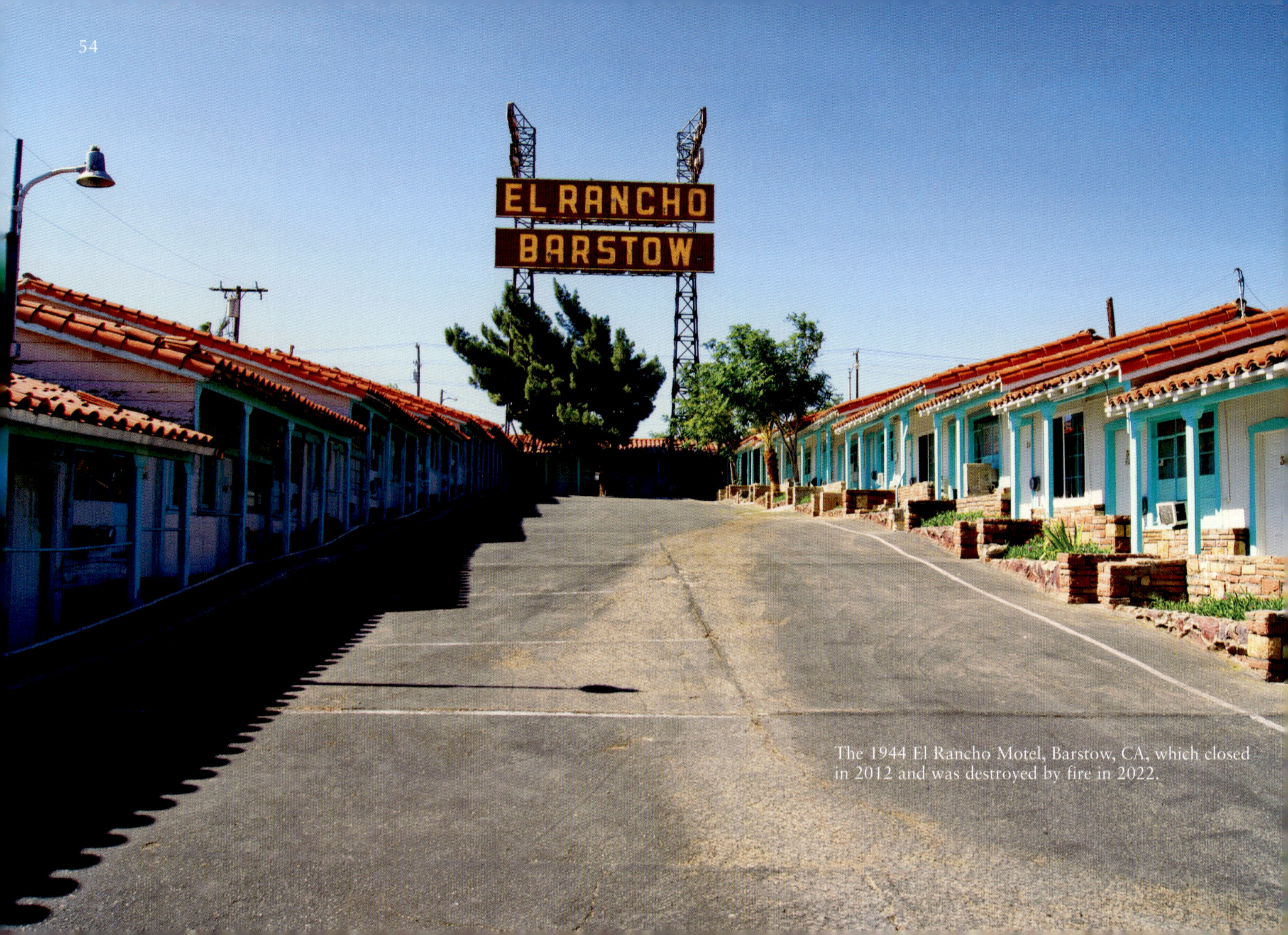

The 1944 El Rancho Motel, Barstow, CA, which closed in 2012 and was destroyed by fire in 2022.

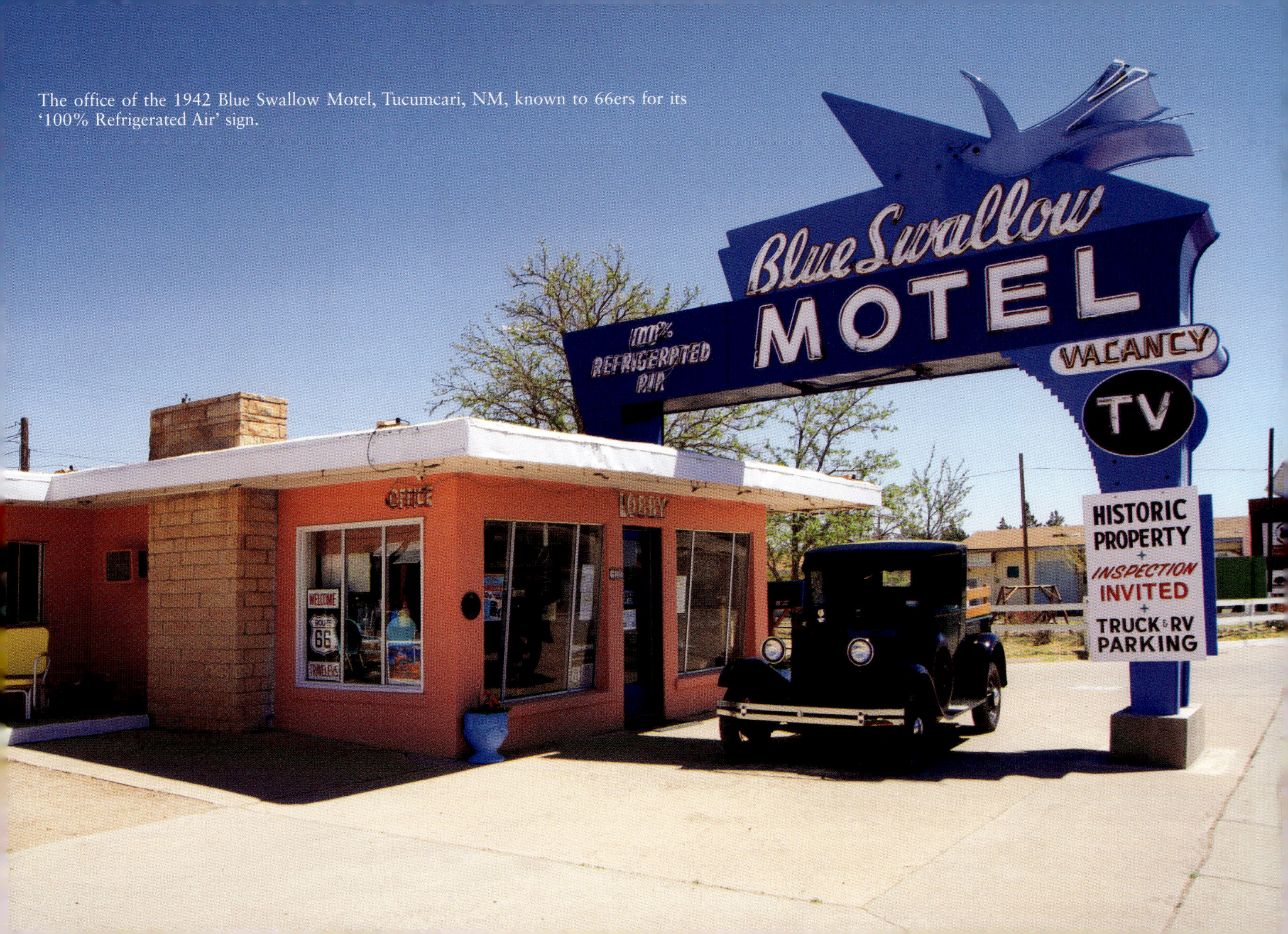

The office of the 1942 Blue Swallow Motel, Tucumcari, NM, known to 66ers for its '100% Refrigerated Air' sign.

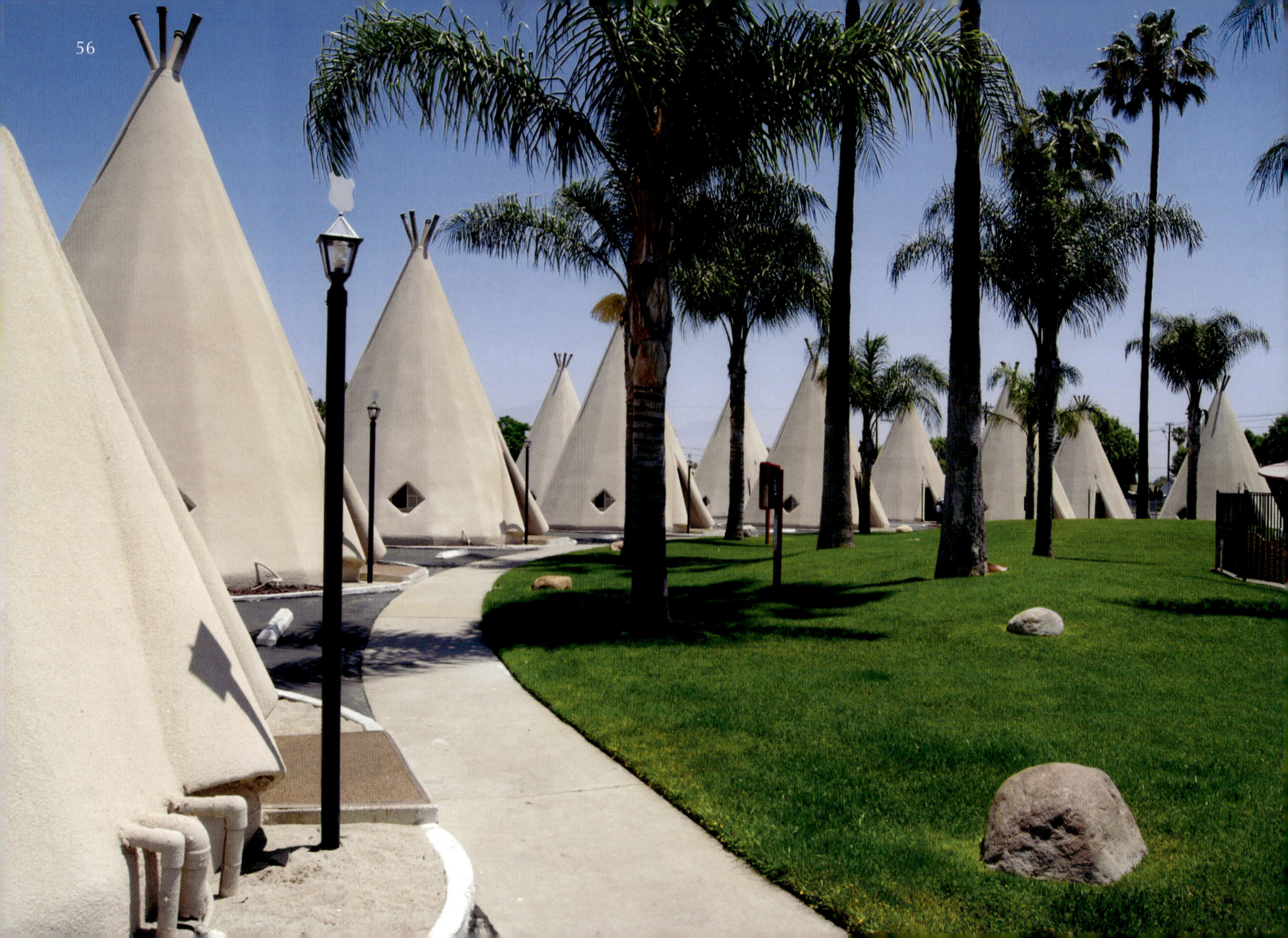

Opposite: About half of the nineteen wigwams comprising the Wigwam Motel on Foothill Boulevard in San Bernadino, CA, which dates from 1949.

Above: The 1937 adobe-style El Vado Motel in Albuquerque, NM, before its renovation.

Below: The pueblo-style De Anza Motor Lodge, Albuquerque, NM.

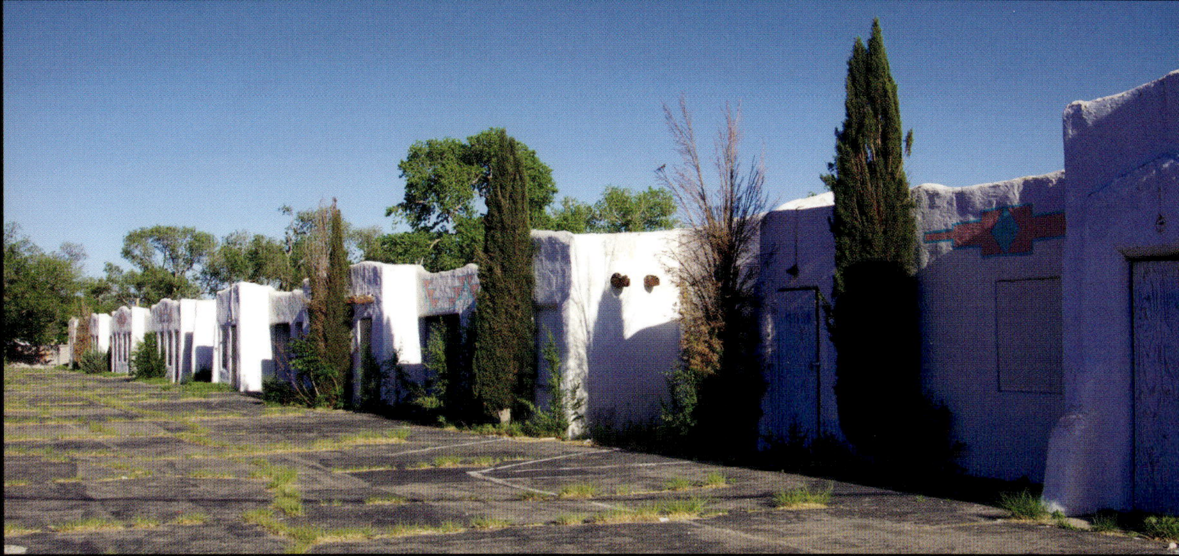

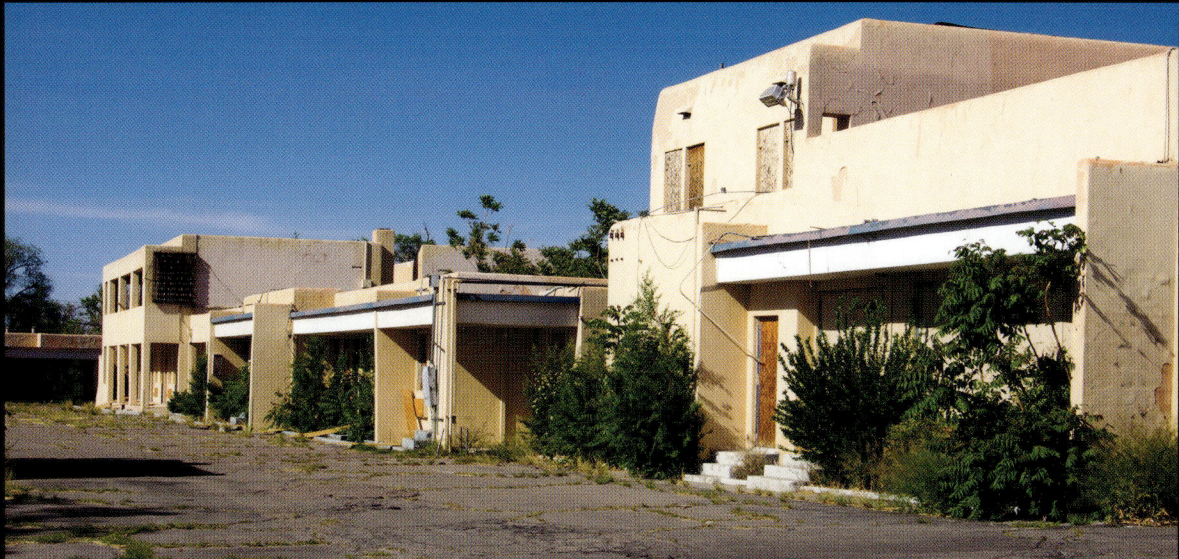

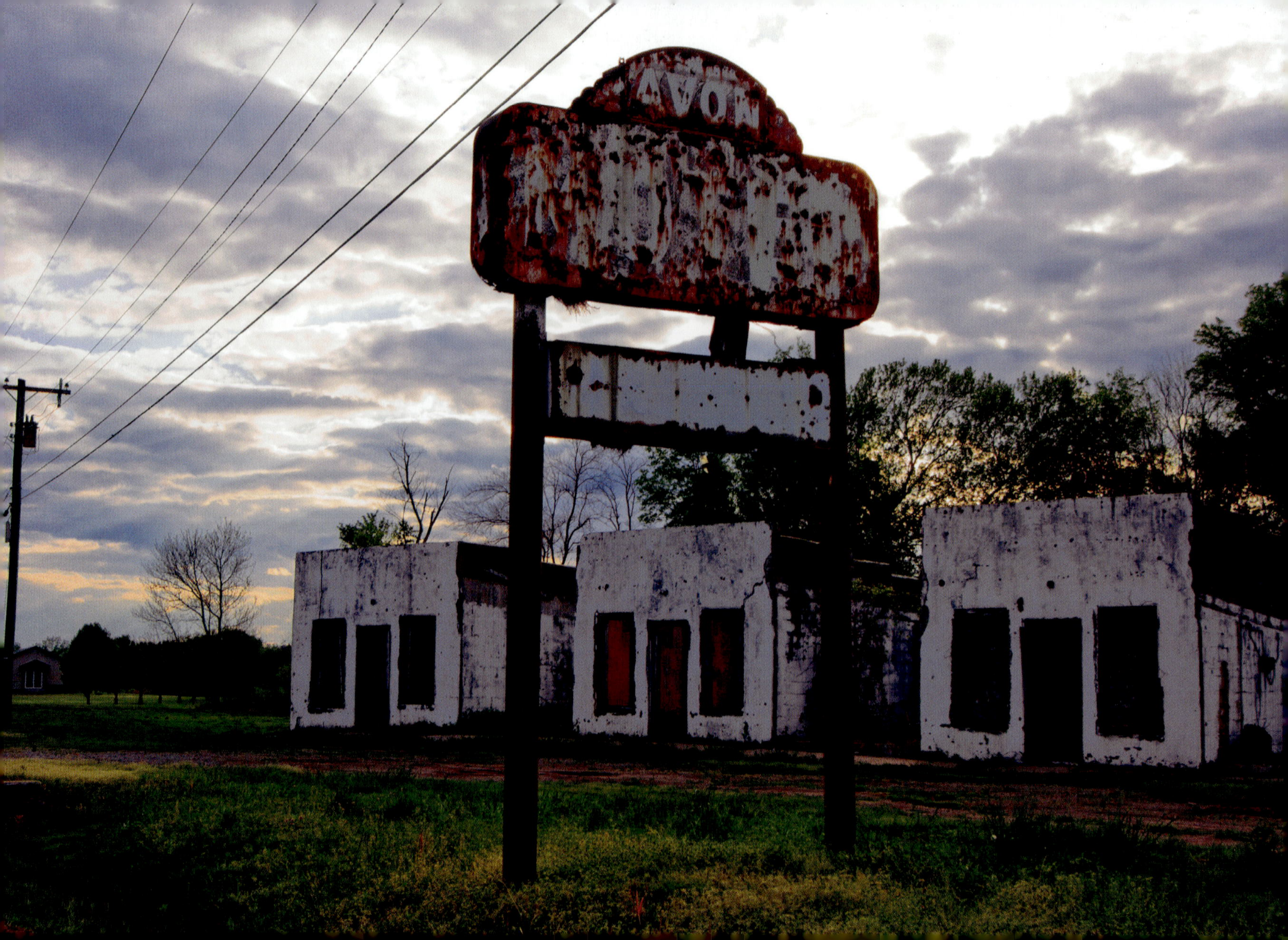
AVON

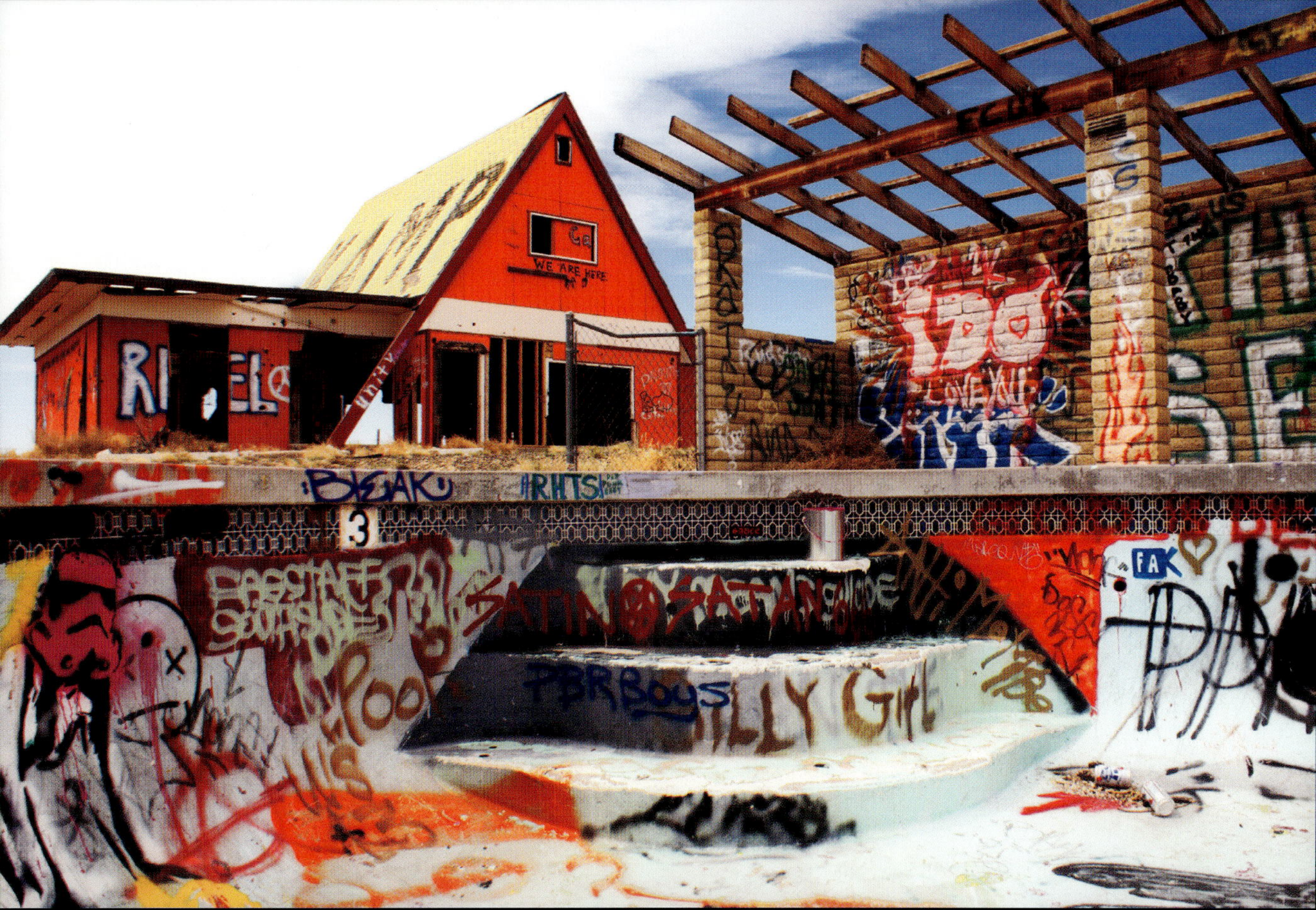

Above: A derelict campsite at Two Guns, AZ, with a swimming pool covered in graffiti.

Opposite: The ruins of the 1936 Avon Motel, Afton, OK, proving that even dilapidated motels have a certain charm (at least for photographers).

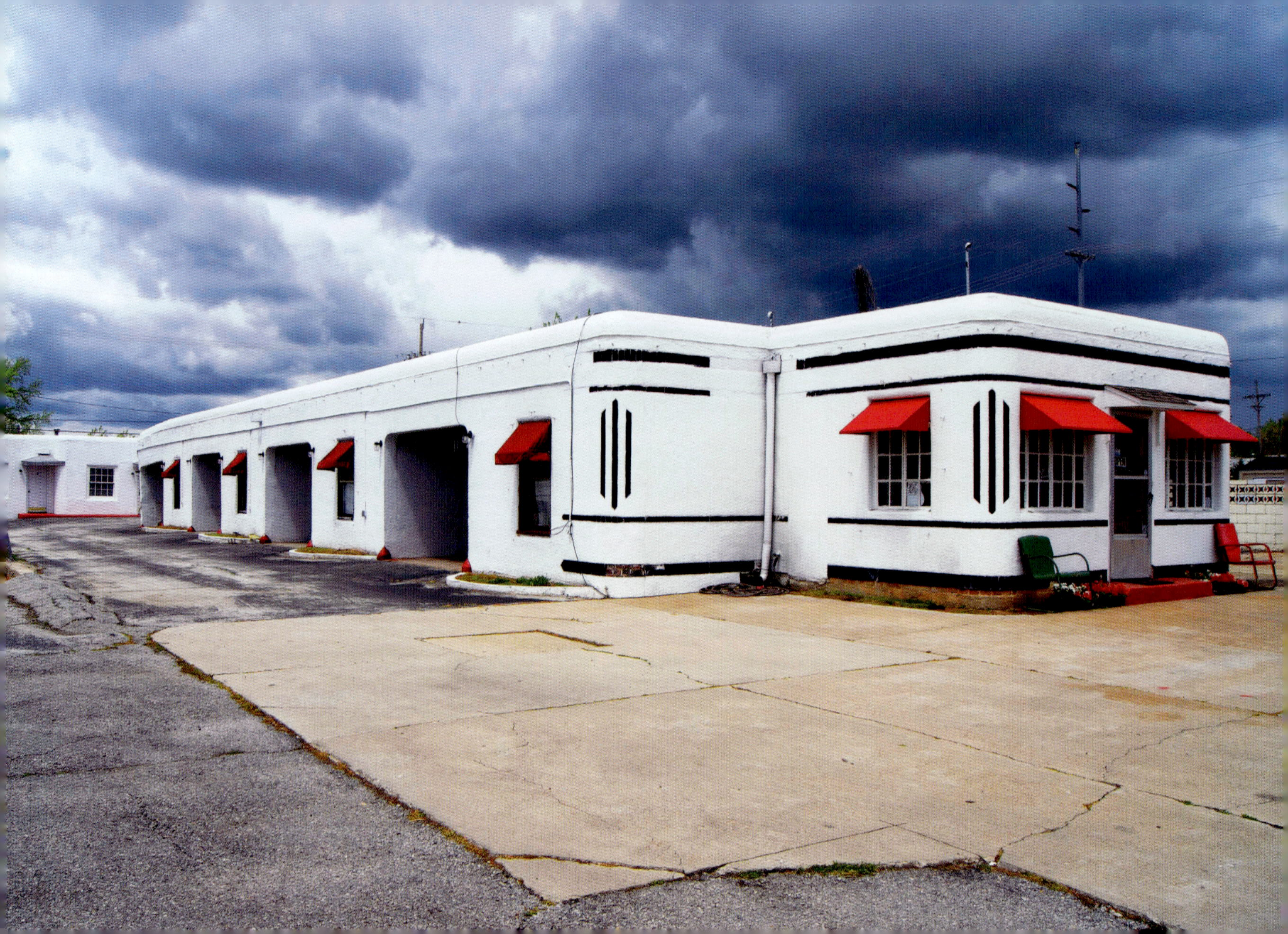

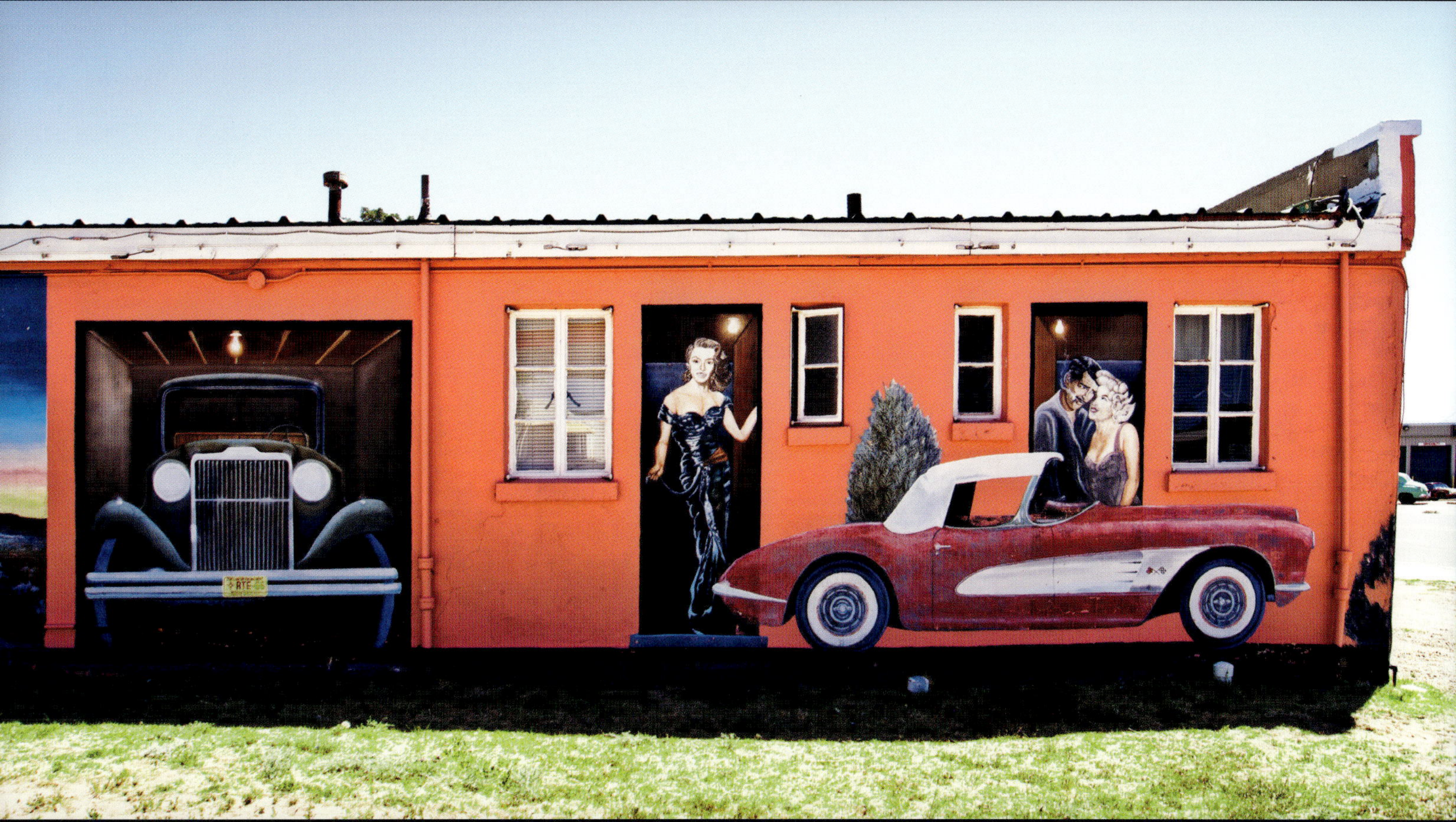

Above: The 'Red Corvette and the Ladies' mural on the Blue Swallow Motel, in Tucumcari, NM, depicts internal garages and references the sleazy aspect of motels as a place for non-marital liaisons.

Opposite: The 1939 Boots Court Motel, Carthage, MO, unusual in its provision of integrated garages.

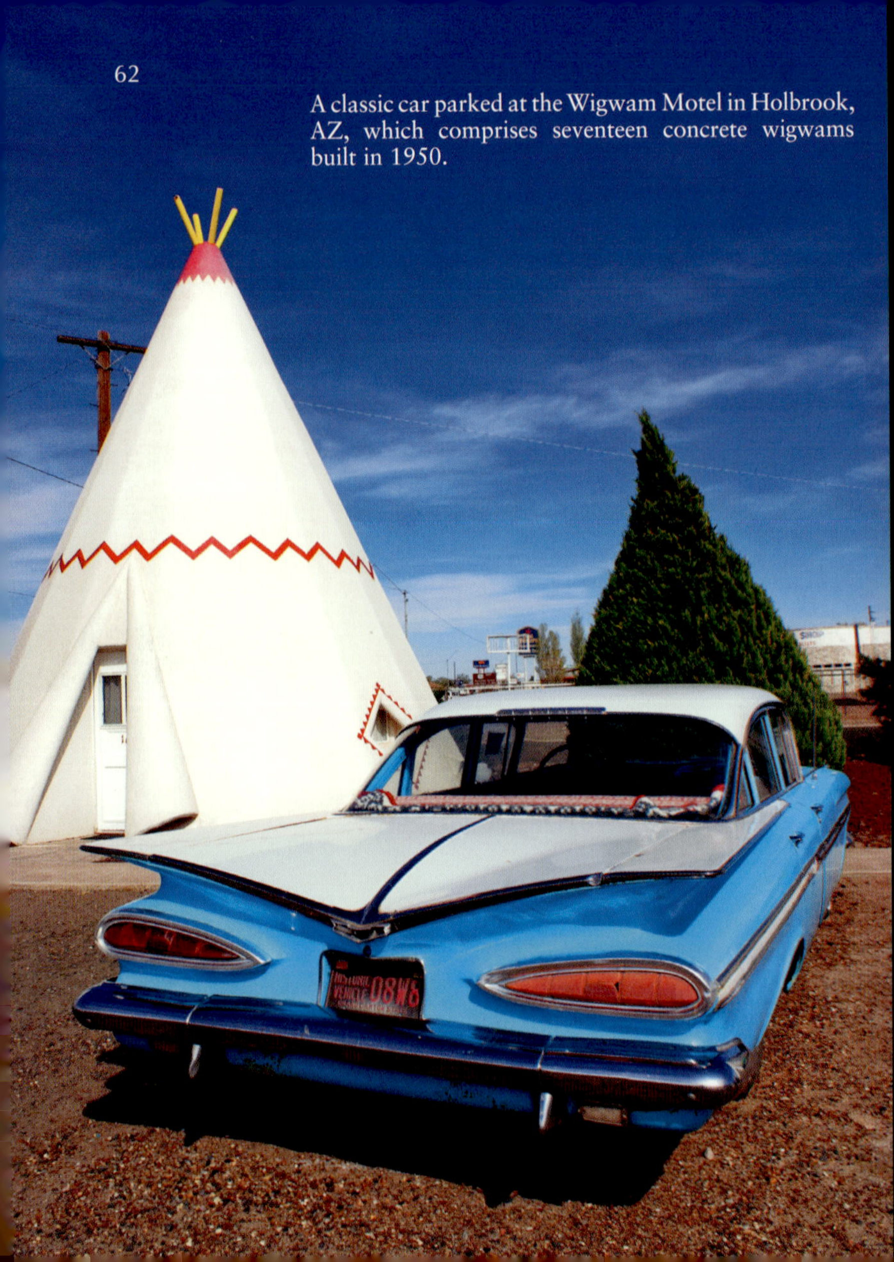

A classic car parked at the Wigwam Motel in Holbrook, AZ, which comprises seventeen concrete wigwams built in 1950.

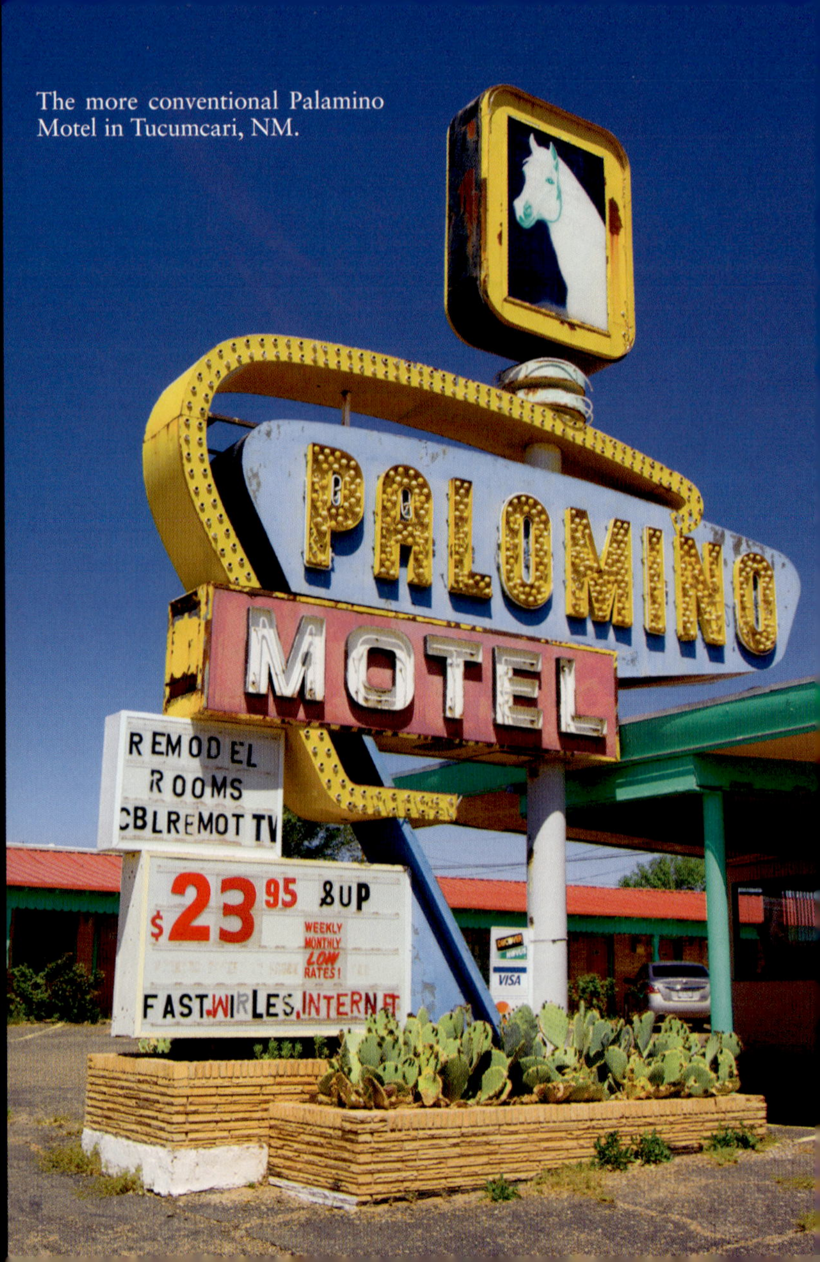

The more conventional Palamino Motel in Tucumcari, NM.

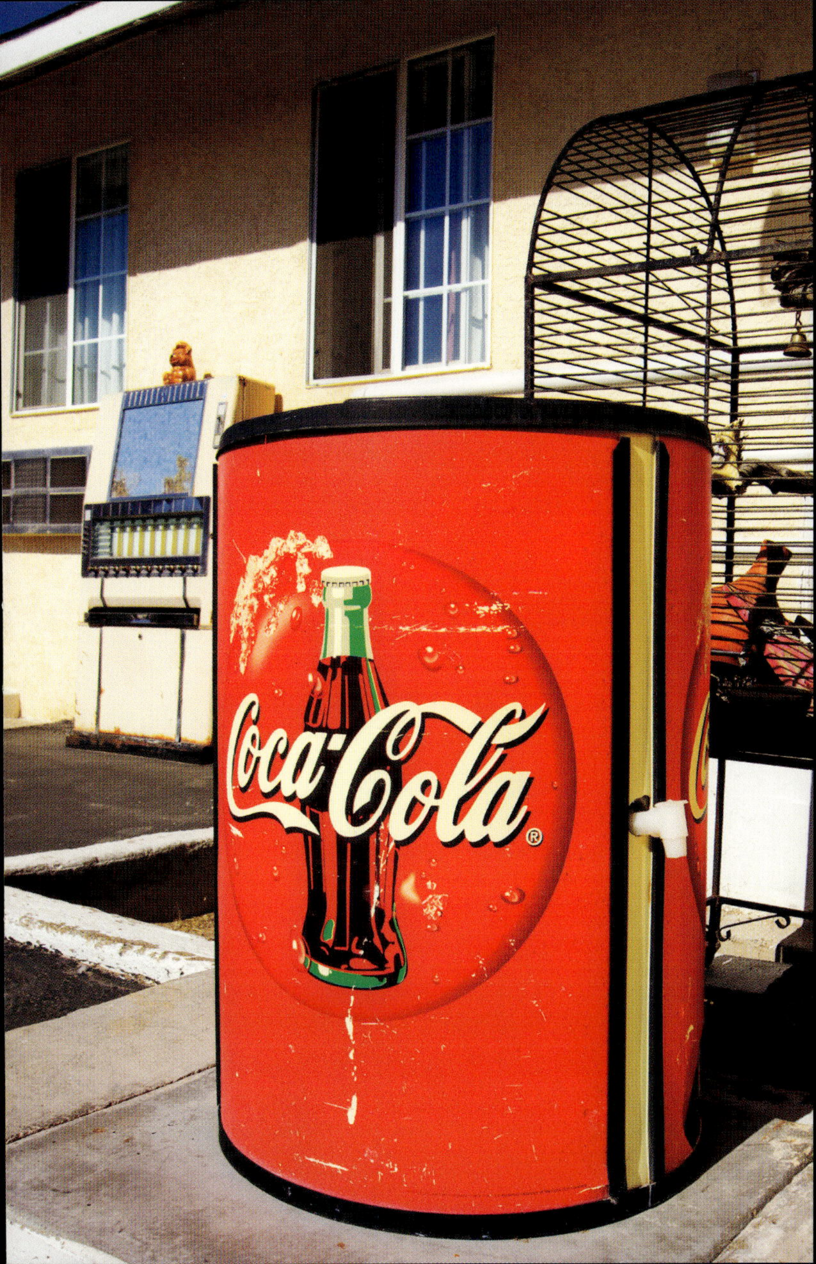

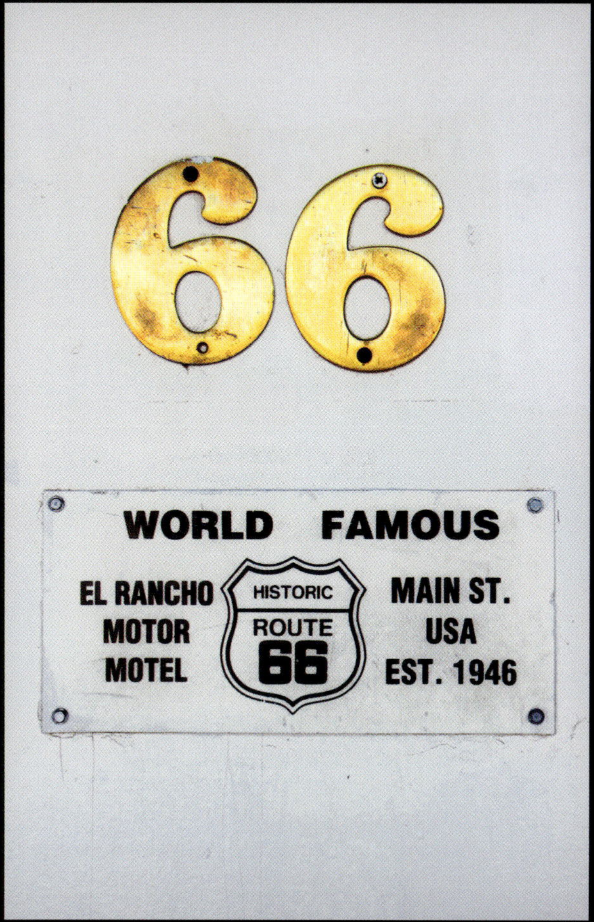

Above: The door to Room 66 at the former El Rancho Motel, Barstow, CA.

Left: A Coca-Cola dispenser outside the Route 66 Motel in Barstow, CA.

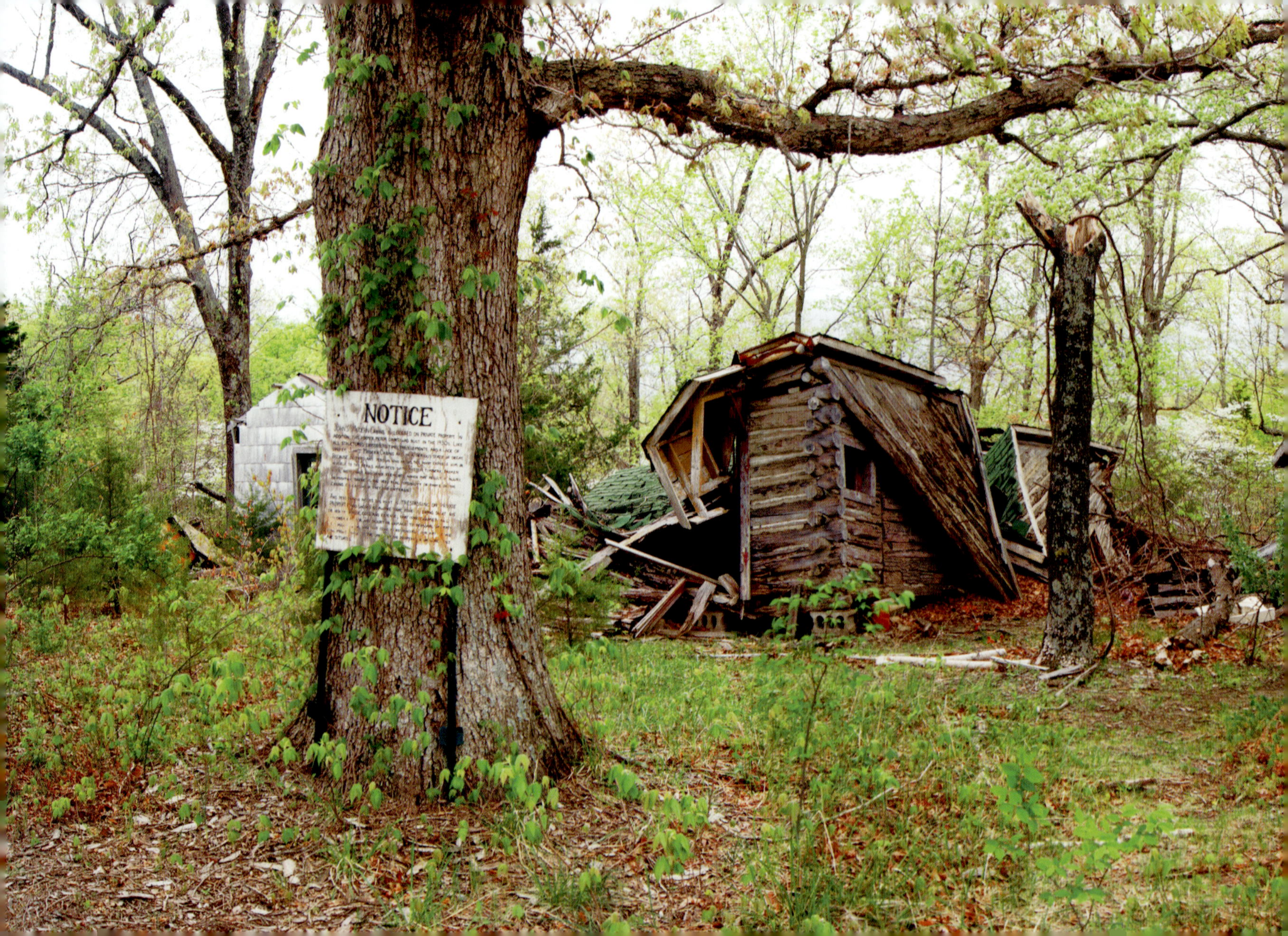
NOTICE

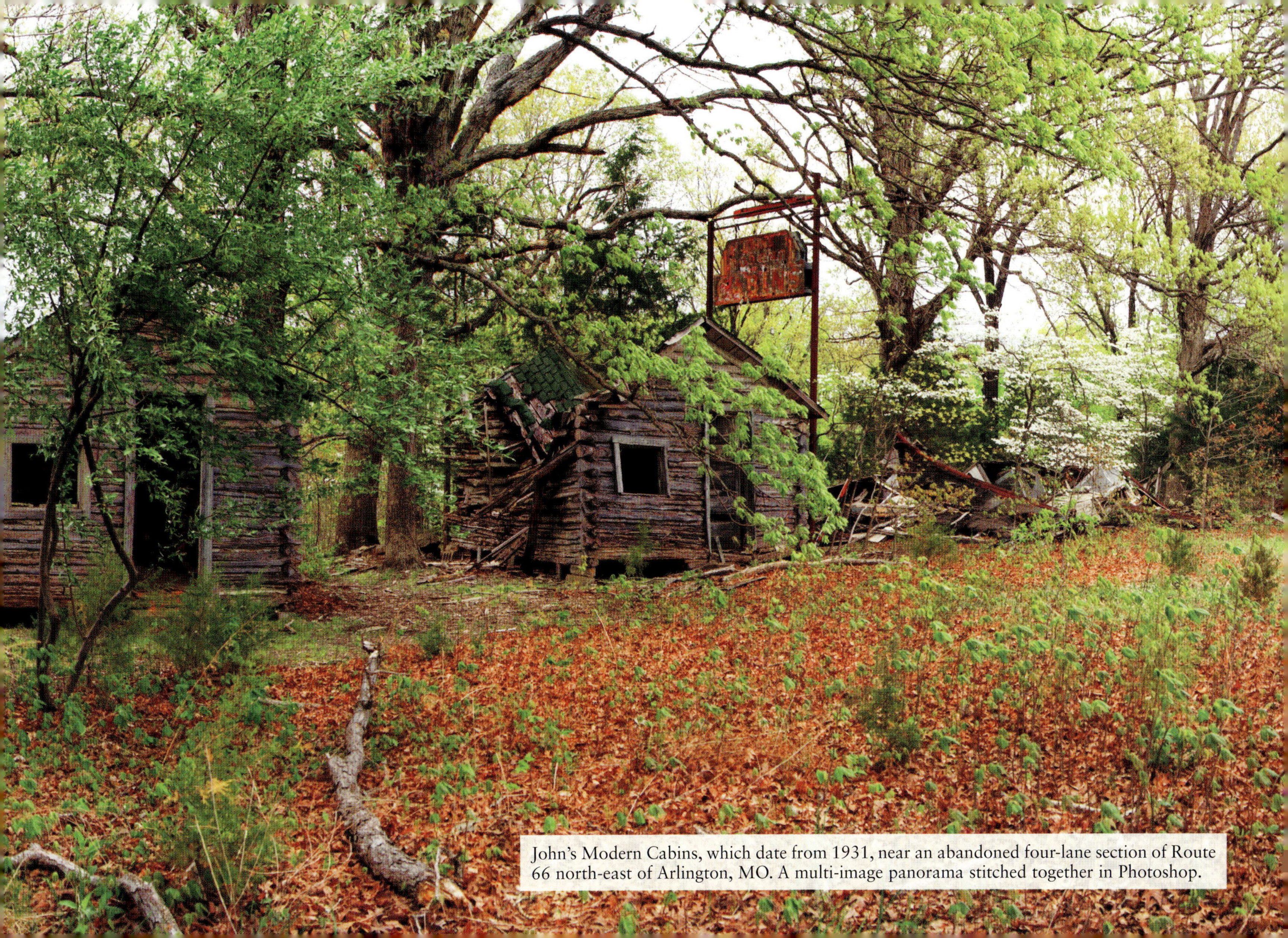

John's Modern Cabins, which date from 1931, near an abandoned four-lane section of Route 66 north-east of Arlington, MO. A multi-image panorama stitched together in Photoshop.

Chapter 6

DINERS

In the same way that cars on Route 66 needed fuel, the people in those cars needed food; and it was the diner that met that need. The history of the American diner has been traced back to 1872, when an entrepreneur from Rhode Island decided to sell food from a horse-drawn wagon; the wagon had serving windows down each side and is considered by some to be the first diner with 'walk-up service'. These 'lunch wagons' were commercially produced from 1887, and the design was even awarded a patent in 1893.

By 1913, however, most diners had become 'static', some of them repurposed from railroad dining cars and delivered – by road – to their final resting place. From the 1920s onwards, standardised, purpose-built diners were prefabricated in factories, fully fitted out with cooking facilities and seating along a counter. An example is the Valentine Diner – built by the Valentine Manufacturing Company of Wichita, Kansas, between 1938 and 1974 – which was supplied with five to ten stools around an L-shaped counter [pp. 68, 70–71]. This early example of the 'plug-and-play' concept made it easier to establish a new small business along the growing transport infrastructure, including Route 66, since all that was needed was a suitable base or foundation and hook-ups to whatever services were available at the time. As a result, the culture of the diner spread gradually west from the eastern cities and became a feature on the open road.

As America entered the art deco period, diners increasingly adopted the 'aluminium aesthetic'. Although this was mainly a reflection of the 'modern look' (typified by the Airstream trailer from 1927), it was also a reference to the shiny railroad dining cars that preceded the prefabs. As the need for diners grew, much like motels, regional or national diner chains appeared and grew alongside the independent 'mom and pop' diners.

This led to the smorgasbord of diner types and architectures that we see today. Indeed, the diner as a species is so common that it becomes difficult to define – it's more of a case of 'knowing one when you see it'. Beyond this, it is sometimes a matter of personal preference or self-definition on the part of the owner, so we find diners named as cafés or restaurants, which to the objective eye look pretty much the same. All that said, diners on Route 66 fit into two main types: derelict and operational, both of which are prime targets for photographers.

Example types include 'historic diners', such as the Maid-Rite sandwich shop in Springfield, Illinois, which has been preserved for posterity and has a National Register of Historic Places plaque to prove it! The Eat-Rite Diner in St Louis [p. 68] is equally historic, having been an eatery since the 1930s, but its future is less certain. At the other end of the scale are the modern-day diners built to evoke the historic vibe, which may be art deco-styled and neon-enhanced or simply brightly painted. Then there are the quirky examples, like the Java Stop in Dwight, Illinois, constructed from a couple of stacked transport containers covered in an eye-catching mural [p. 73].

Signage is, of course, an important part of the mix. Like gas stations and motels, diners sought to attract travellers to their establishments with a gaudy array of brightly-painted, sometimes flag-adorned signs on high poles. In fact, the clutter of signage allowed along the major routes is an aspect of American road travel noticed by foreign visitors: diners and other businesses are advertised many miles in advance and, as you pass a centre of population on the freeway, the horizon is punctuated by a forest of competing signage.

Surviving (or reimagined) examples on Route 66 include wooden painted signs, metal (sometimes neon-lit) signs and everything in between. One of the most unusual is the clock that advertised the Polk-a-Dot Drive-In in Braidwood, Illinois, which served burgers from a painted school bus from 1956 before opening as a restaurant in 1962 [p. 77].

Then we come to the famous fibreglass figures used across the nation to advertise local businesses. The first of the type – made in 1962 by International Fiberglass of Venice, California, for the Lumberjack Café in Flagstaff, Arizona – was a facsimile of the North American folklore character Paul Bunyan carrying an axe. It was from garage businesses, however, that the 5-to-7-metre-tall figures gained their fame: because they served to advertise tyres or car exhausts (known in the US as mufflers), they became known collectively as 'Muffler Men'.

Of the few remaining figures on Route 66, my personal favourite is the Gemini Giant, erected in Wilmington, Illinois, to advertise the Launching Pad restaurant. Having opened in 1960, the owners decided to celebrate the American space programme – in particular the Gemini missions of that decade – by rebranding the restaurant and installing a repurposed Muffler Man holding a silver rocket. Once you realise the figure was designed to hold an exhaust, you notice how clumsily he supports the rocket; this is even more the case for the man holding a hot dog in Atlanta, Illinois [pp. 76–77]. The Gemini Giant became an icon of Route 66 and has, surely, attracted many more people to the restaurant than would otherwise have been the case for a small town in Illinois. Unfortunately, the restaurant had to close, but the giant was saved and, in 2024, moved to a nondescript location in town.

Taking a retrospective overview of these three key elements of roadside Americana – gas stations, motels and diners – there seem to be very few examples of combined or integrated businesses. Of course, the exceptions break the rule, such as the once-fine art deco-influenced diner in Glenrio, Texas [p. 79], with matching gas station immediately adjacent. Also of note is Roy's in Amboy, California, which opened as a gas station in 1938, but was expanded to include a café and auto court in the 1940s.

Exceptions aside, gas stations rarely had diners attached and motels rarely incorporated gas stations. Today, it seems obvious that the 'captive market' for a motel would also require feeding and, since they arrived in a car, might also be tempted to fill the tank before moving on. Perhaps it was simply that the three types of business attracted different types of owner; perhaps it was the fact that the other elements were always available nearby. It's all part of the enigma of Route 66.

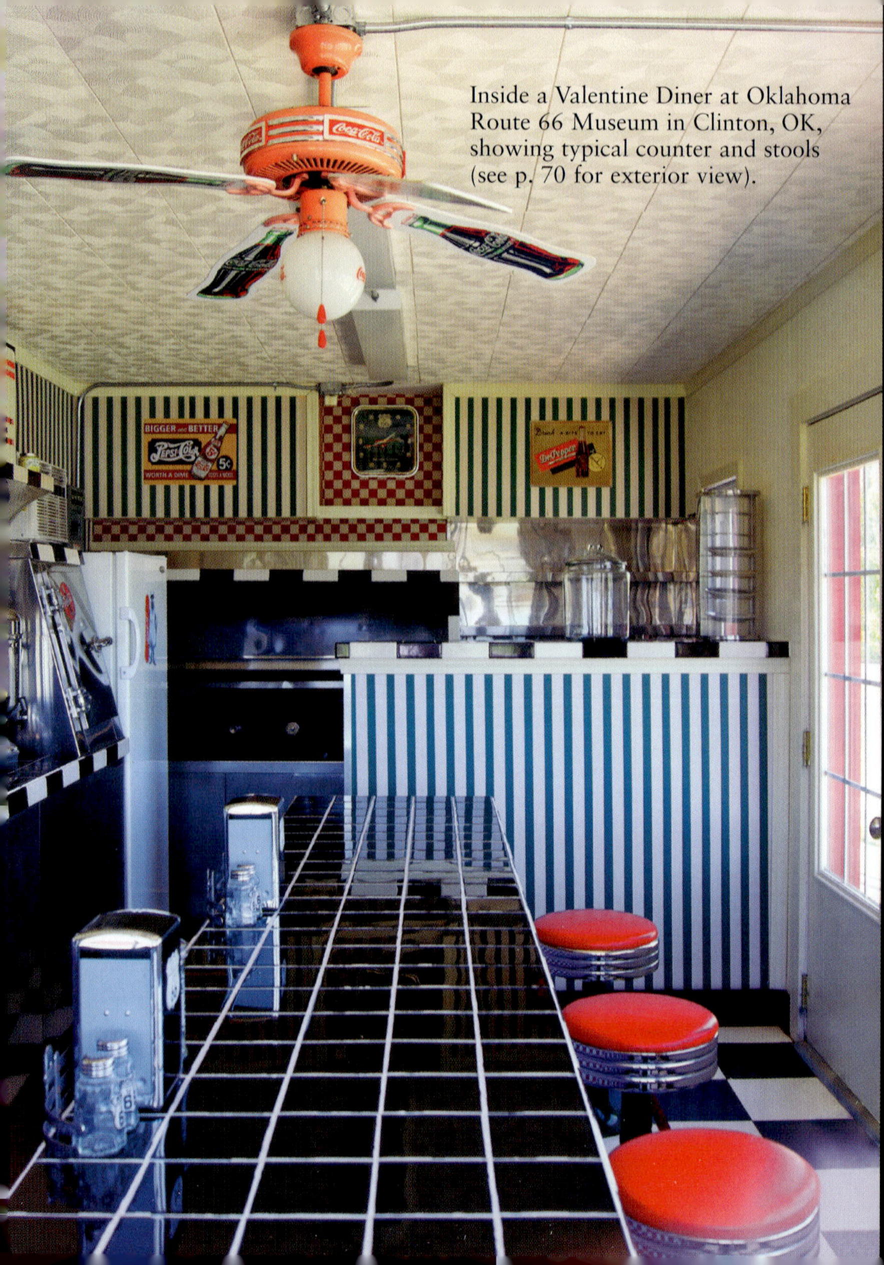

Inside a Valentine Diner at Oklahoma Route 66 Museum in Clinton, OK, showing typical counter and stools (see p. 70 for exterior view).

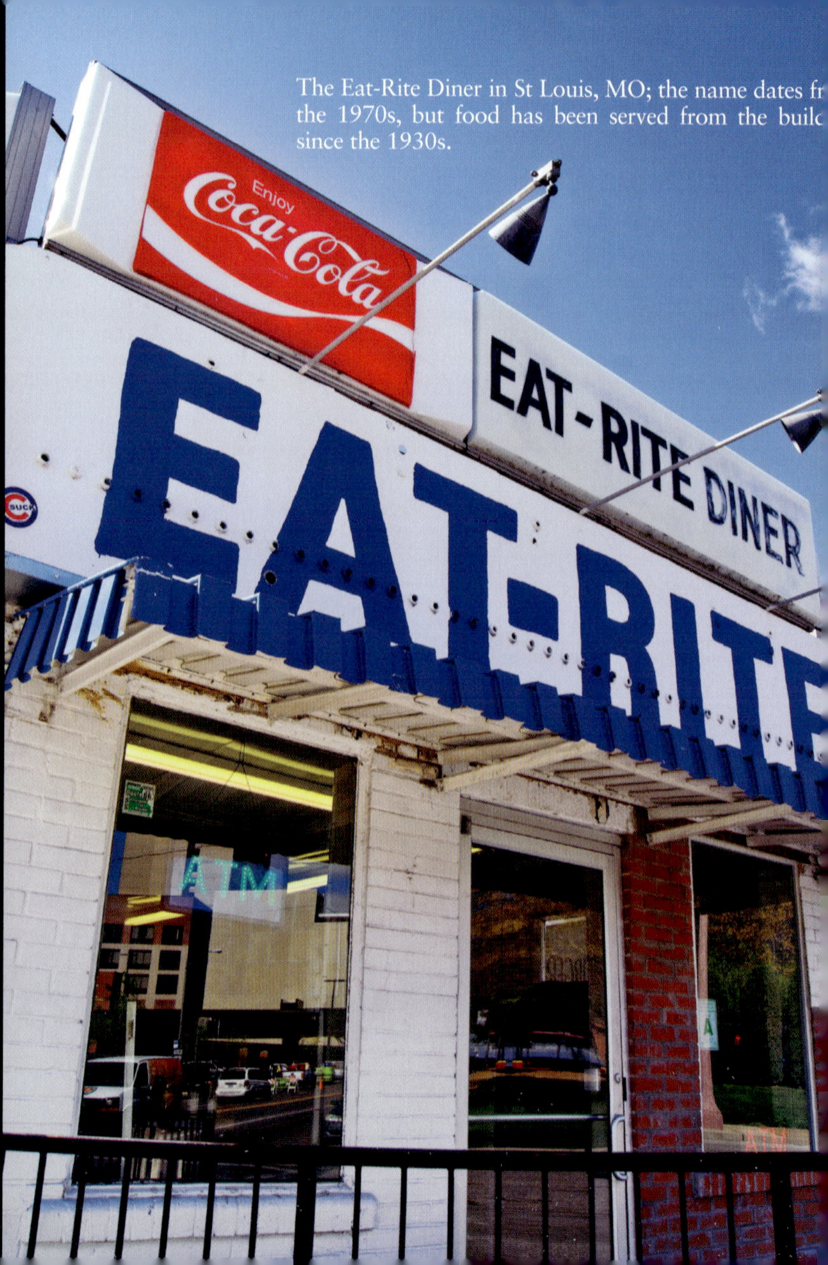

The Eat-Rite Diner in St Louis, MO; the name dates fr the 1970s, but food has been served from the builc since the 1930s.

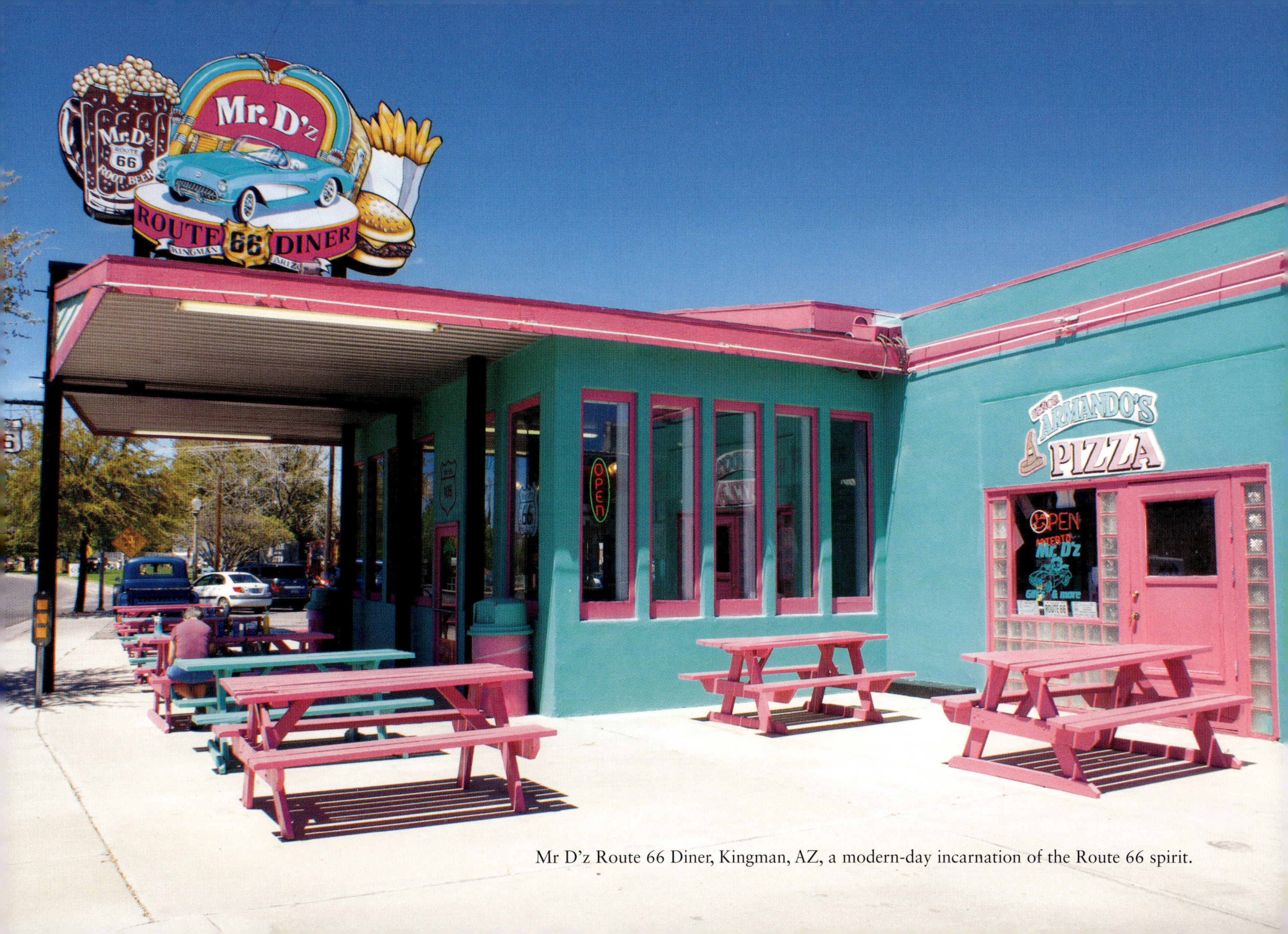

Mr D'z Route 66 Diner, Kingman, AZ, a modern-day incarnation of the Route 66 spirit.

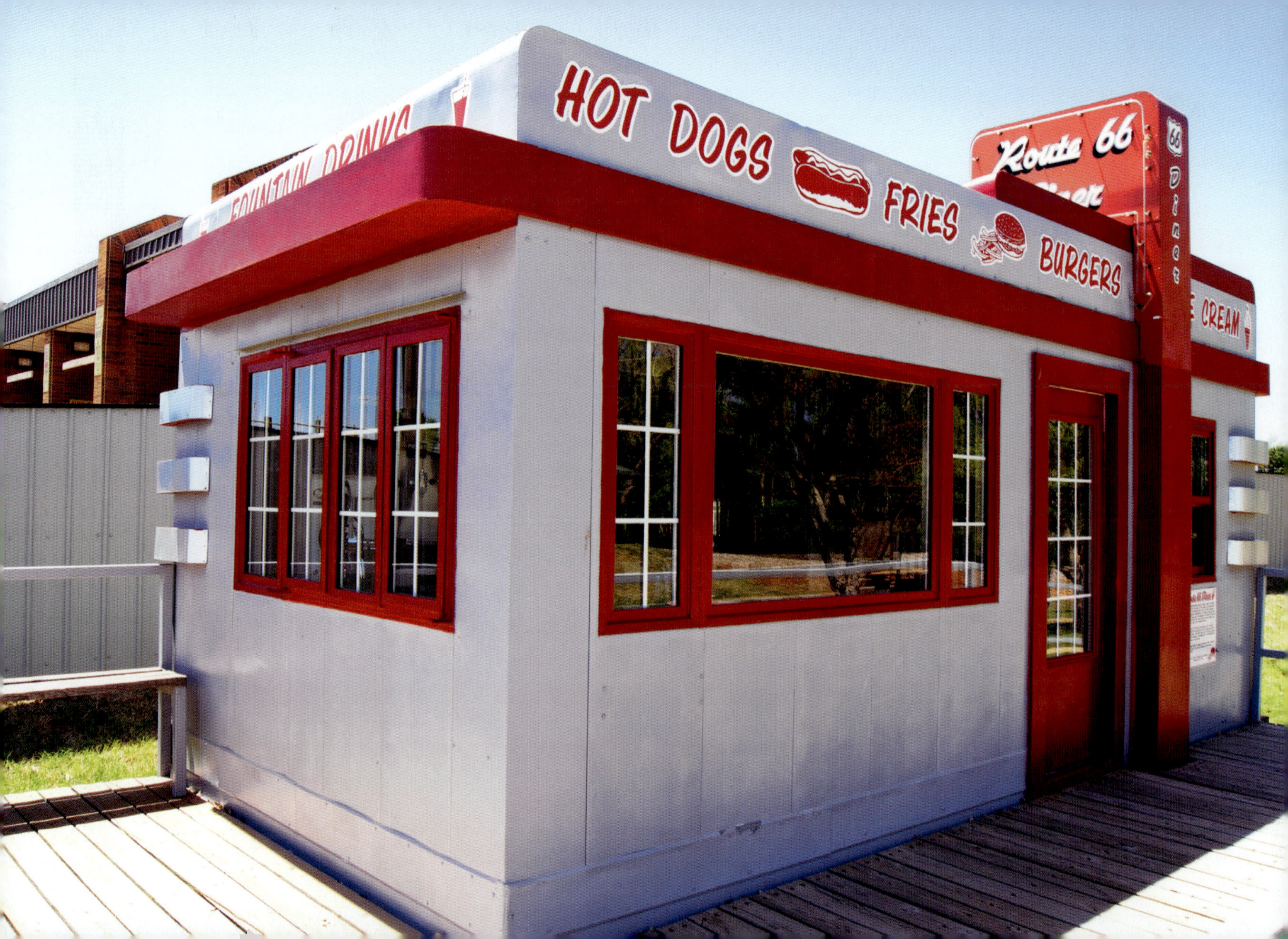
HOT DOGS
FRIES
BURGERS
Route 66
Diner

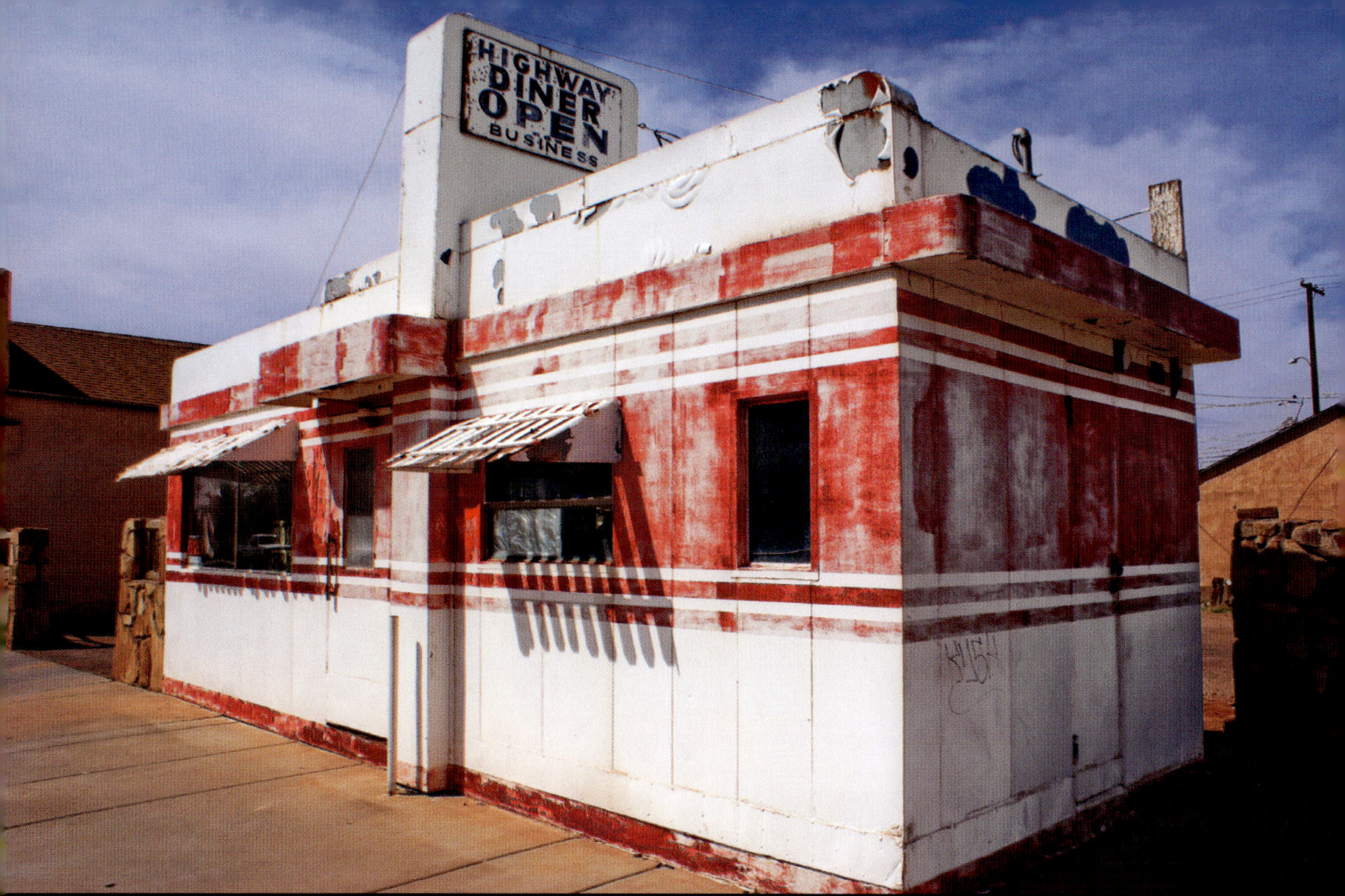

Above: The Highway Diner in Winslow, AZ (corner of E 2nd and Colorado). A prime example of the transitory nature of Route 66, i
was nicely refurbished in the years before this image was captured in 2011, but by 2025 it was whitewashed, future uncertain.

Opposite: A Valentine Diner at Oklahoma Route 66 Museum in Clinton, OK, originally sited in Shamrock, TX, where it operated as

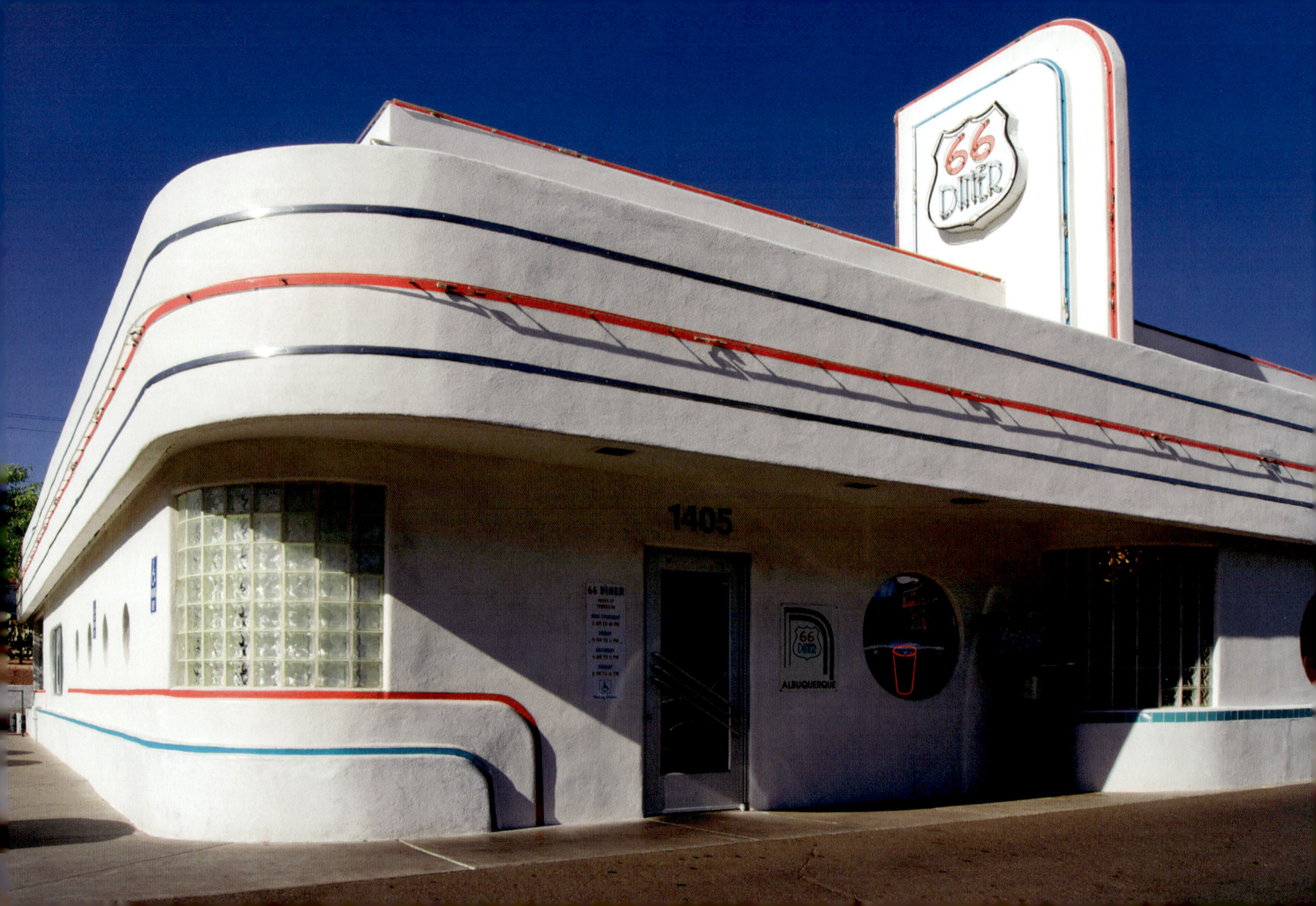
66
DINER
1405
66 DINER
66
DINER
ALBUQUERQUE

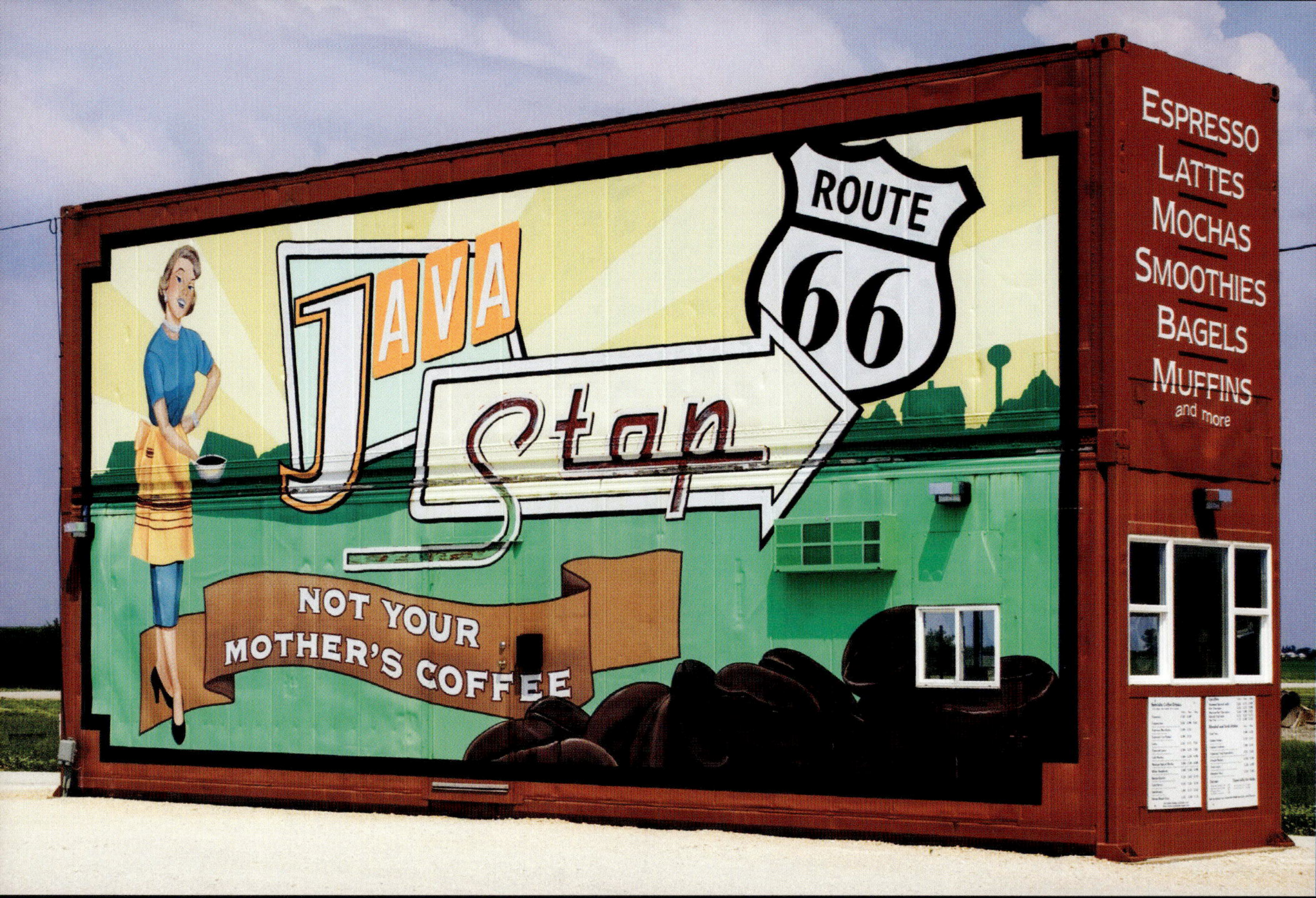

Above: The temporary Java Stop in Dwight, IL, an inventive use of two transport containers.

Opposite: The art deco-style 66 Diner on Central Avenue, Albuquerque, NM, which was built around the shell of a 1940s gas station in 1987, then rebuilt after a fire in 1995.

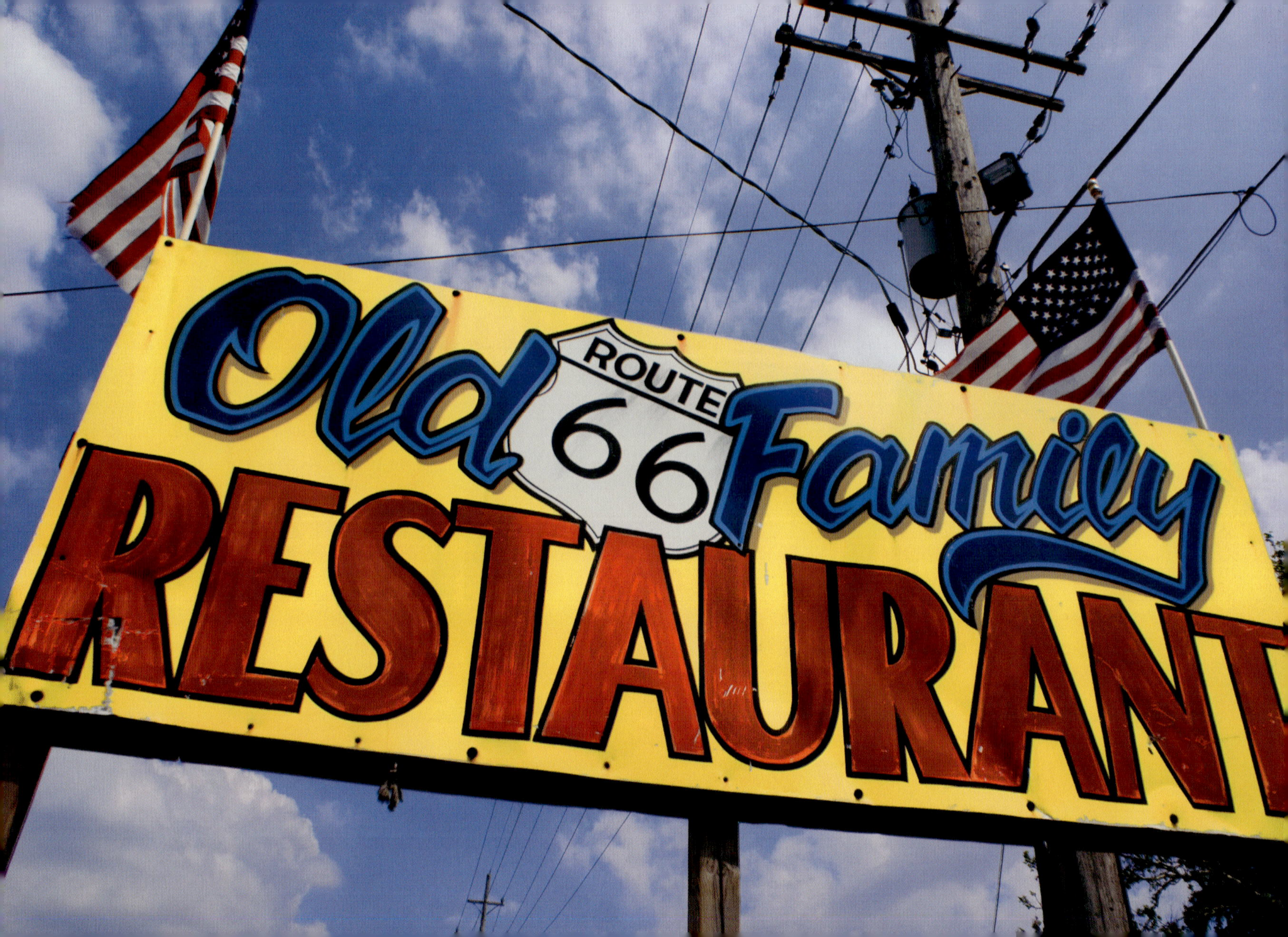
Old Family
ROUTE
66
RESTAURANT

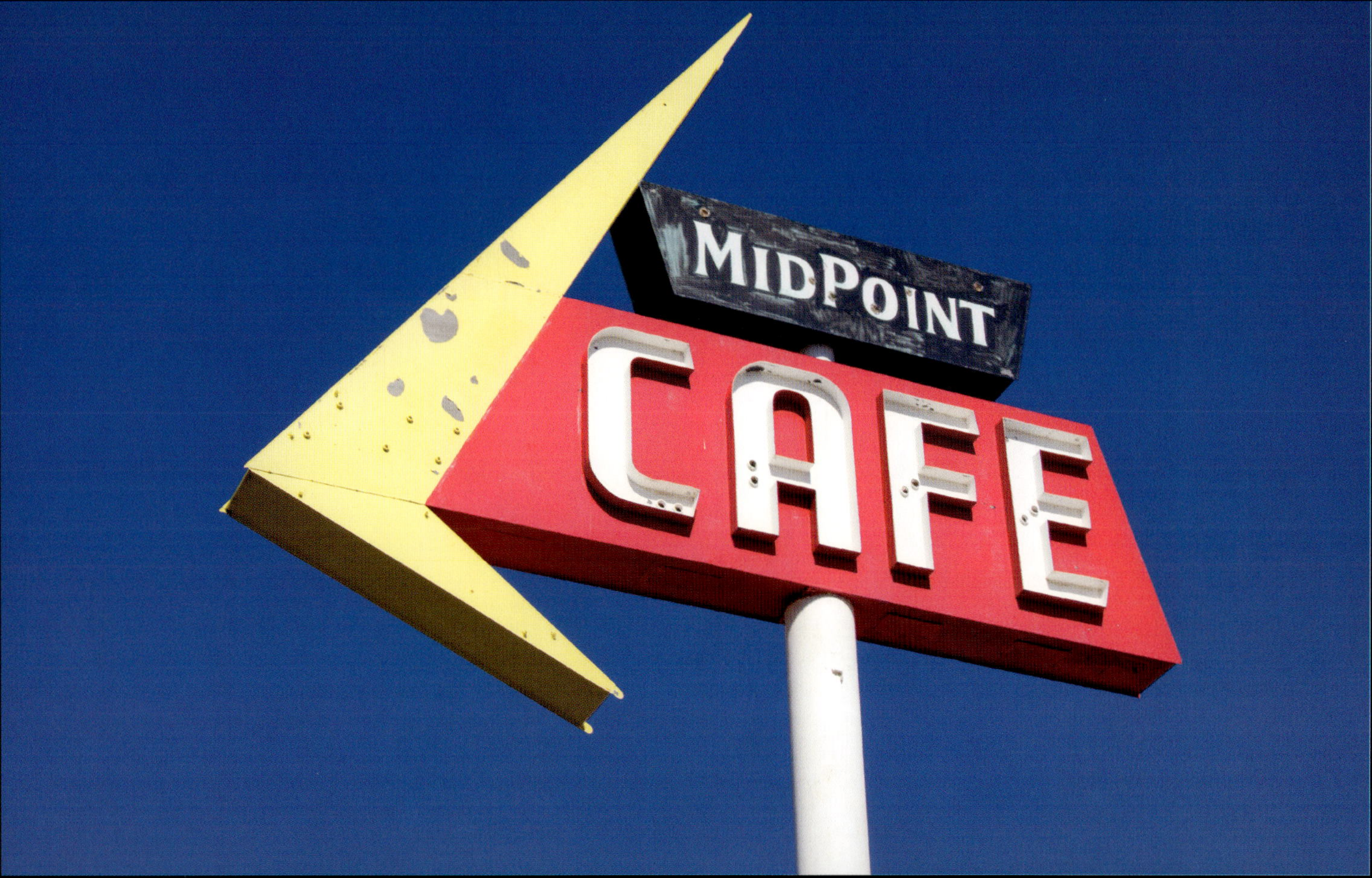

Above: The Midpoint Café in Adrian, TX, was built in 1928 and is one of the oldest continuously-operated cafés along Route 66.

Opposite: A sign for the Old Route 66 Family Restaurant, Dwight, IL, evokes an earlier age.

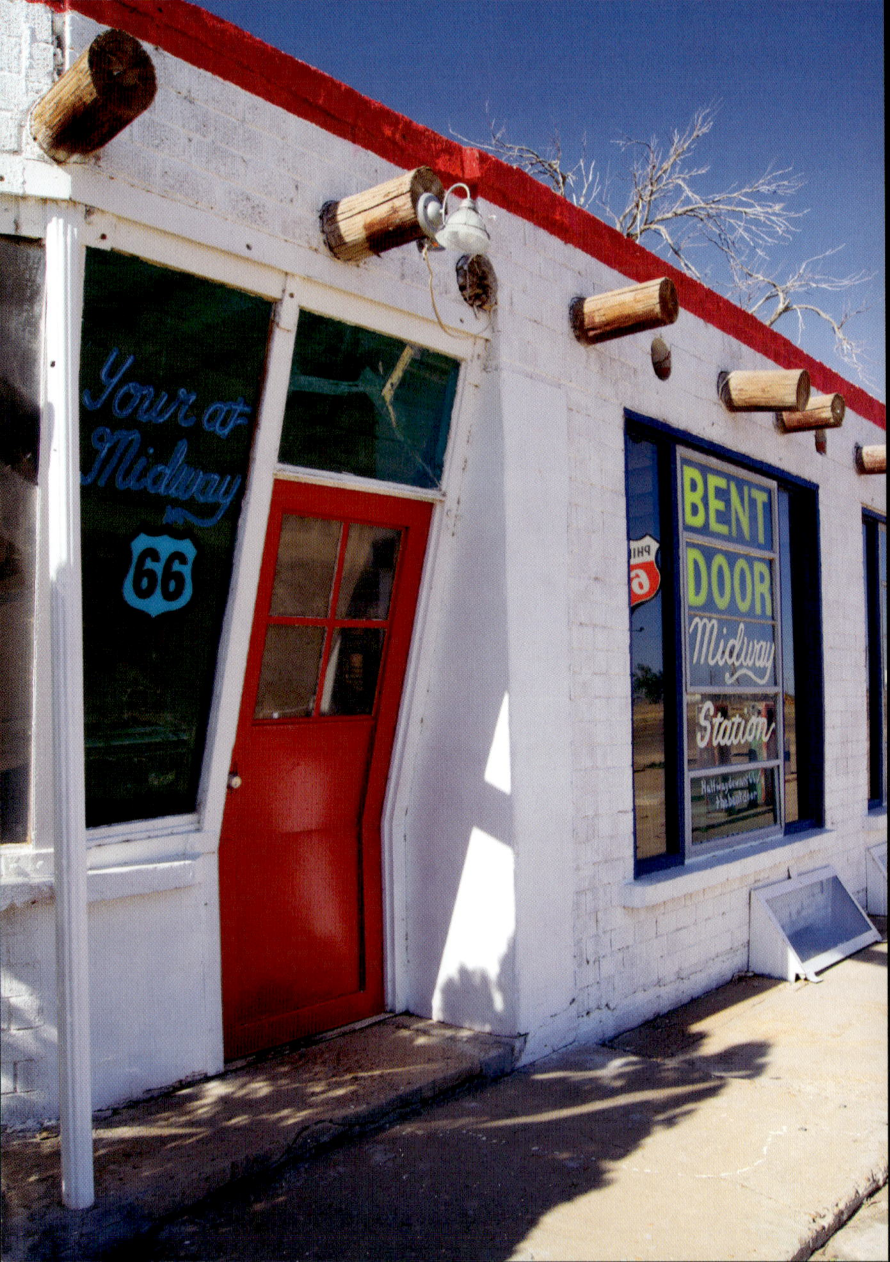

Your at
Midway
66
BENT
DOOR
Midway
Station

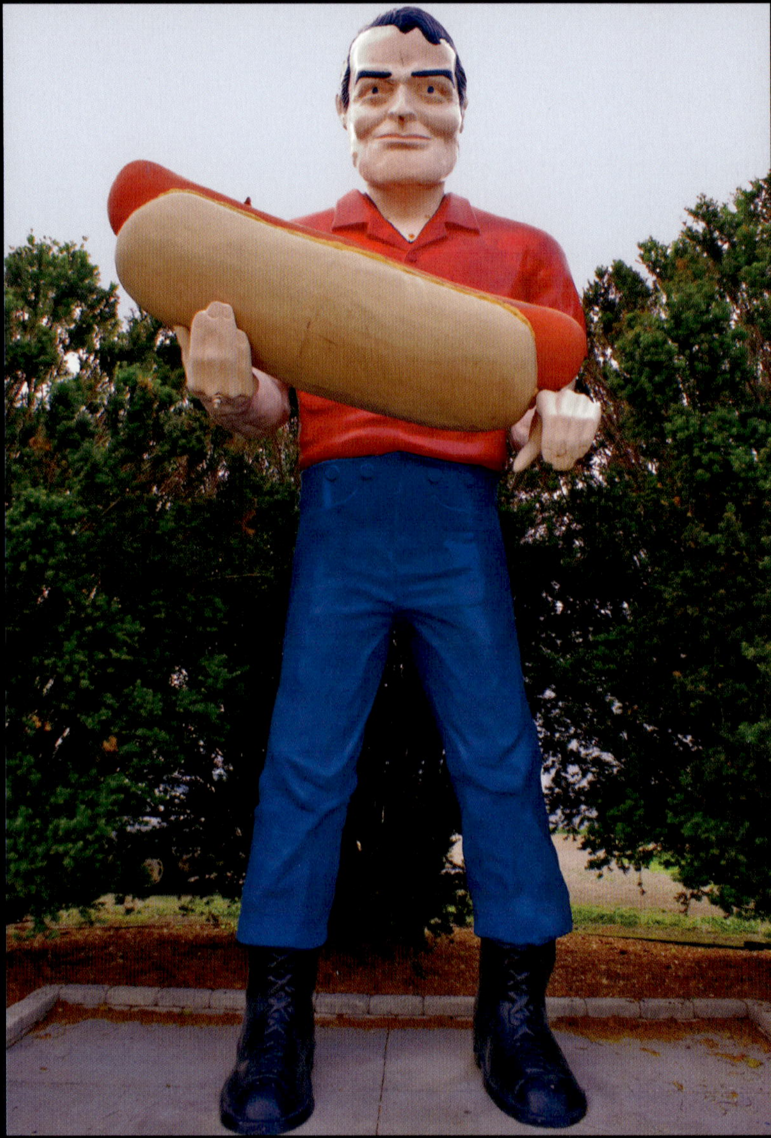

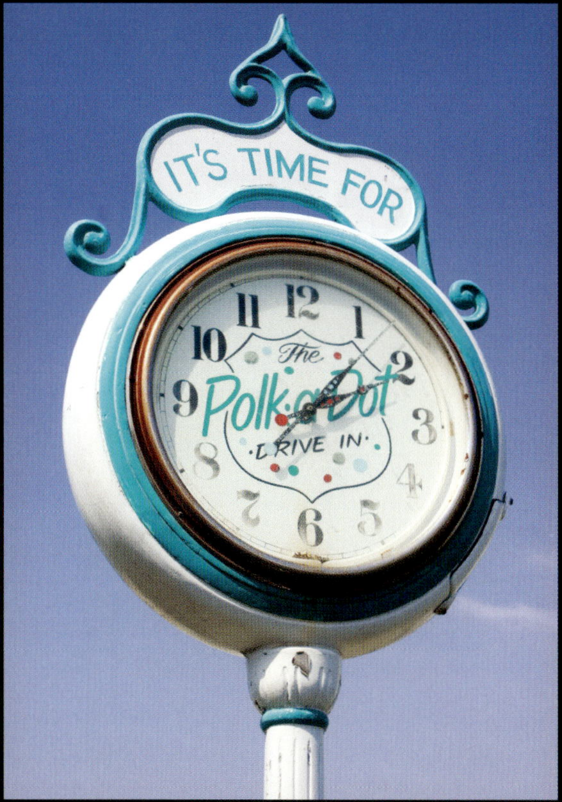

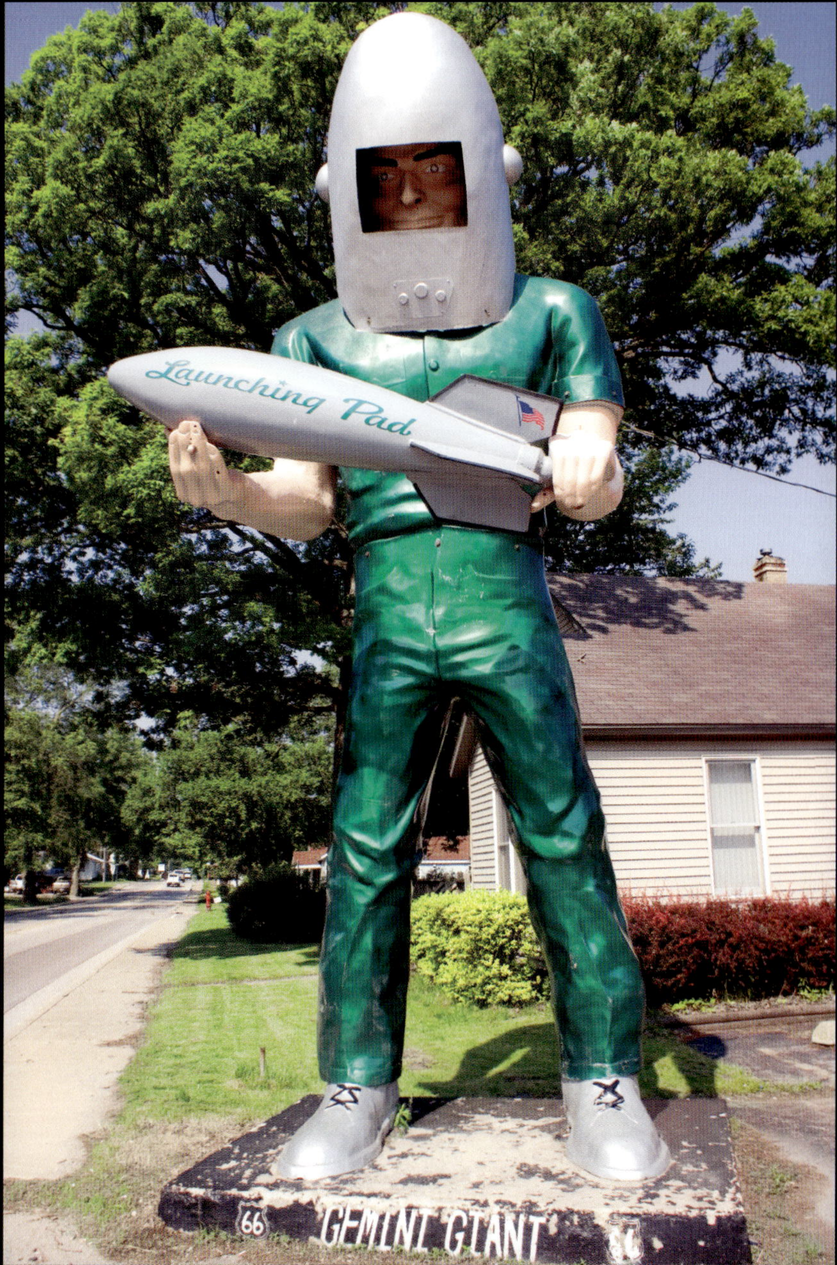

Above: A clock advertising The Polk-a-Dot Drive-In in Braidwood, IL, which includes the tagline: 'It's Time For … Polk-a-Dot'.

Right: The Gemini Giant 'Muffler Man', which formerly advertised the Launching Pad restaurant in Wilmington, IL.

Opposite left: The Phillips 66 Bent Door Diner at the 1947 Midway Station, Adrian, TX, said to have made use of a surplus control tower.

Opposite right: A repurposed 'Muffler Man' in Atlanta, IL, which was previously the 'Bunyon Giant' outside Bunyon's restaurant in Cicero, IL (the Paul Bunyan axe was exchanged for a hotdog).

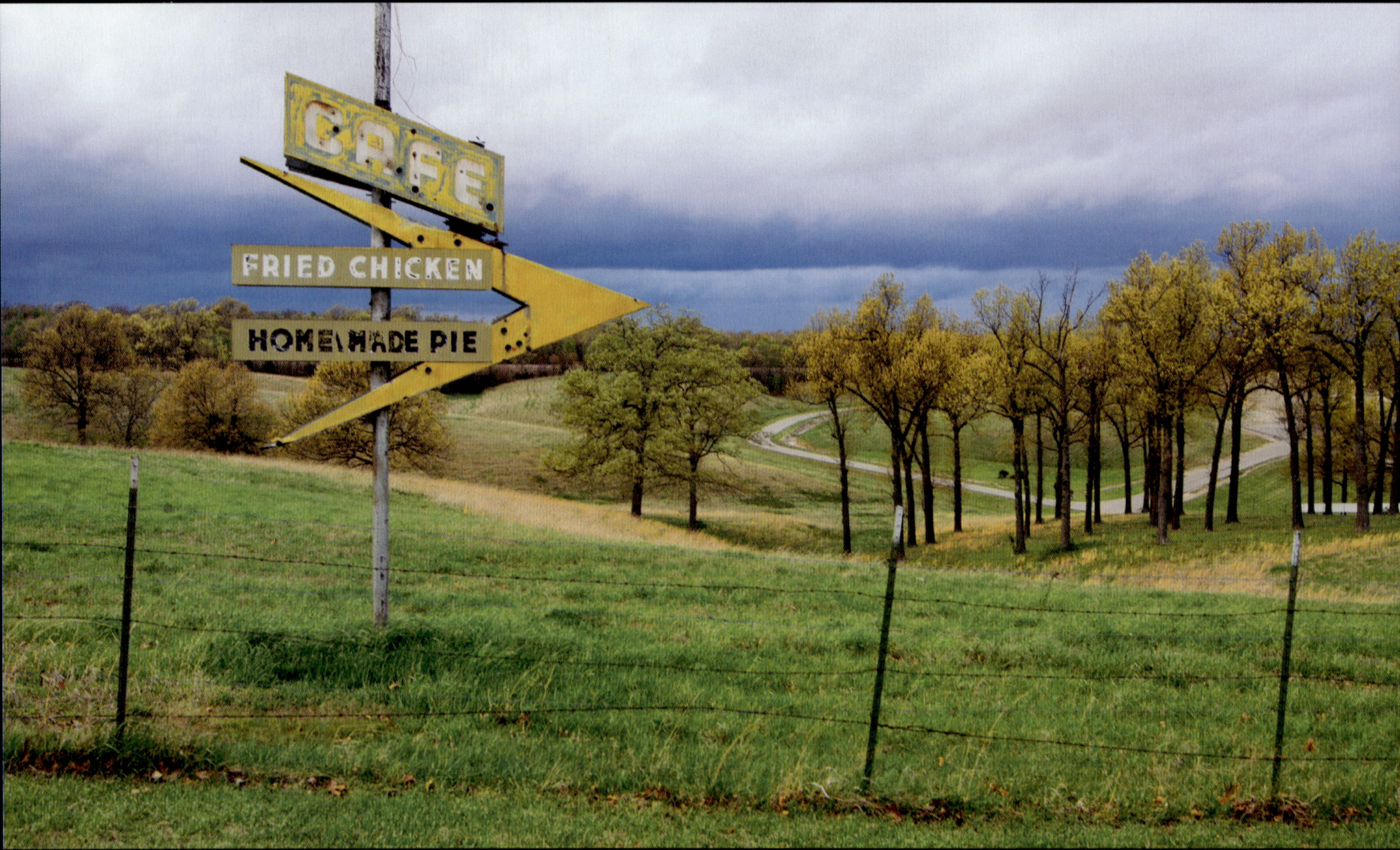

Above: All that remains of the sign for the Satellite Café and Phillips 66 space station (*c.* 1955) on Pecos Drive near the Lebanon Speedway, MO.

Opposite: A once-fine art deco-influenced diner in the ghost town of Glenrio, TX.

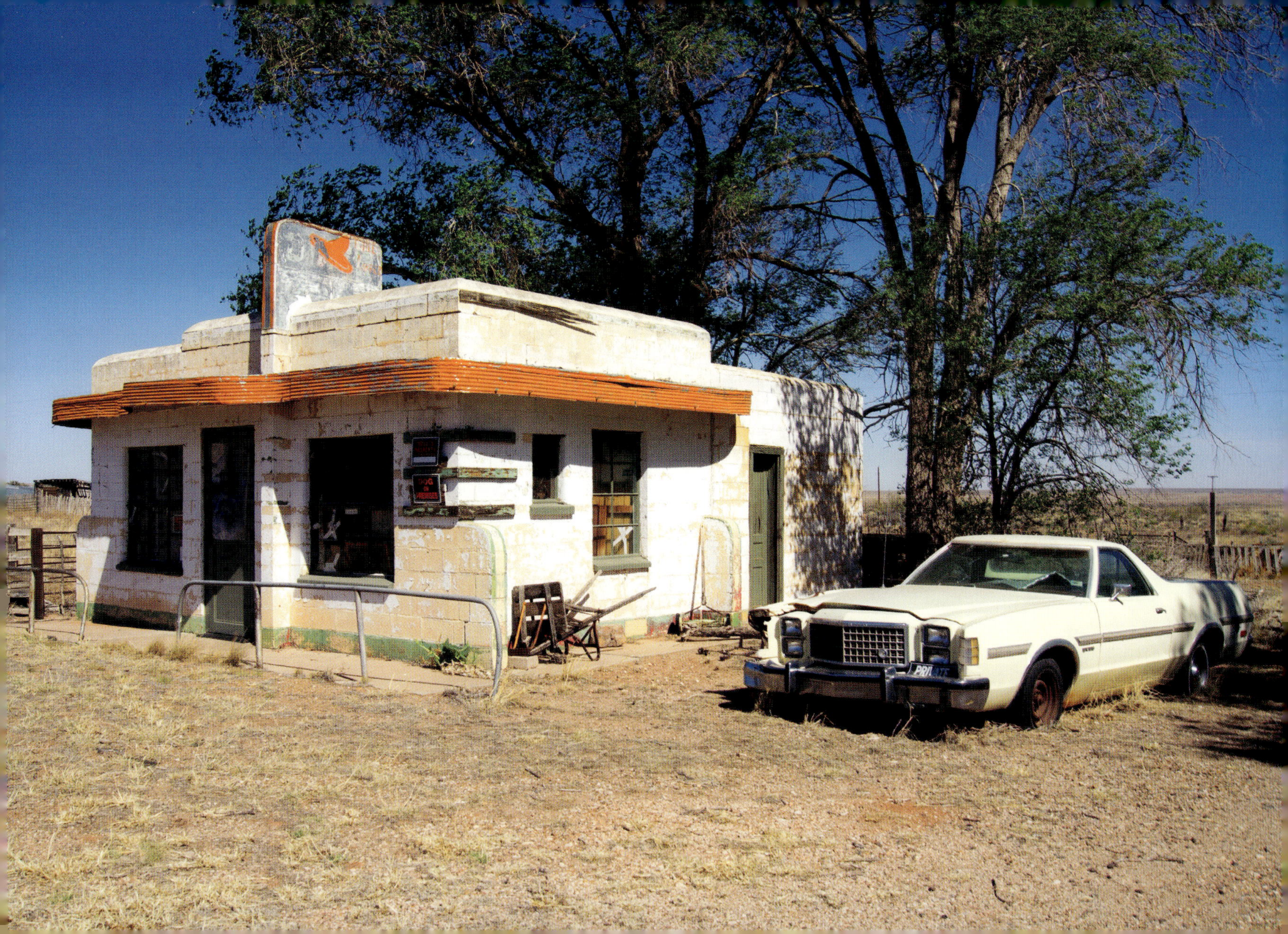

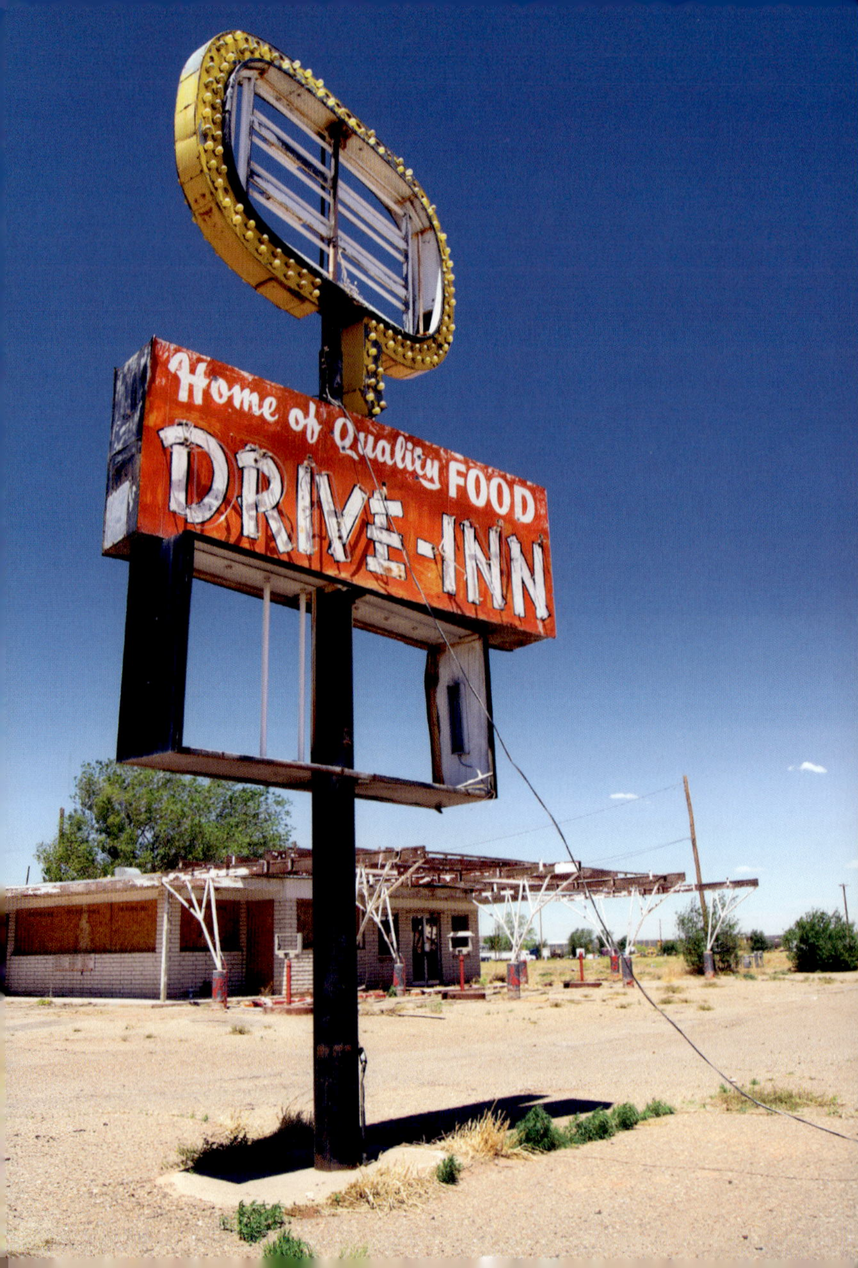

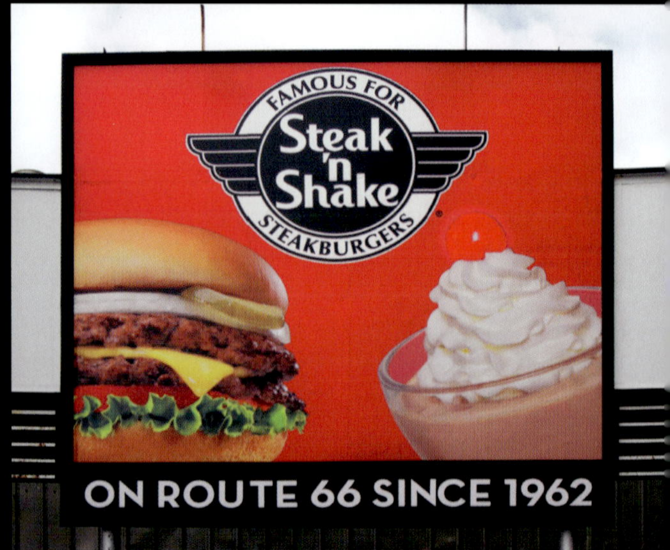

Left, above and below: The long-abandoned Drive-Inn restauran in Tucumcari, NM; the sign for a Steak 'n Shake in Springfield MO; and Bono's 1936 Old Route 66 Deli in Fontana, CA (in the 1920s, Bono's Giant Orange stand offered 'all the orange juic you can drink – 10c').

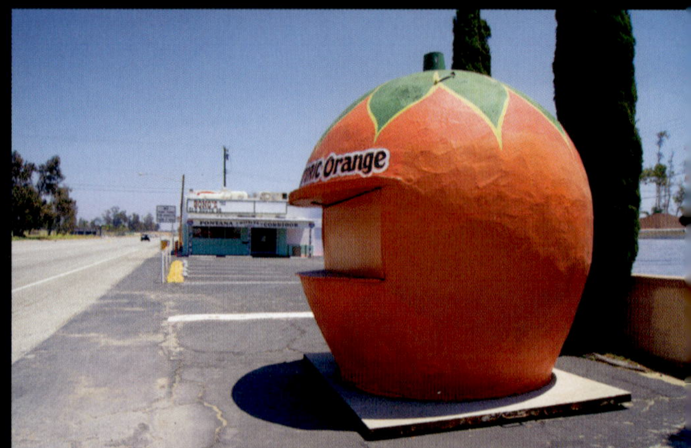

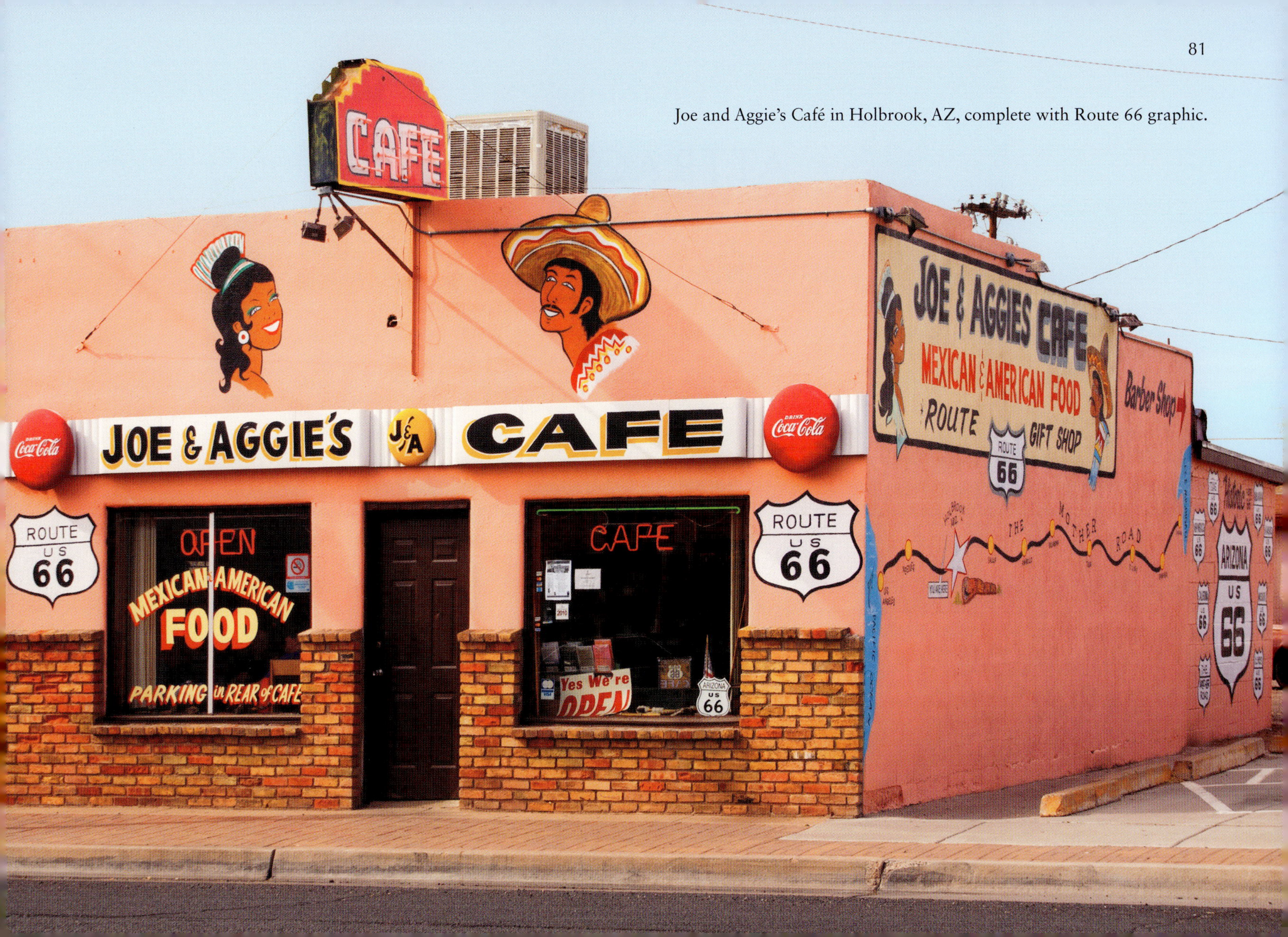

Joe and Aggie's Café in Holbrook, AZ, complete with Route 66 graphic.

Chapter 7

ATTRACTIONS

Given the long distances involved in travelling along Route 66, it was likely that tourists – especially those with families on their great American road-trip vacation – would welcome a break from time to time. So, it was inevitable that attractions were developed along the Route.

One of the best-known among Route 66ers is the 24-m-long Blue Whale at Cartoosa, Oklahoma, which was constructed in the early 1970s as an anniversary gift and turned into a swimming park. Another is the Route 66 Rocker at the Outpost Store in Fanning, Missouri, allegedly the largest rocking chair in the world [p. 85].

Sometimes, though, an item's status as a Route 66 icon is accidental. For example, when truck-stop owner Ralph Britten bought a derelict water tower and planted it purposely at an angle in a field outside Groom, Texas, he did so to advertise his business, but it has since become part of Route 66's 'manufactured history' as the road's iconic 'leaning tower of Texas' [p. 86].

An attraction with more obvious links to a highway is the Cadillac Ranch, a 1974 art installation by the San Francisco-based Ant Farm group; graphic in its simplicity, it comprises ten old Cadillacs half-buried in a muddy field with their tail fins in the air [pp. 88–89]. Part of the attraction appears to be the facility to bring a spray-paint can and redecorate the cars with your own 'artwork' or girlfriend's name. Whatever the standard of the art, attempting to capture an original image of the group, or simply match what has already been done is almost de rigeur for passing photographers. I advise getting there early in the morning, before the first bus party arrives.

Among the more 'historic' roadside attractions for tourists is Tee Pee Curios in Tucumcari, which saw life as a 1940s gas station, grocery store and trading post before it became a curio shop around 1960. Meanwhile, the Meramec Caverns, not content with its natural, limestone attractions, advertised itself as the 'World Famous' Jesse James hideout [pp. 84, 85].

Certainly, in its heyday, American travellers were well aware of the Route's attractions, an awareness reinforced by abundant signage. Sometimes, it was all about the signage, as demonstrated by the Jack Rabbit Trading Post, in Joseph City, Arizona. The convenience store was founded in 1949 and quickly became famous for a string of billboards featuring the silhouette of a jack rabbit; the string, which stretched from Missouri to Arizona, reached its end outside the trading post with a large sign that read 'Here It Is' (or in satnav terminology, 'you have reached your destination'). It may only have been a curio shop with snacks and restrooms, but it became as well known on Route 66 as the Blue Whale and the Cadillac Ranch.

Today's travellers should also look out for the sponsored blue-and-white signs declaring a site as a 'Route 66 Roadside Attraction ... Recognized by Hampton Hotels Save-A-Landmark program as a sight worth seeing'. This quirky marketing ploy is not confined to Route 66, but it certainly helps to highlight and preserve its history.

Preservation is the stock-in-trade of museums large and small along the Route. Some are glossy, professional and well-designed while others are dusty, amateur and haphazard ... and there is a place for both. While the former exist to document, archive and present the past, the latter help to preserve the less tangible elements of Route 66 – the ethos, the emotion and the essence of the Mother Road. Indeed, Route 66ers never seem to tire of seeing yet more original signage (rusty or not) and reading another fact (or factoid) about the road. Take the Devil's Rope Museum – a 'Tribute to Barbed Wire' – as an example. According to one website, the US government has issued patents for more than 800 types of barbed wire, while collectors (yes, there are barbed-wire collectors) have identified more than 2,000 different types! Now, that is a factoid in the true 66 spirit.

The growing need to preserve historic sites and celebrate the nation's heritage is nowhere more evident than on Route 66. It is why the Hackberry General Store was reopened in the 1990s, by Robert (Bob) Waldmire, an artist and cartographer known for his whimsical maps of Route 66. It's also why the Arcadia Round Barn, which dates from 1898, was refurbished in 1992 [p. 87]. Of course, it's impossible to preserve everything, so there are far more dilapidated structures than refurbs – luckily, both are fodder for the creative photographer.

In the context of all this manufactured interest, one should also celebrate the natural attractions of the geographical features near the Route, which are part of the highway's history simply because they were there for the original 66ers to visit. Arguably, the most incredible examples occur once the weary westbound traveller has reached Arizona. Just beyond the border with New Mexico lie the Painted Desert and Petrified Forest and, about 50 miles further on, the unexpected spectacle of Meteor Crater. Just beyond Flagstaff and worthy of the detour is the marvellous Grand Canyon, as fantastic a Route 66 attraction as anyone could hope for.

Nor should one forget the cities along the Route, which are attractions in their own right. From east to west, the most significant, at least in terms of size, are Chicago, St Louis, Tulsa, Oklahoma City, Amarillo, Albuquerque and Los Angeles, but 66ers will be more interested in the smaller conurbations with particular relevance to the Road. These include Springfield, Missouri (the birthplace of Route 66), Adrian, Texas (the midpoint), Tucumcari, New Mexico (unheard of but for Route 66), and Seligman and Kingman in Arizona (where every other sign and attraction seems to relate to the road). In fact, the longest original remaining segment of Route 66 is in Arizona – between Ash Fork and Topock – and links Seligman, Hackberry, Kingman and Oatman. For attractions both natural and manufactured, this section is a 'must drive'.

Taking a nationwide view of Route 66, it seems that tourists and photographers alike are spoilt for choice on the eastern sections – particularly in Illinois – where attractions and photo opportunities abound. Once you cross the Mississippi at St Louis, however, the opportunities become fewer and further between, and the roads across the Great Plains can seem interminable. Driving the vast distances, you begin to feel a little of how the Joad family in *The Grapes of Wrath* felt as they shook off the dust bowl of Oklahoma and dreamed about the orange groves of California.

For the modern traveller who is open to emotional influences and impressions, the Route 66 experience gradually becomes less about where the road takes you and more about staying power. At some point in the continuum that is Route 66, the driver or biker begins to understand and enjoy the concept of the 'open road' and, ultimately, the greatest attraction is the road itself.

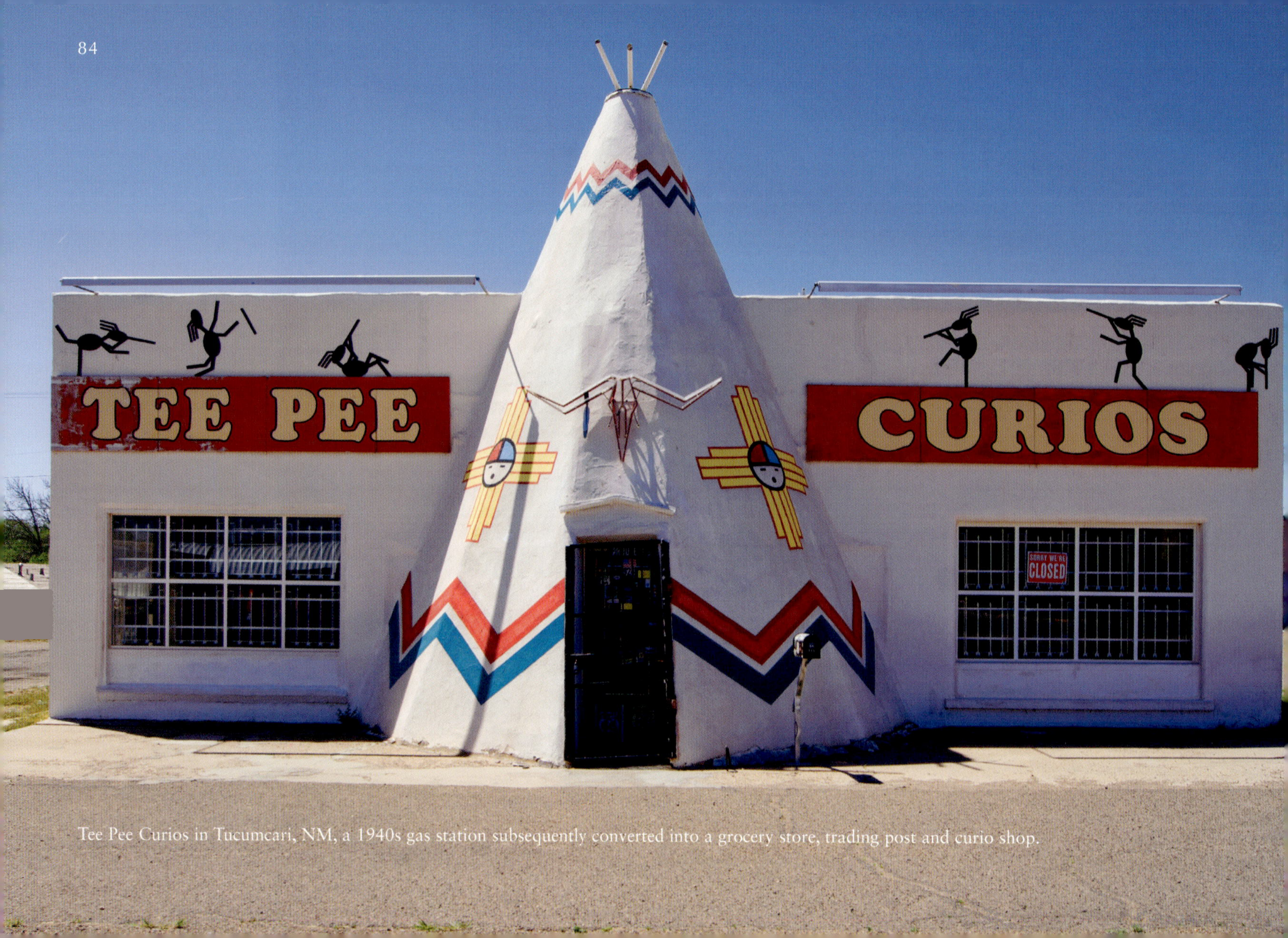

Tee Pee Curios in Tucumcari, NM, a 1940s gas station subsequently converted into a grocery store, trading post and curio shop.

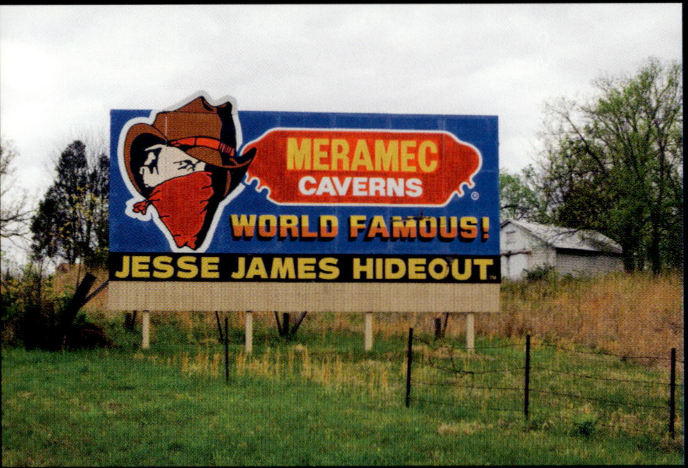

Above: A sign near Pontiac, IL, advertising Meramec Caverns.

Right: The Route 66 Rocker at the Outpost Store, Fanning, MO, allegedly the largest rocking chair in the world.

Below: The Blue Whale in Cartoosa, OK, well known as a Route 66 icon despite dating back only to the 1970s.

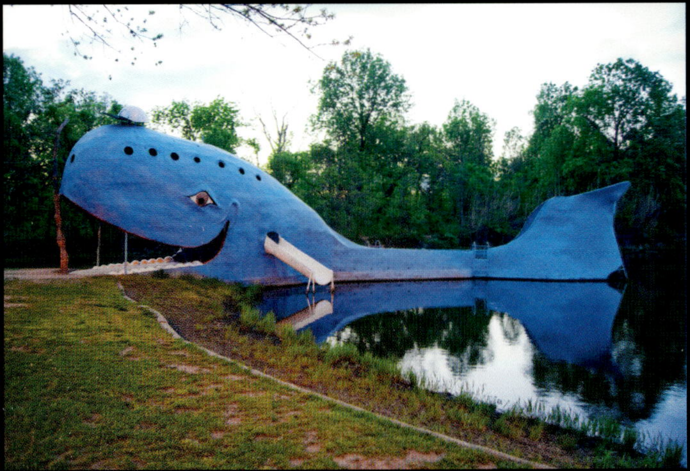

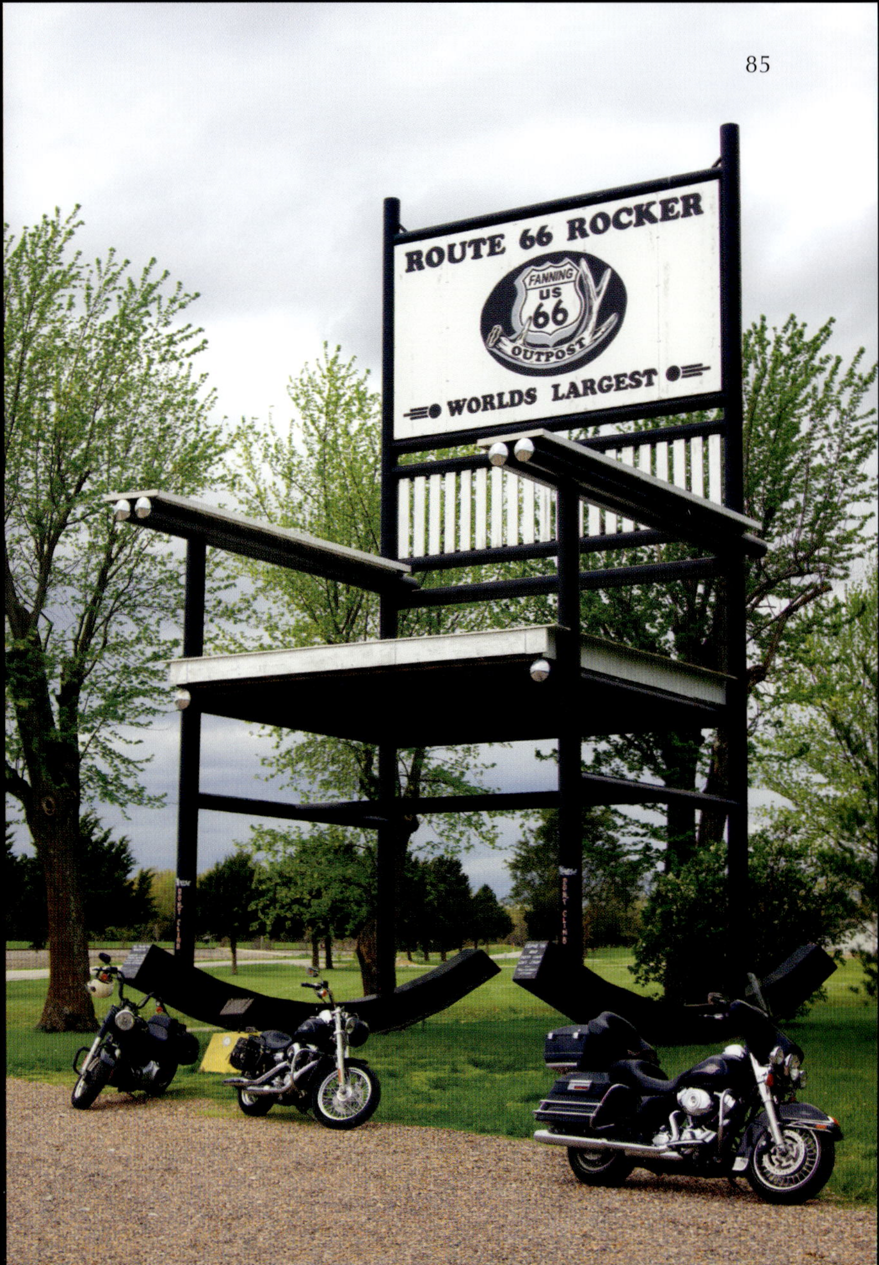

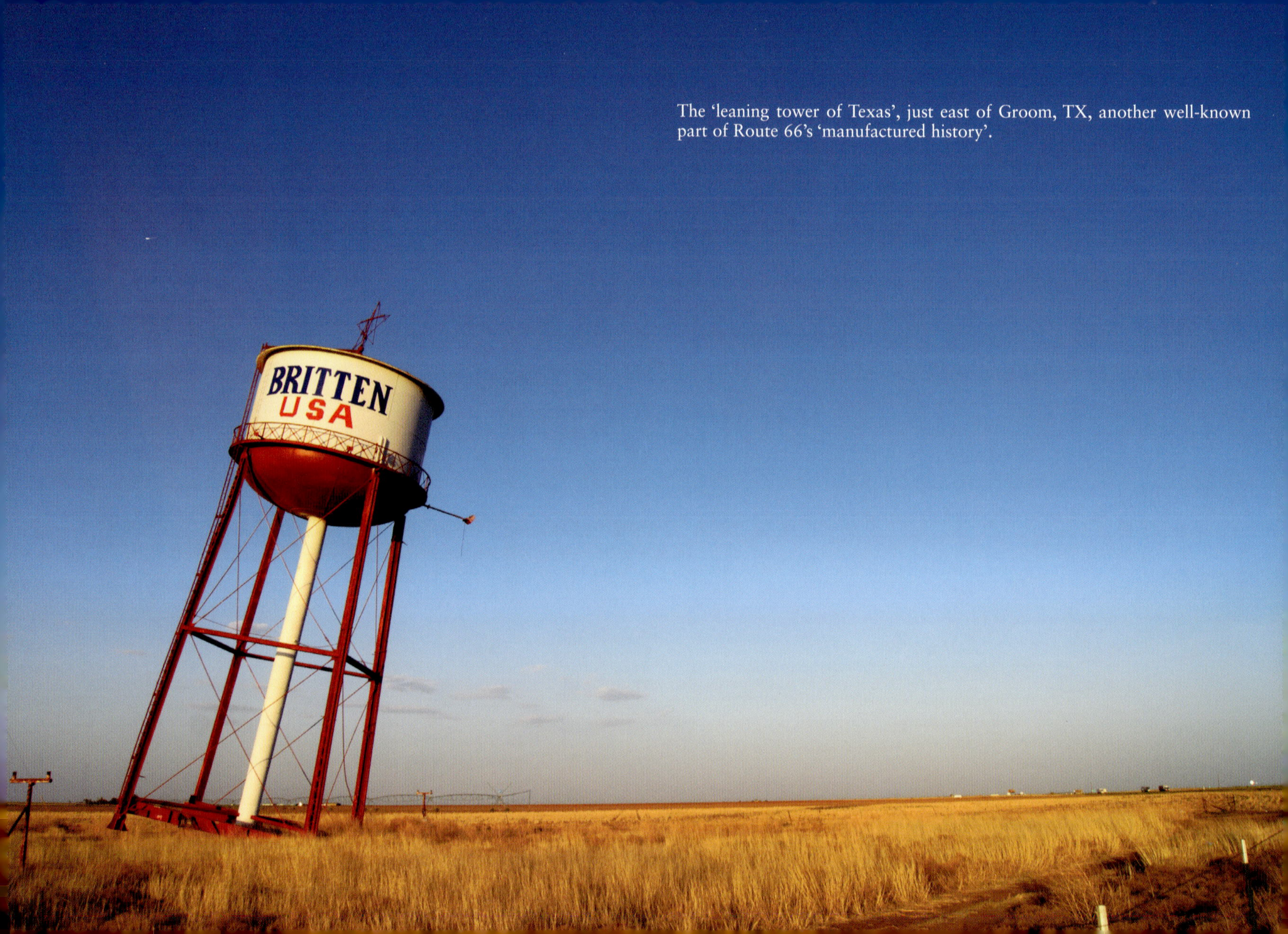

The 'leaning tower of Texas', just east of Groom, TX, another well-known part of Route 66's 'manufactured history'.

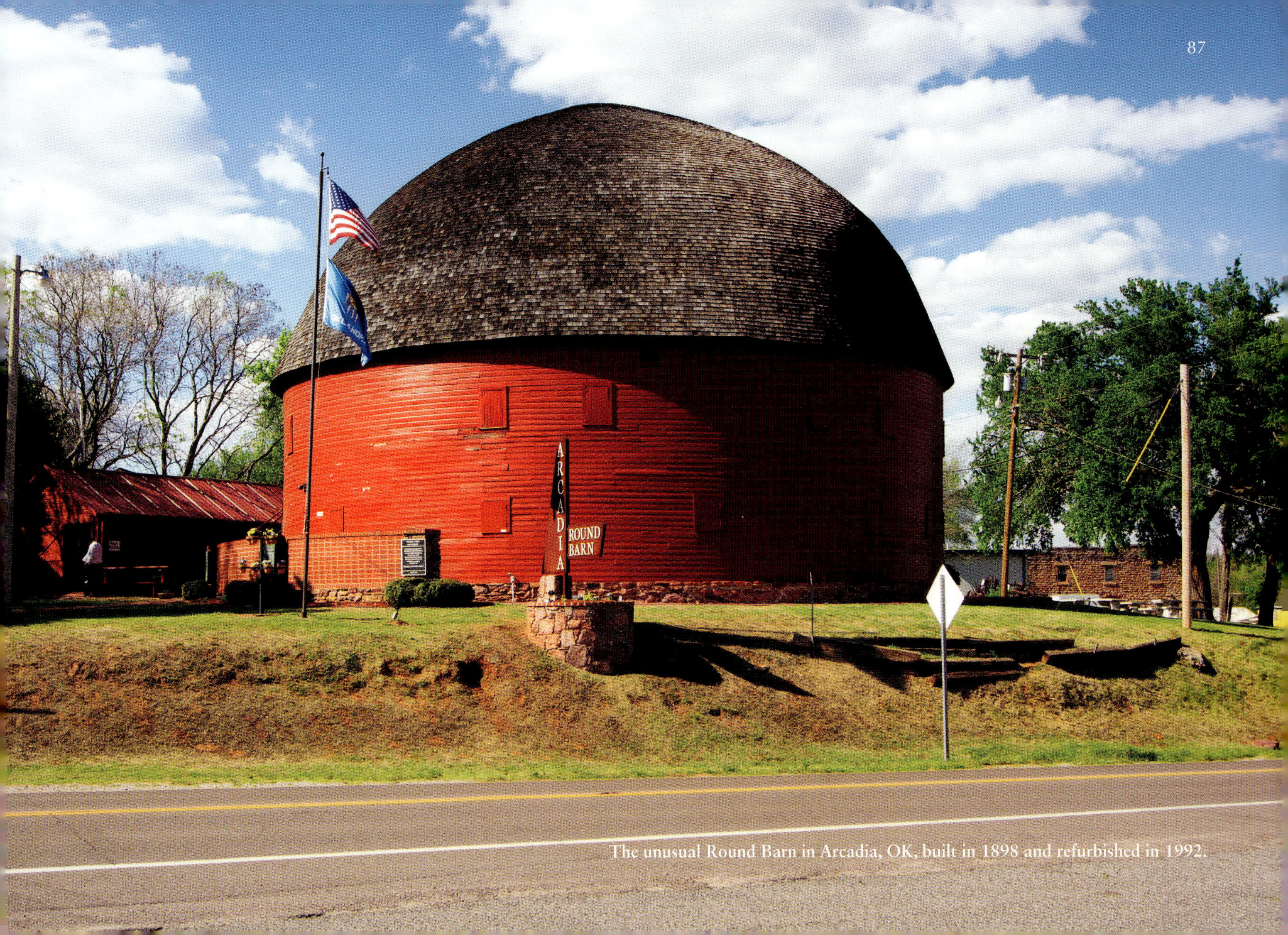

The unusual Round Barn in Arcadia, OK, built in 1898 and refurbished in 1992.

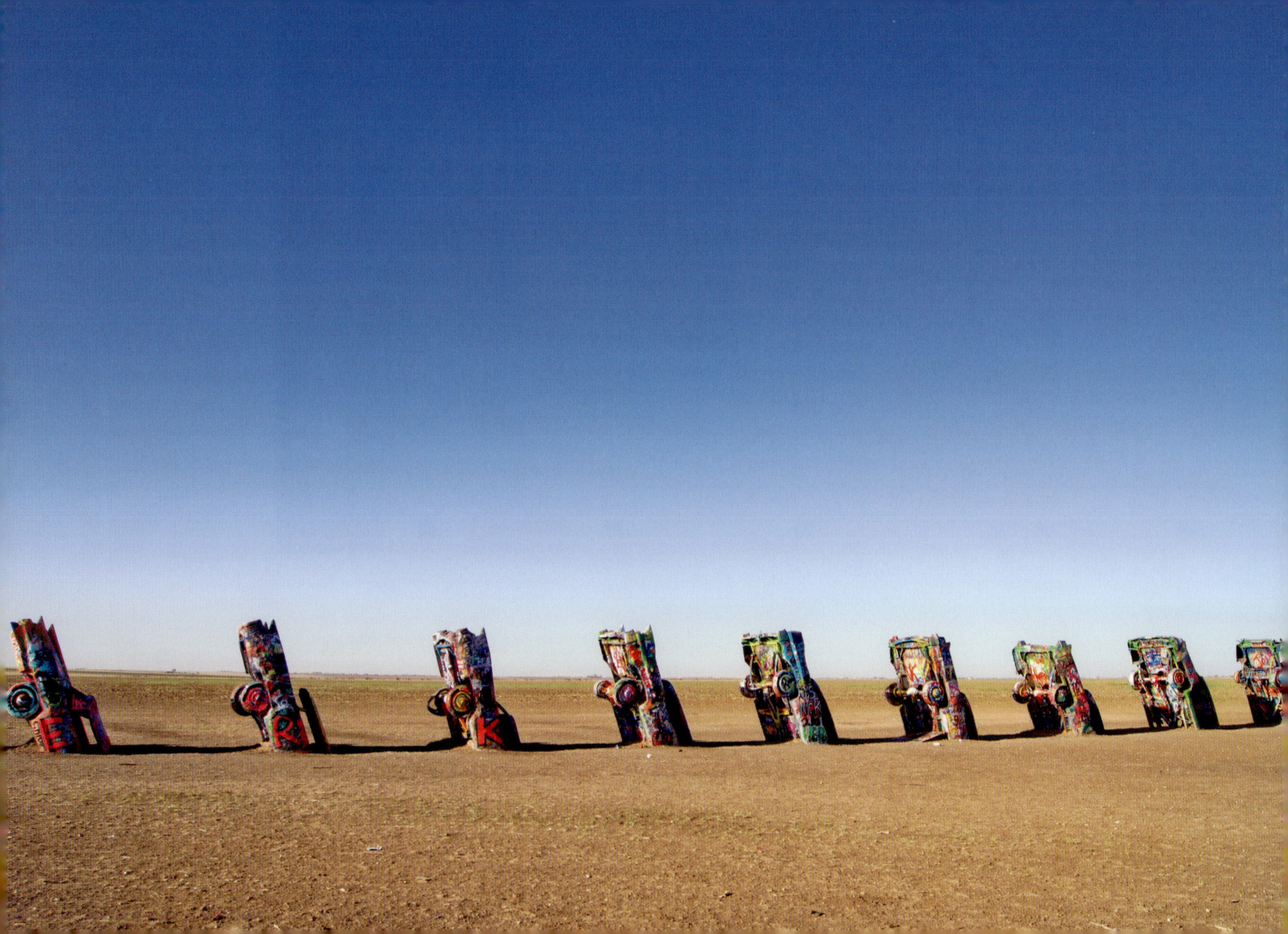

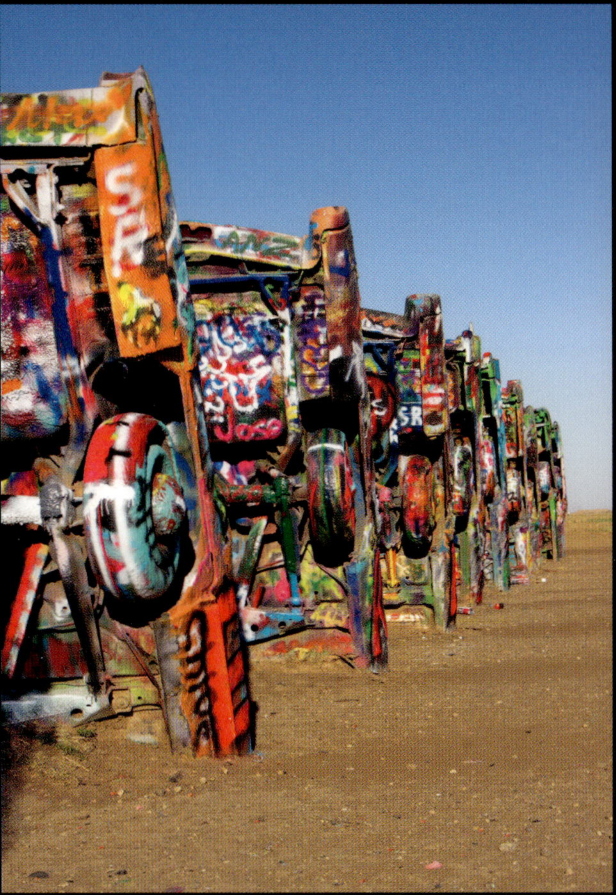

Opposite and above: Cadillac Ranch, west of Amarillo, TX, a 1974 art installation commissioned by rancher/art collector Stanley Marsh III and based on ten 1949–64 Cadillac cars set at the same angle as sides of the Great Pyramid in Egypt. Parodied by the 'Bug Ranch' in Conway, TX, among others.

Right: Angel & Vilma Delgadillo's store in Seligman, AZ, a pilgrimage destination for many Route 66ers.

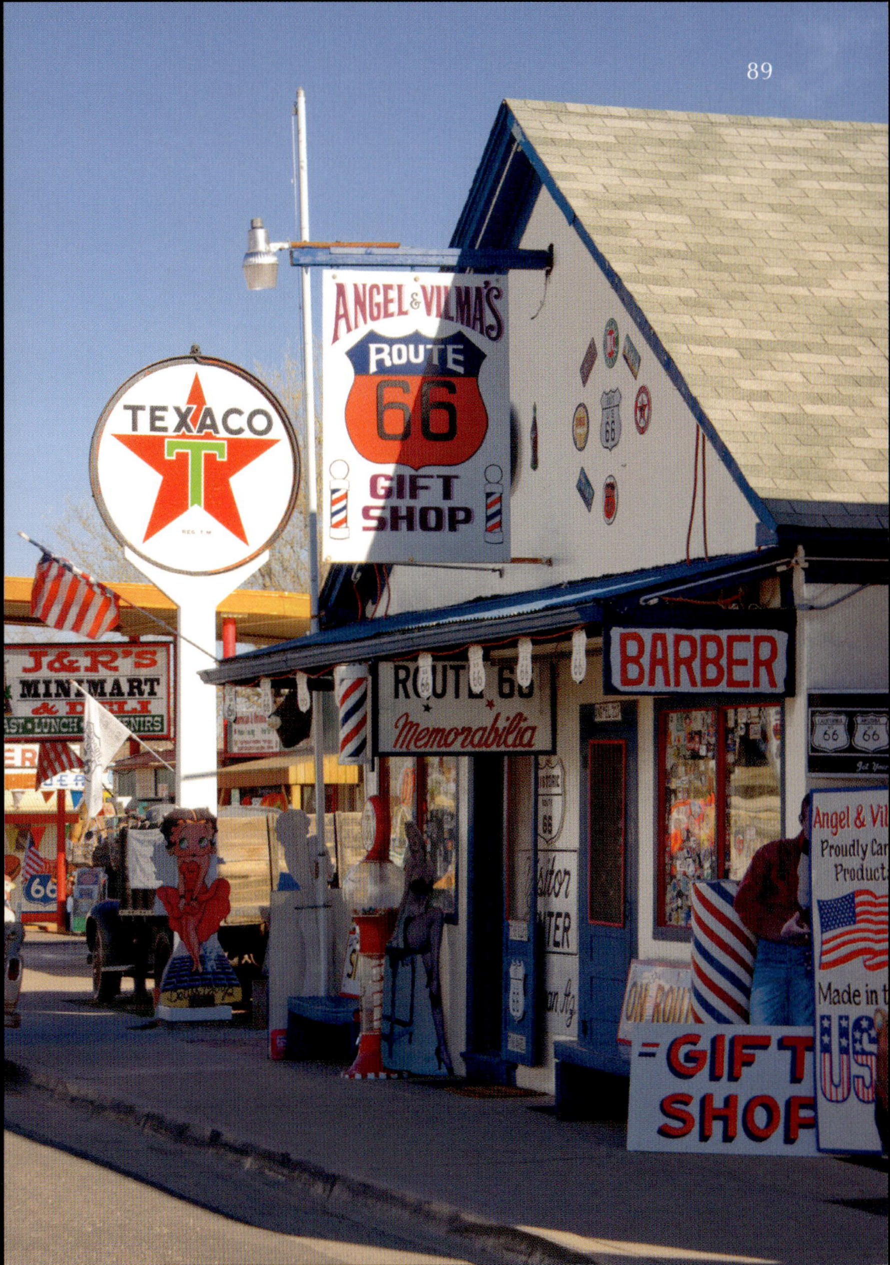

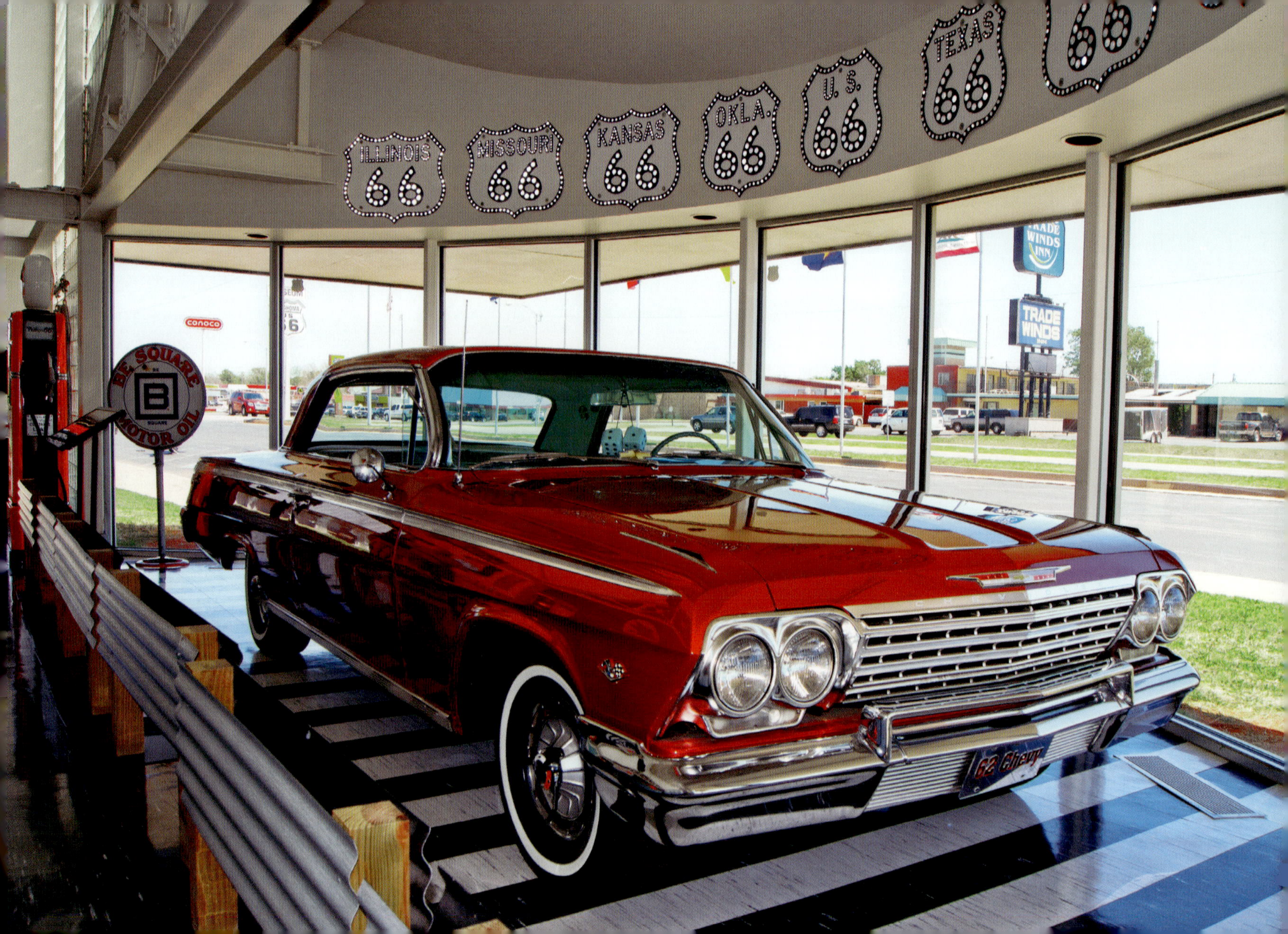
ILLINOIS 66
MISSOURI 66
KANSAS 66
OKLA. 66
U.S. 66
TEXAS 66
66
CONOCO
BE SQUARE MOTOR OIL
B
TRADE WINDS INN
TRADE WINDS
'62 Chevy

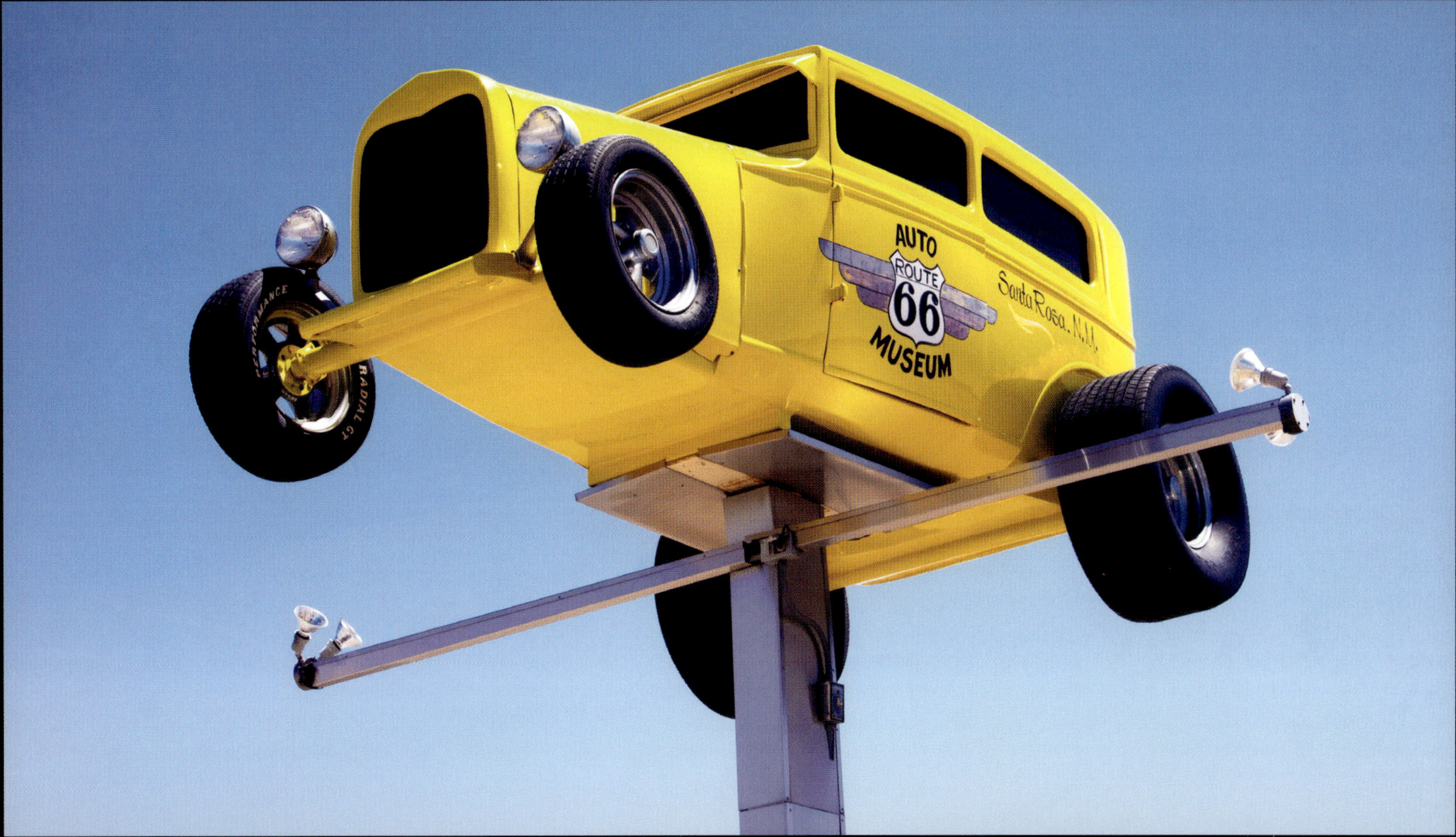

Above: An elevated hot-rod announces the Route 66 Auto Museum in Santa Rosa, NM.

Opposite: A 1962 Chevrolet in the window of the Oklahoma Route 66 Museum in Clinton, OK.

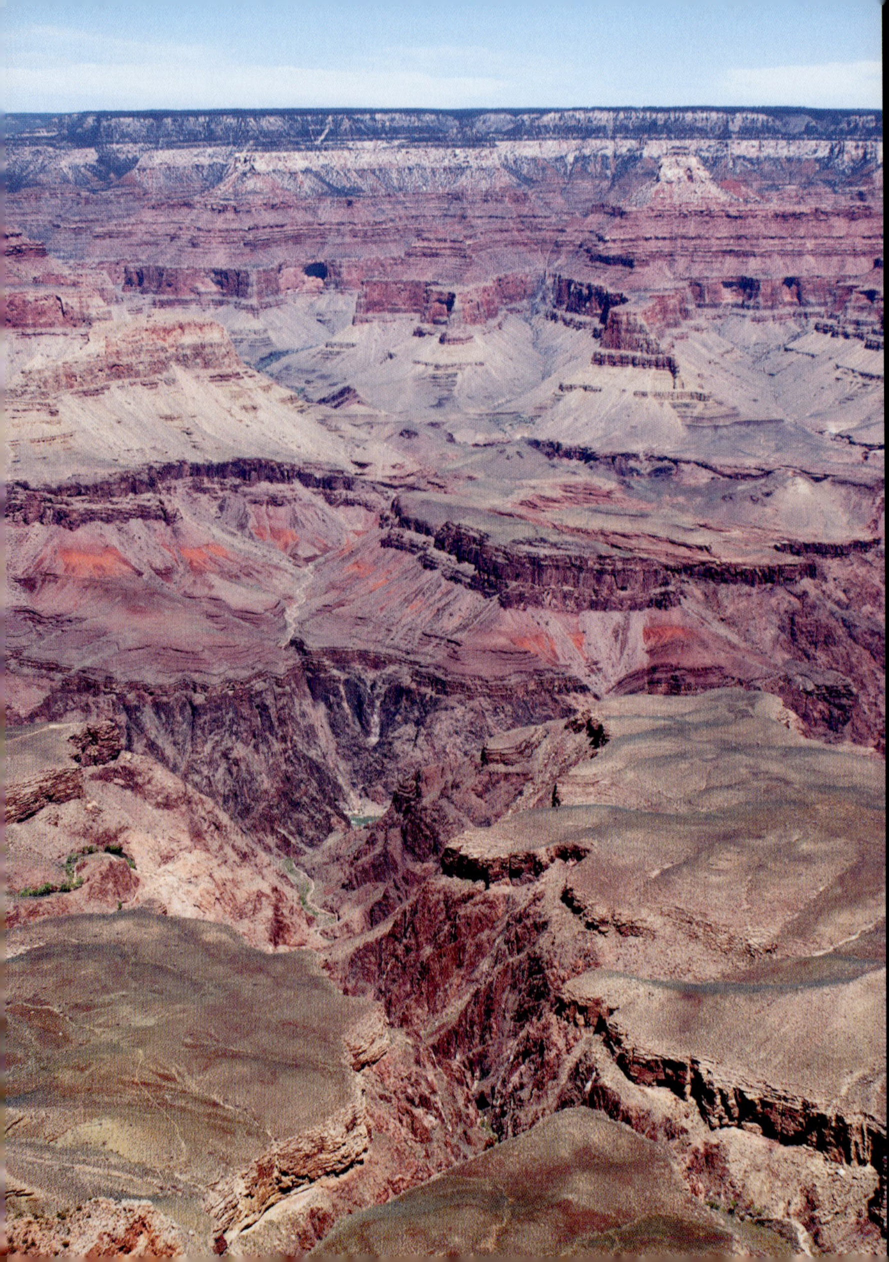

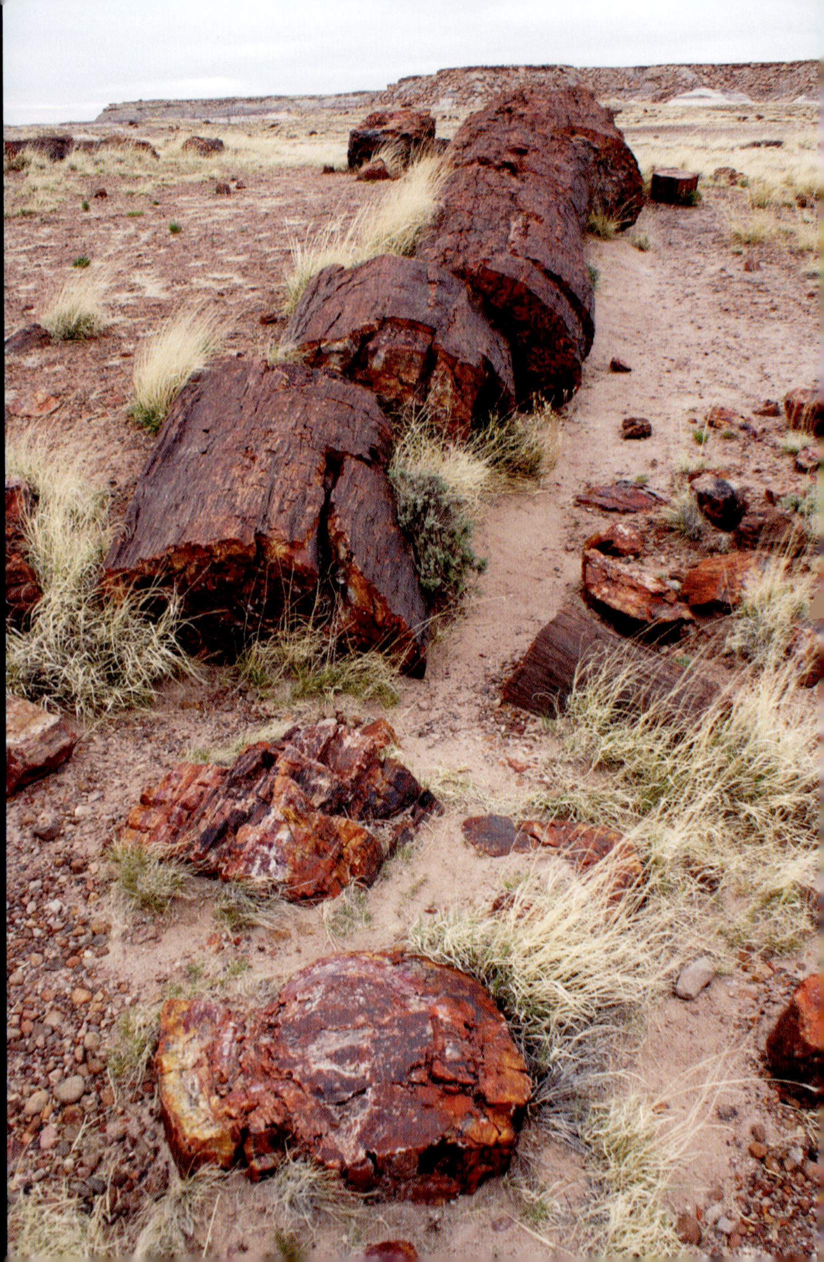

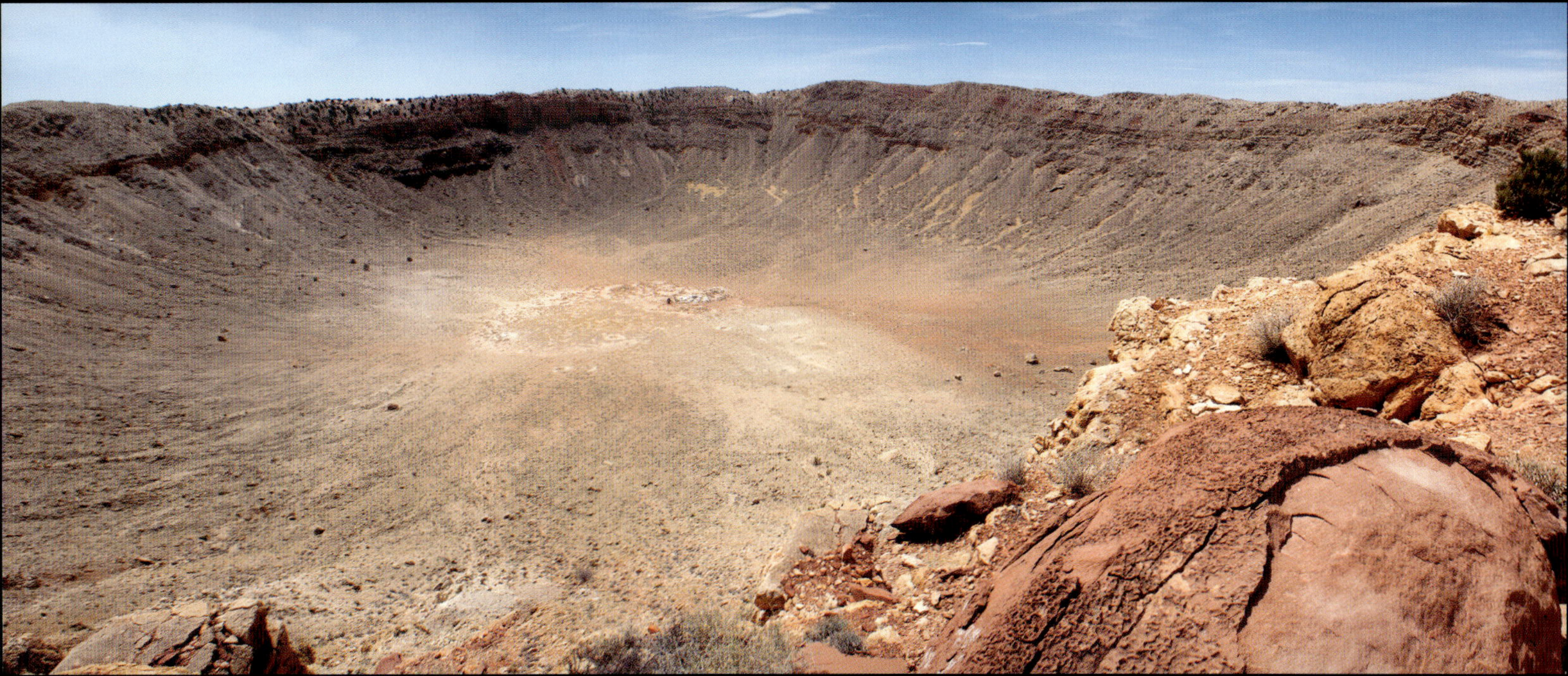

Opposite and above: Natural tourist attractions in Arizona: Grand Canyon, Petrified Forest and Meteor Crater.

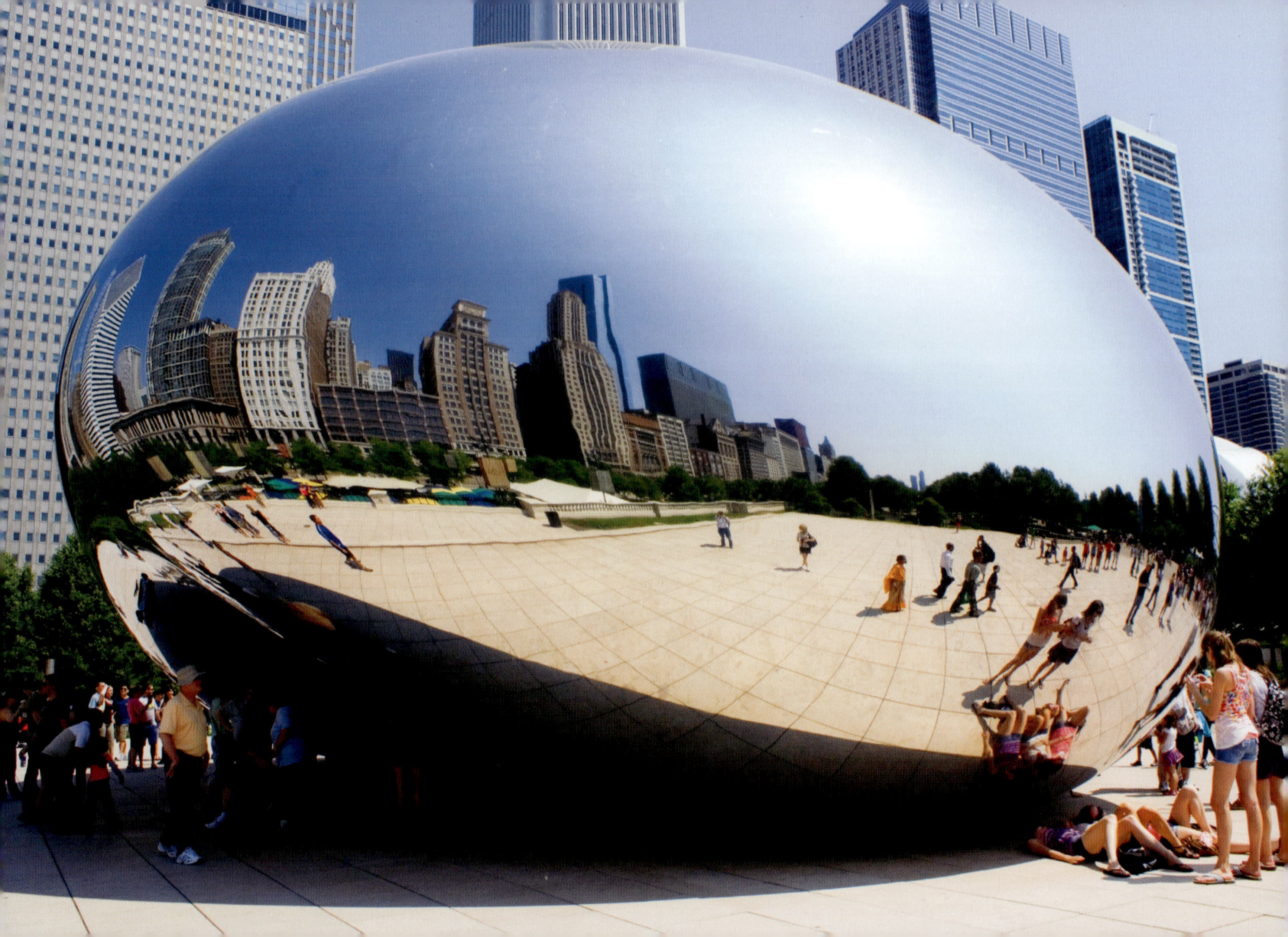

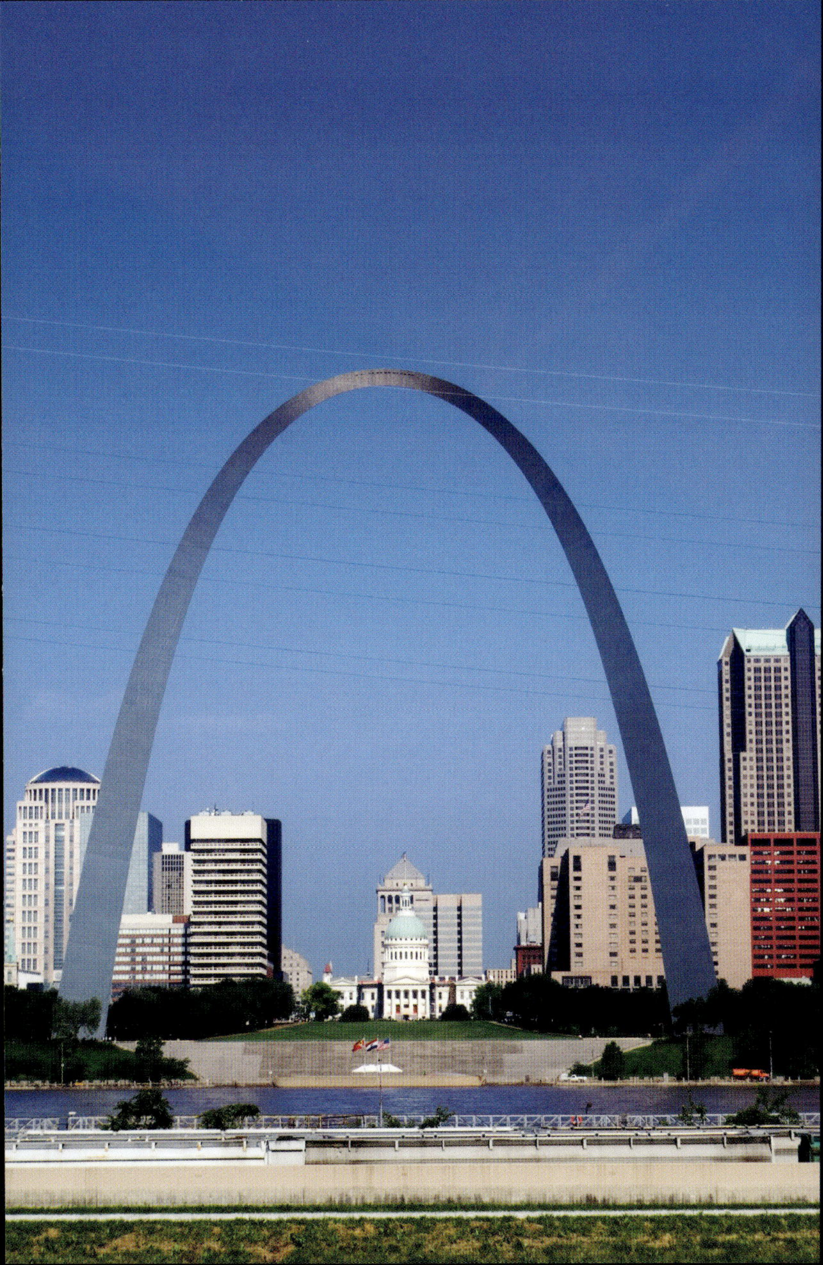

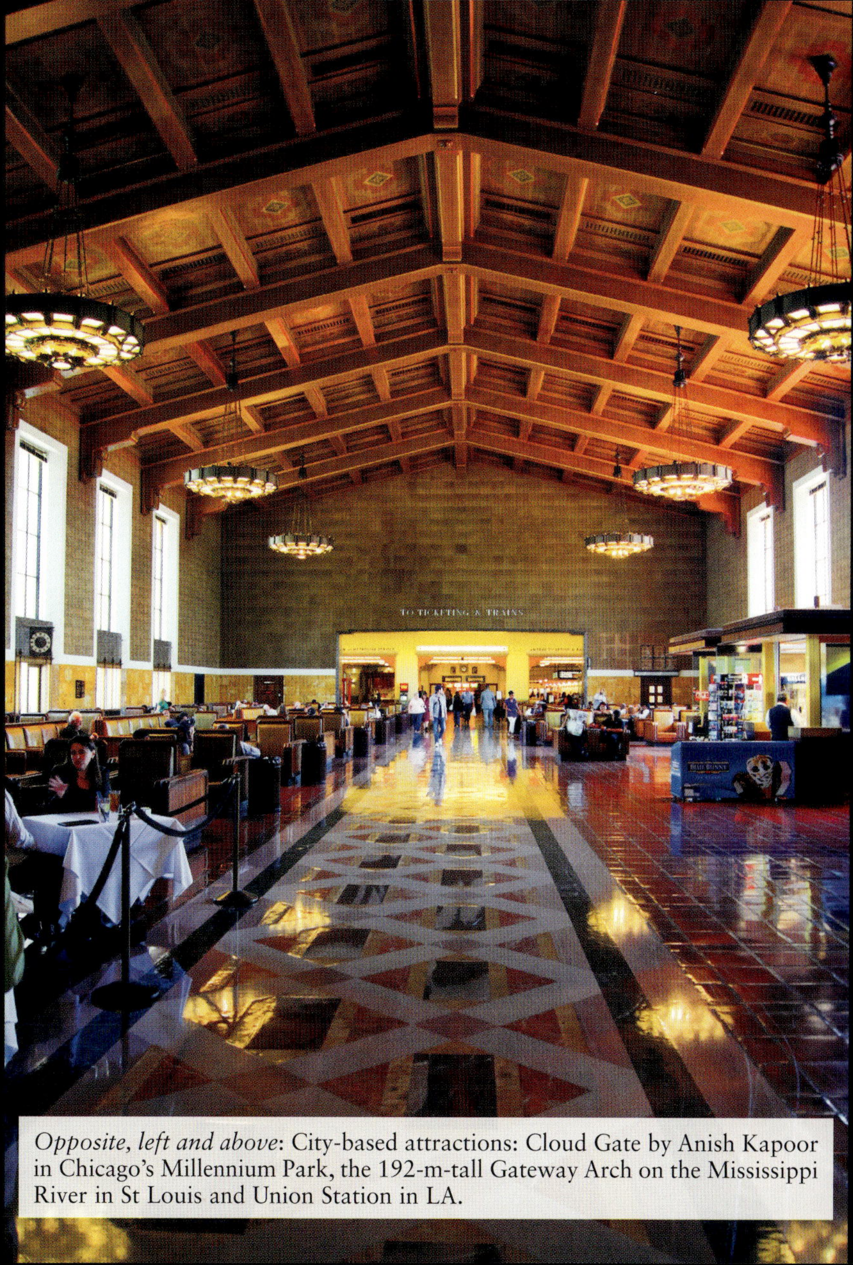

Opposite, left and above: City-based attractions: Cloud Gate by Anish Kapoor in Chicago's Millennium Park, the 192-m-tall Gateway Arch on the Mississippi River in St Louis and Union Station in LA.

Chapter 8

MURALS

Route 66 aside, murals are big in America (literally) and the decoration of otherwise blank walls with paint seems to have been escalated to a cultural artform. Route 66, in particular, has adopted the culture of the mural not only as a marketing ploy, but also as a confirmation of its unique iconography, from cars and shields to well-known phrases.

It seems probable that, for as long as there have been walls and paint, people have been painting pictures on walls – from the early cave paintings onwards. Although the practice of painting large advertisements on walls is thought to date back to the late nineteenth century, it undoubtedly reached its heights in the twentieth century. If you look carefully at old buildings in an urban environment, usually on the side elevations at first-floor level (second storey in America), you can still see the faded remnants of this advertising. In fact, they are sufficiently common in American cities to have been given a name: 'ghost signs'.

Route 66 has its fair share of ghost signage, some of which has been restored to its former glory. For example, in many towns, one can find adverts for Coca-Cola, Pepsi and other products, alongside local advertising for shops and attractions [pp. 98–99]. For this photographer, murals exist in a special category, because they are only two-dimensional. With three-dimensional objects, one can alter the viewpoint for effect – exaggerate the perspective of a motel sign, highlight the chrome front bumper of a Cadillac – but a mural is best-viewed as the artist intended: from a distance perpendicular to its centre line.

However, a sub-clause of Murphy's Law states that whenever a photographer is desperate to take a street mural straight-on, there will be a car or dumpster in the way! In some cases, images can be adjusted for perspective using editing software, but in others it might be worth considering a stitched panorama at the shooting stage. I did this for one of the largest murals dedicated to Route 66 – *The Legendary Road* – an impressive artwork by Doug and Sharon Quarles on the side of a Lowe's supermarket in Tucumcari, New Mexico [pp. 102–03]. The 35-m-long, 4-m-tall mural is effectively a triptych of three stretches of tarmac separated by steer skulls, featuring the obligatory diner, biker and Route 66 shield. Rather than stand at the centre to shoot a number of images from left to right, it is worth shooting from several positions in front of the mural to produce successive straight-on images – this reduces distortion and, as long as there is sufficient overlap, gives the software a better chance of making a decent panorama.

All that said, as with any other subject, it is always possible to crop the mural and that can produce a satisfying image, albeit one the original artist did not intend. Another side note concerns the predominantly 2D nature of the mural, a rule occasionally broken by the *trompe l'oeil* technique. A great example is the *Pontiac on Route 66* mural (by Tom and Kathy Durham) in downtown Pontiac, Illinois – the right-hand tail fin really hits you in the eye [p. 100].

Other notable Route 66 murals are the *Crossroads of America* in El Reno, Oklahoma, and the *Arizona* 66 mural in Kingman, Arizona, both of which feature the classic car that has itself become an icon of Route 66 – a red 1957 Chevrolet Corvette convertible with a white side panel [pp. 104–05]. The same Chevy can also be seen on the side of the General Store in Fanning, Missouri, on the wall of the Blue Swallow Motel in Tucumcari [p. 61] and in the *El Camino de Los Caminos* mural in downtown Albuquerque [p. 101]. If you're really lucky, you might see a real one outside the Hackberry General Store, a popular attraction in Arizona.

Unfortunately, popular though the Route 66 murals are, they are as transitory as the urban advertisements of yesteryear and there is no better example than the *Deep in the Heart of Amarillo Texas* mural [pp. 106–07]. It depicted the Route across the eight (differently-coloured) states, with Amarillo taking centre stage, and included the usual Main Street and Mother Road slogans. Back in 2014, when I captured its fast-degrading image, it was already a ghost sign half-obscured by a wooden fence; a decade later it was completely covered by trees rendering it invisible to unsuspecting passers-by. The warning here is obvious: if the culture and heritage of Route 66 is to be retained, it must be actively identified and preserved.

In more recent times, local communities have sought to advertise themselves as being 'on Historic Route 66' by commissioning murals from local artists. In some cases, the murals have become more than adverts to attract tourists to the town or city and are now attractions in their own right. For example, the small town of Cuba, Missouri, styles itself as 'Route 66 Mural City' and has more than a dozen building-sized murals; Tucumcari (of course) and Pontiac, Illinois, are also havens for mural lovers.

Now, although we've concentrated here on walls (that's why it's called wall art, after all), it's worth noting that other surfaces are available! On Route 66, for example, photographers can find murals on wooden barns, window shutters and even picket fences [p. 107].

It is also good to see that the classic, letter-based artworks from the old postcards and posters have been rediscovered by younger street artists who are also Route 66 fans. The 'Greetings From' travel series of postcards was developed by German-born printer Curt Teich, who moved to the USA in 1895. In the 1930s, his company introduced a series of brightly coloured graphic designs that featured the words 'Greetings from' and the name of the place; the unique selling point was that each block letter of the name was illustrated with scenes from the locale. Although the cards covered the whole nation, they seem to typify the quirky, self-confident nature of Route 66 publicity and, for a time at least, became synonymous with the Route.

It is interesting to see that this artform is now being 'recycled'. Wall art may not last forever, but – like Route 66 itself – it will be continually renewed and replaced and, hopefully, will never die.

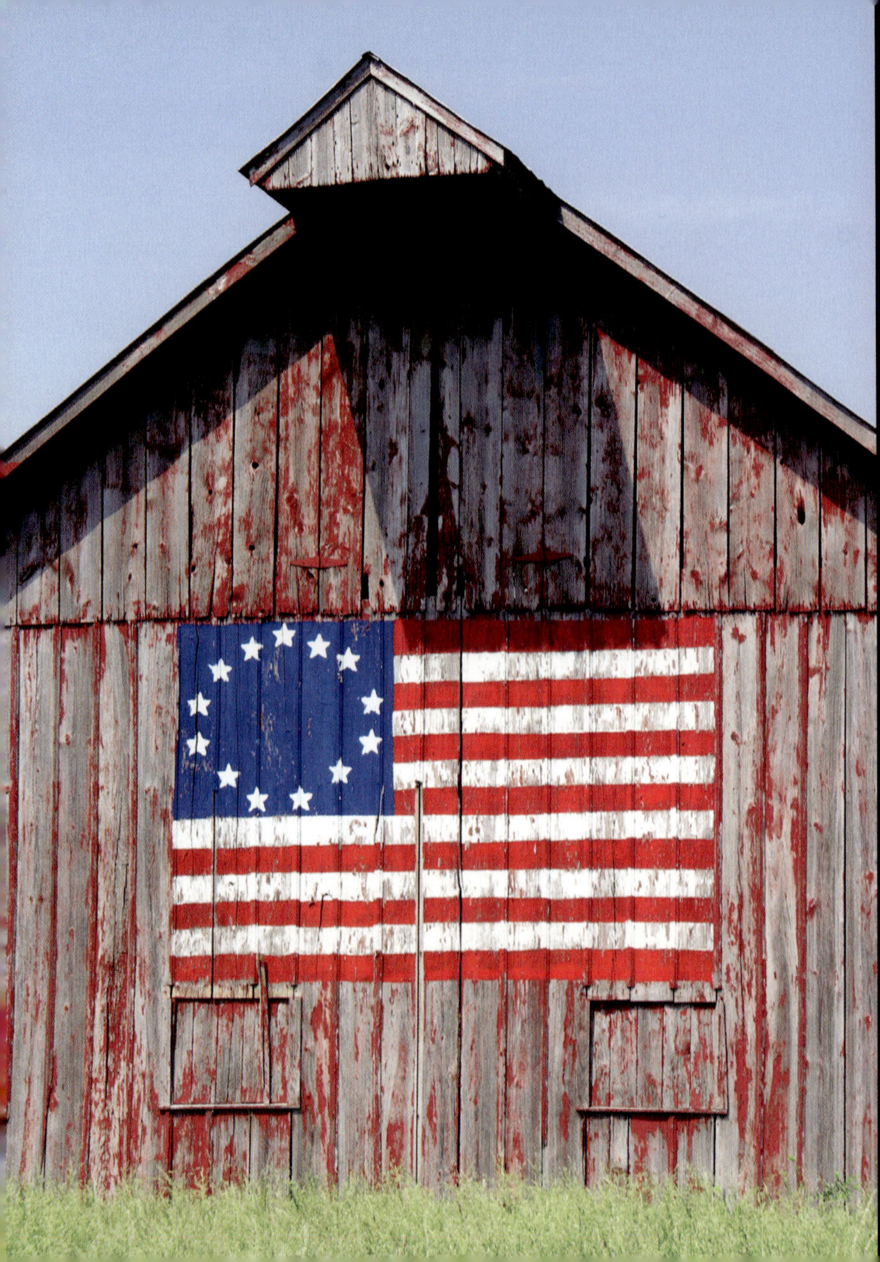

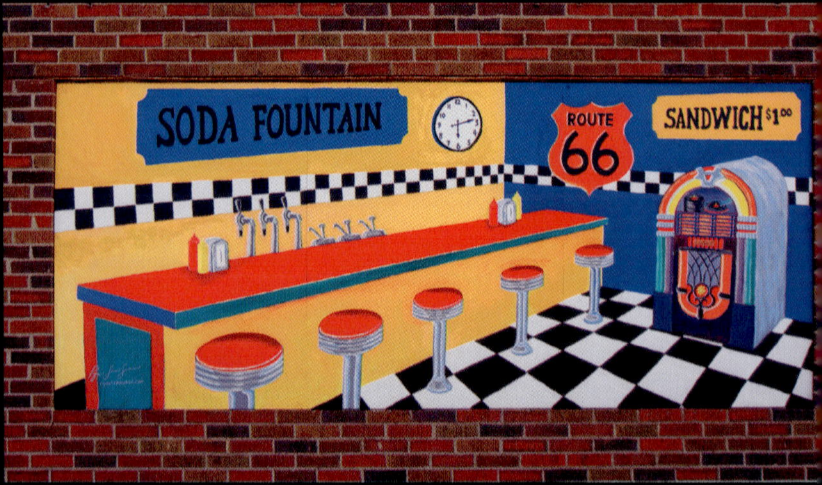
SODA FOUNTAIN
ROUTE
66
SANDWICH $1.00

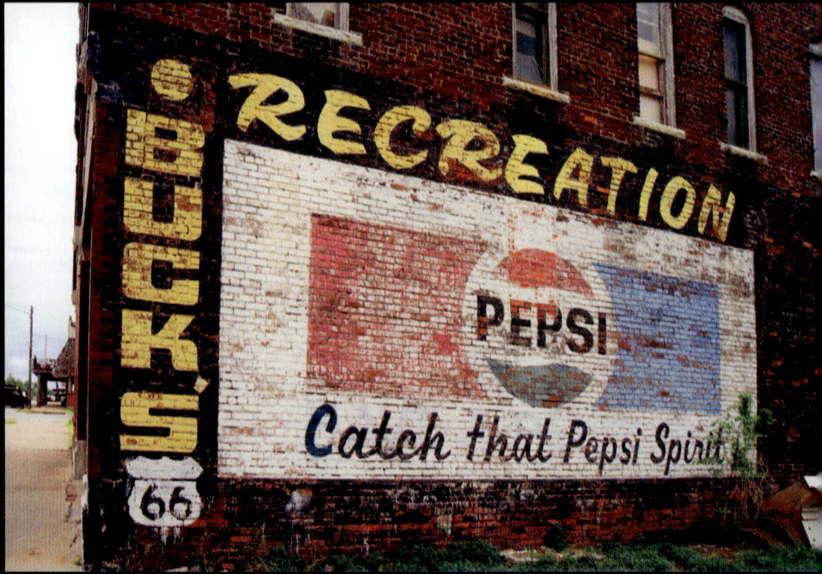
BUCK'S
RECREATION
PEPSI
Catch that Pepsi Spirit
66

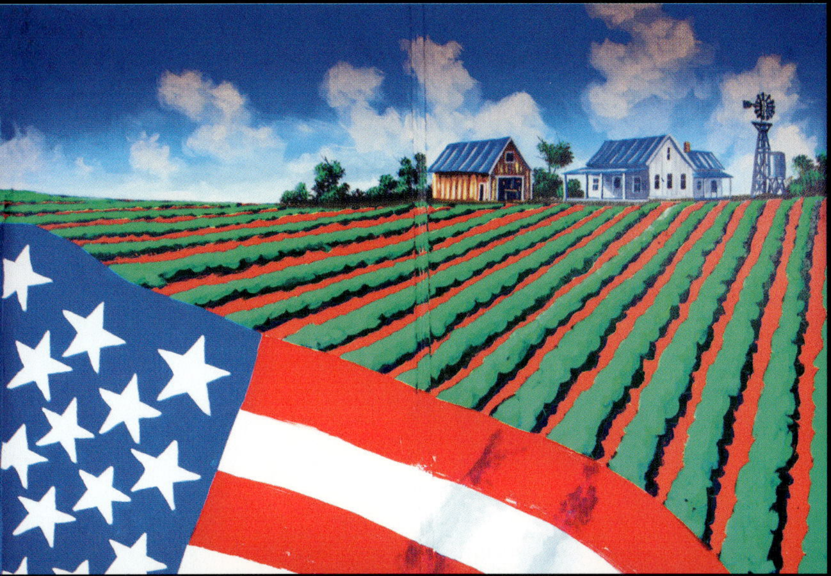

Above: A flag and farm mural in McLean, TX, both patriotic and homespun.

Right: A Coca-Cola bottle advert in Stroud, OK.

Opposite left: A barn in Illinois decorated with an early design for the American flag known as the 'Betsy Ross' (between Nilwood and Carlinville on a Route 66 alignment following Illinois Route 4).

Opposite above right: A modern 'soda fountain' mural in McLean, TX.

Opposite below right: A Pepsi wall advert on Main Street, Galena, KS, fast becoming a ghost sign.

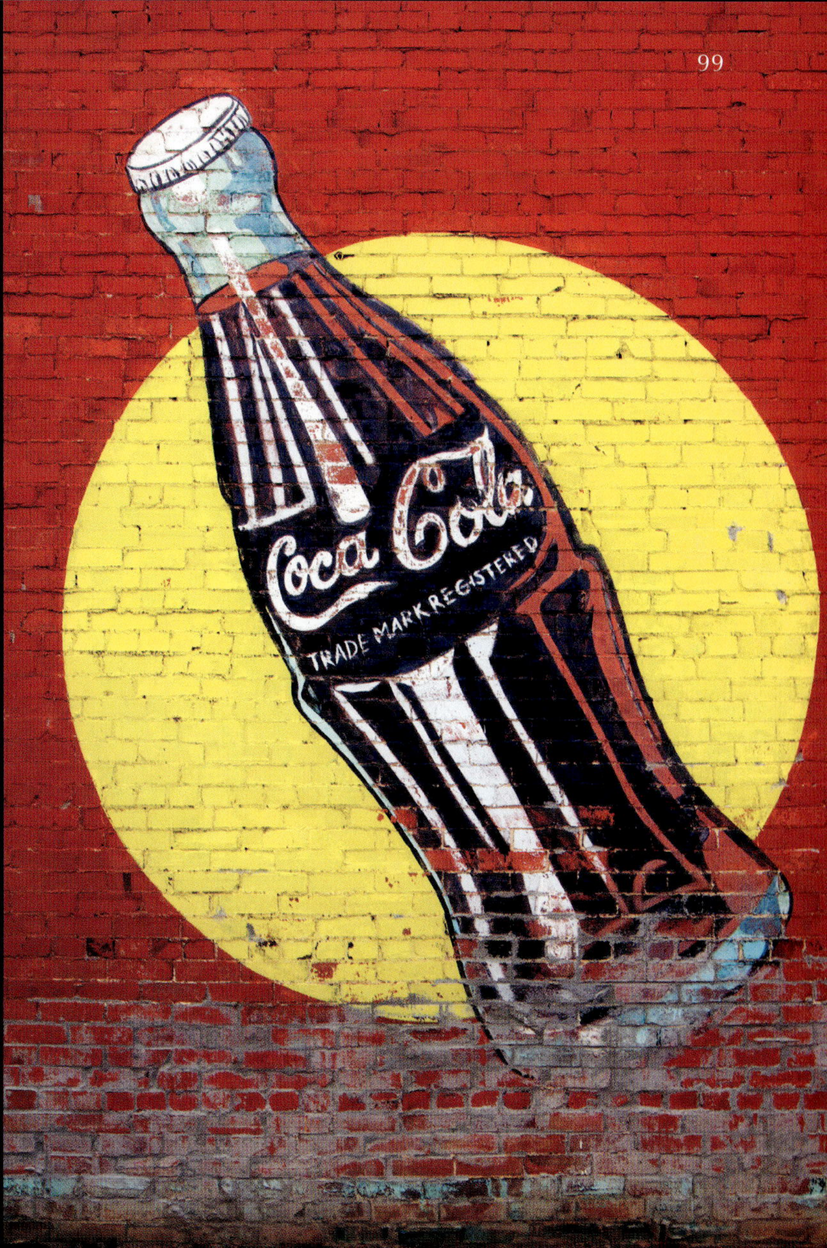

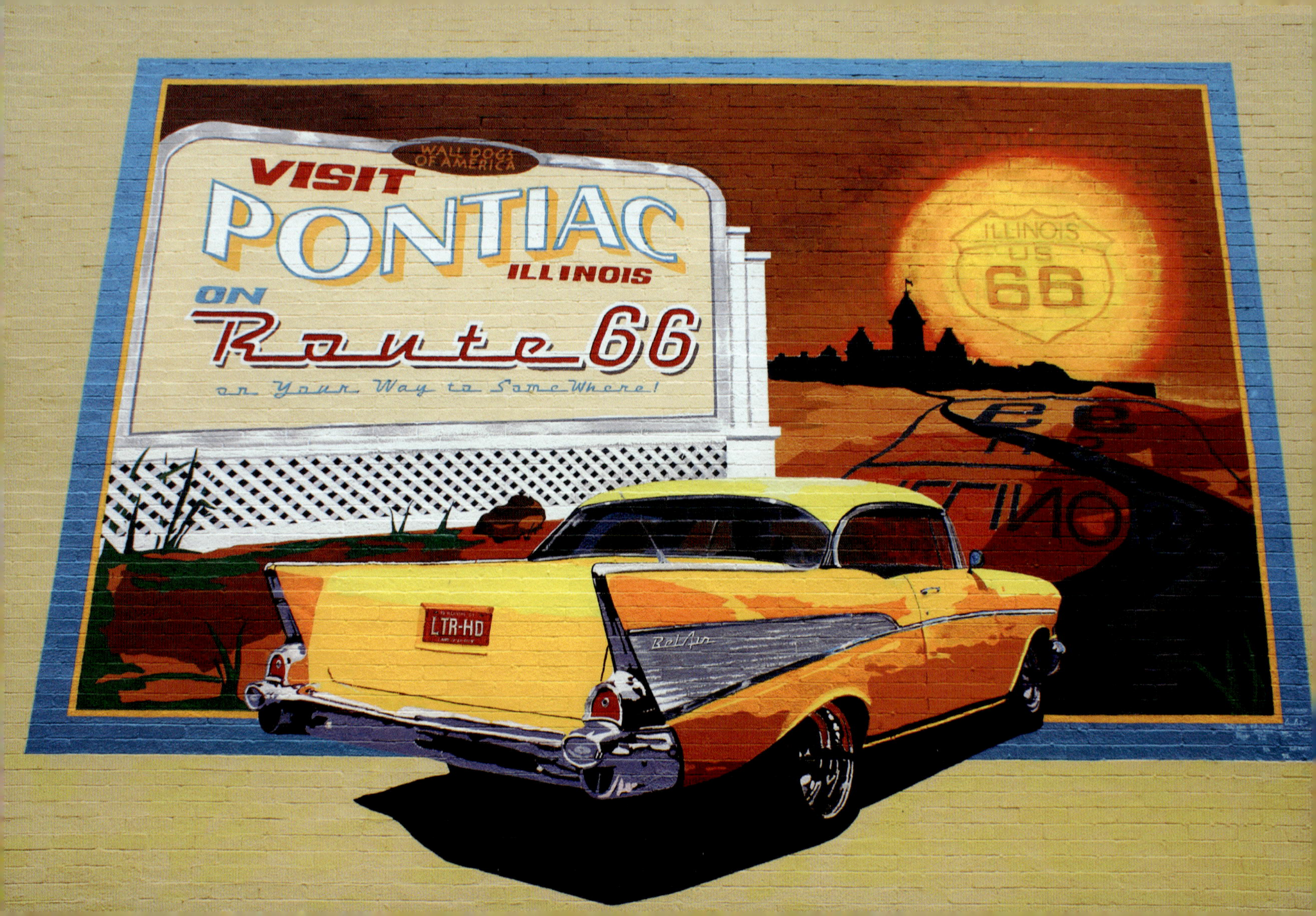
WALL DOGS OF AMERICA
VISIT
PONTIAC
ILLINOIS
ON
Route 66
on Your Way to SomeWhere!
ILLINOIS
US
66
LTR-HD
BelAir

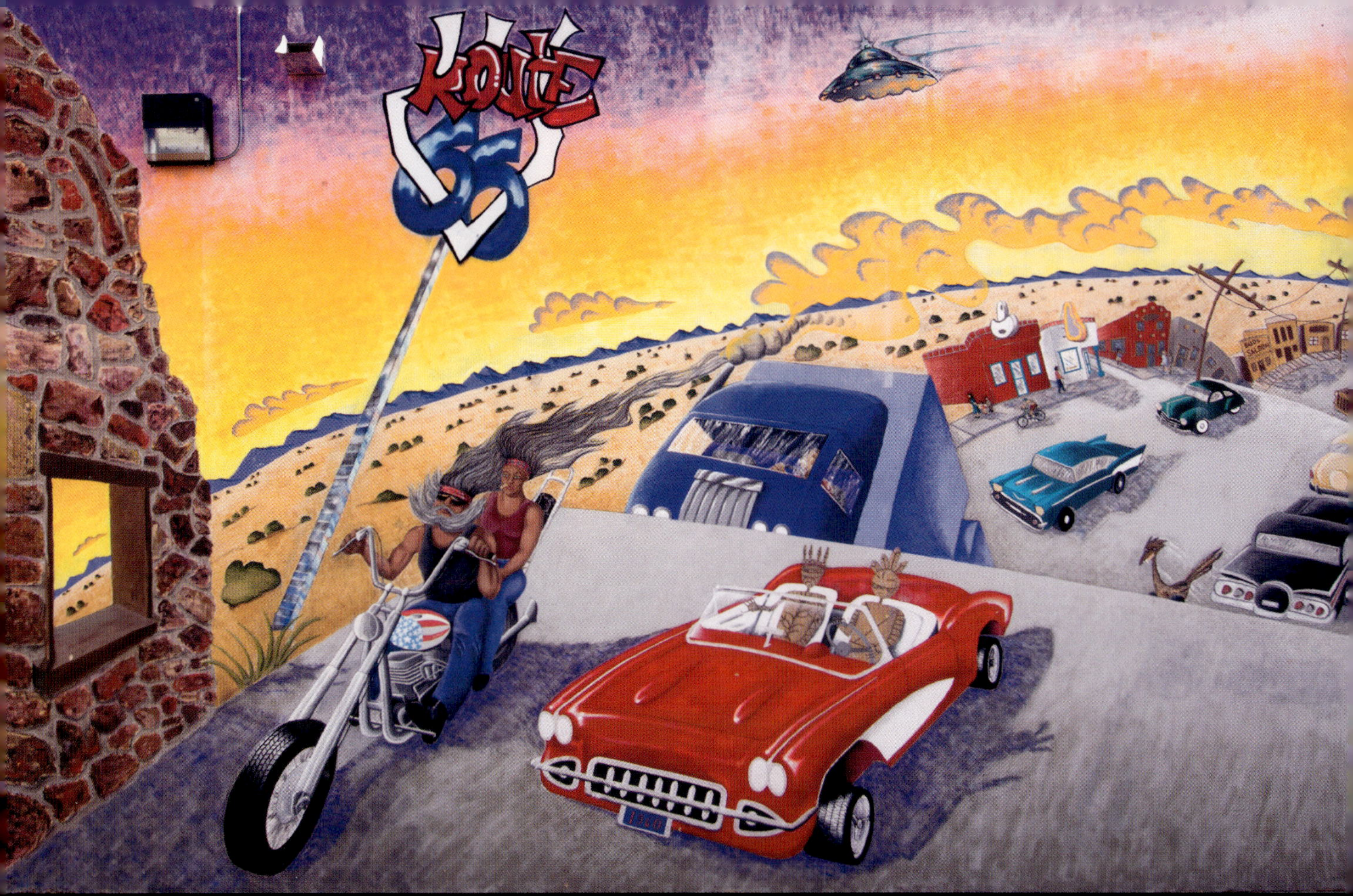

Above: Detail of *El Camino de Los Caminos* mural (designed by Joe Stephenson, 1995) in downtown Albuquerque, NM, including the iconic rec
Corvette.

Opposite: The *Pontiac on Route 66* mural (by Tom and Kathy Durham) in downtown Pontiac, IL, a good example of vehicular *trompe l'oeil*.

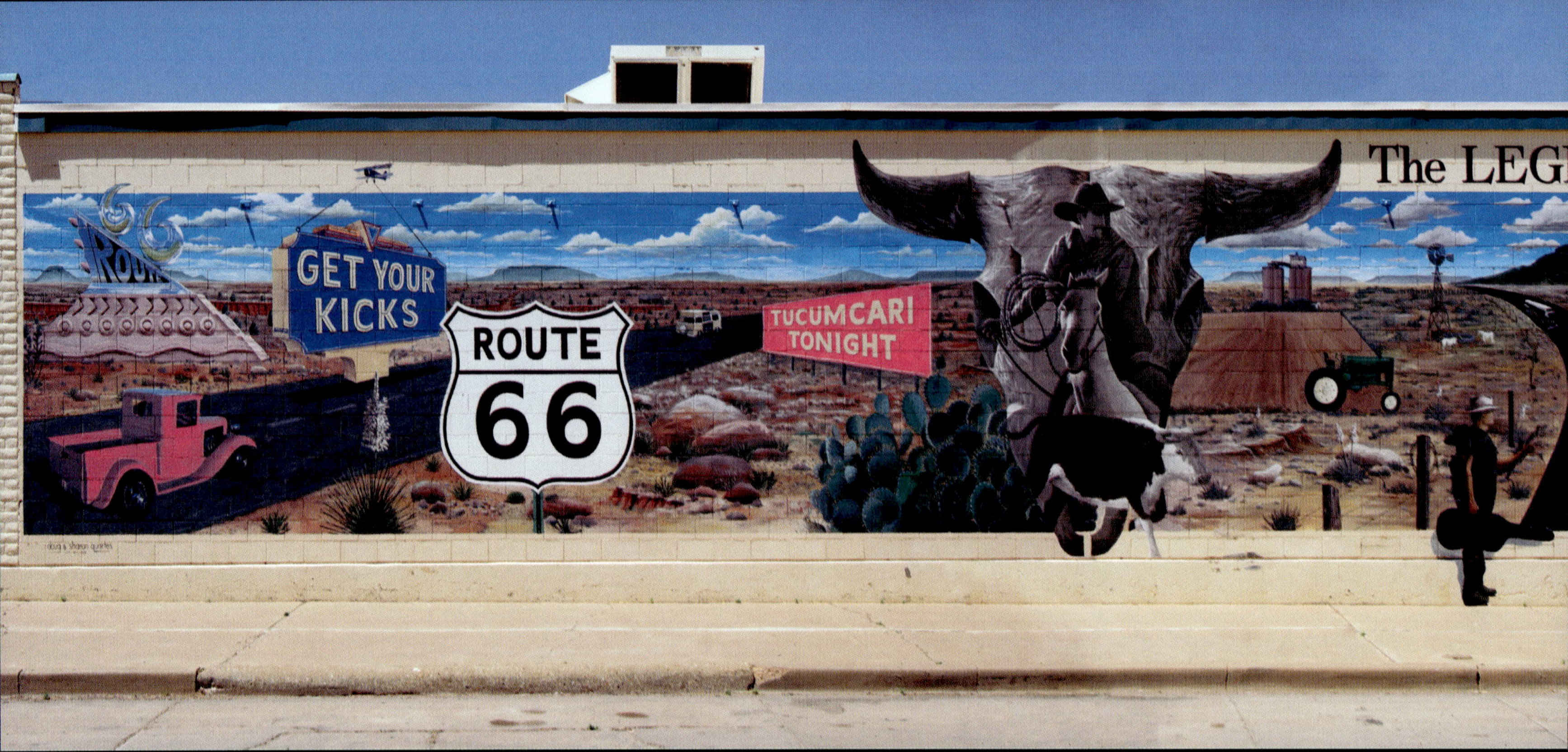

The 35-m-long *The Legendary Road* mural (by Doug and Sharon Quarles) on the side of a Lowe's supermarket on South 2nd Street, Tucumcari, NM.

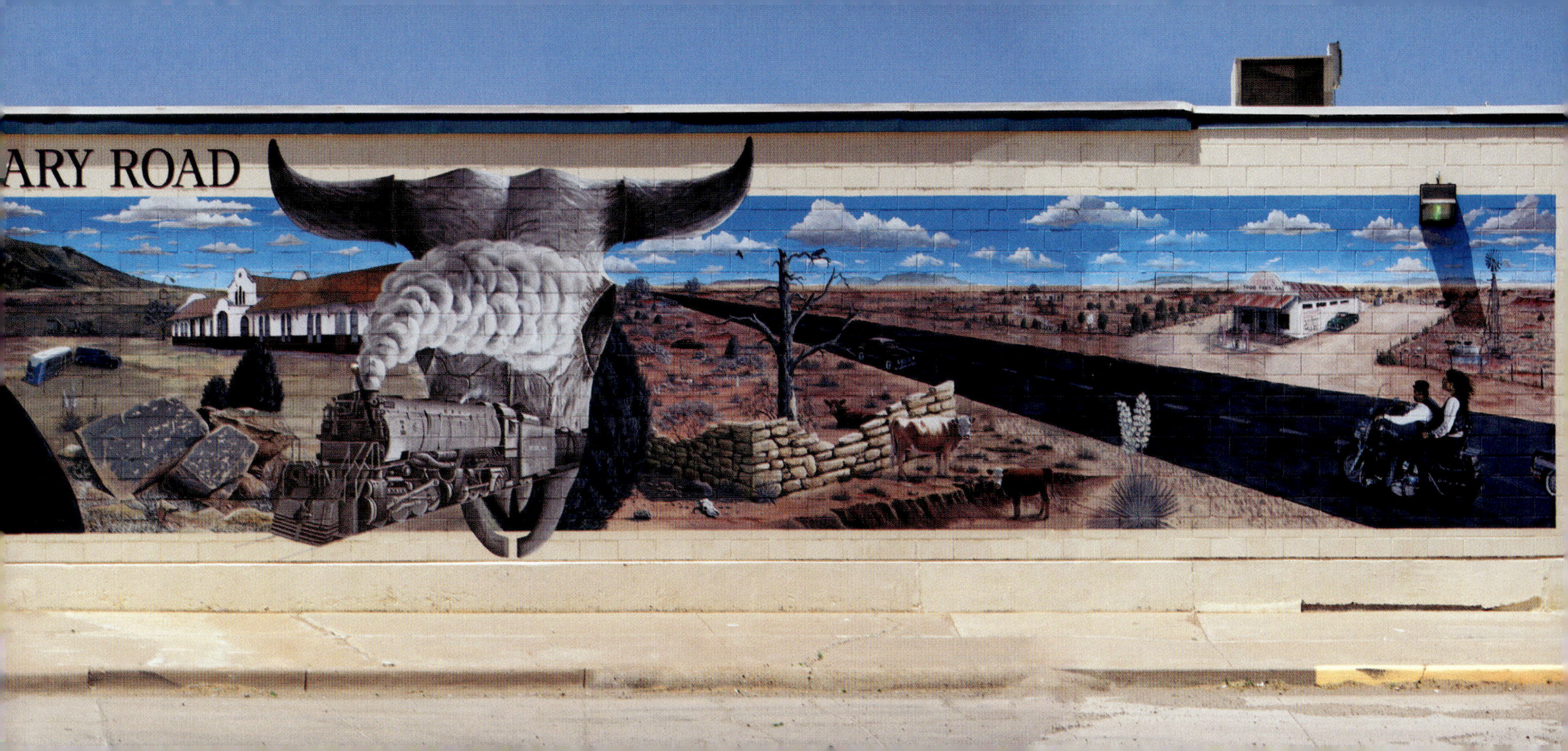
ARY ROAD

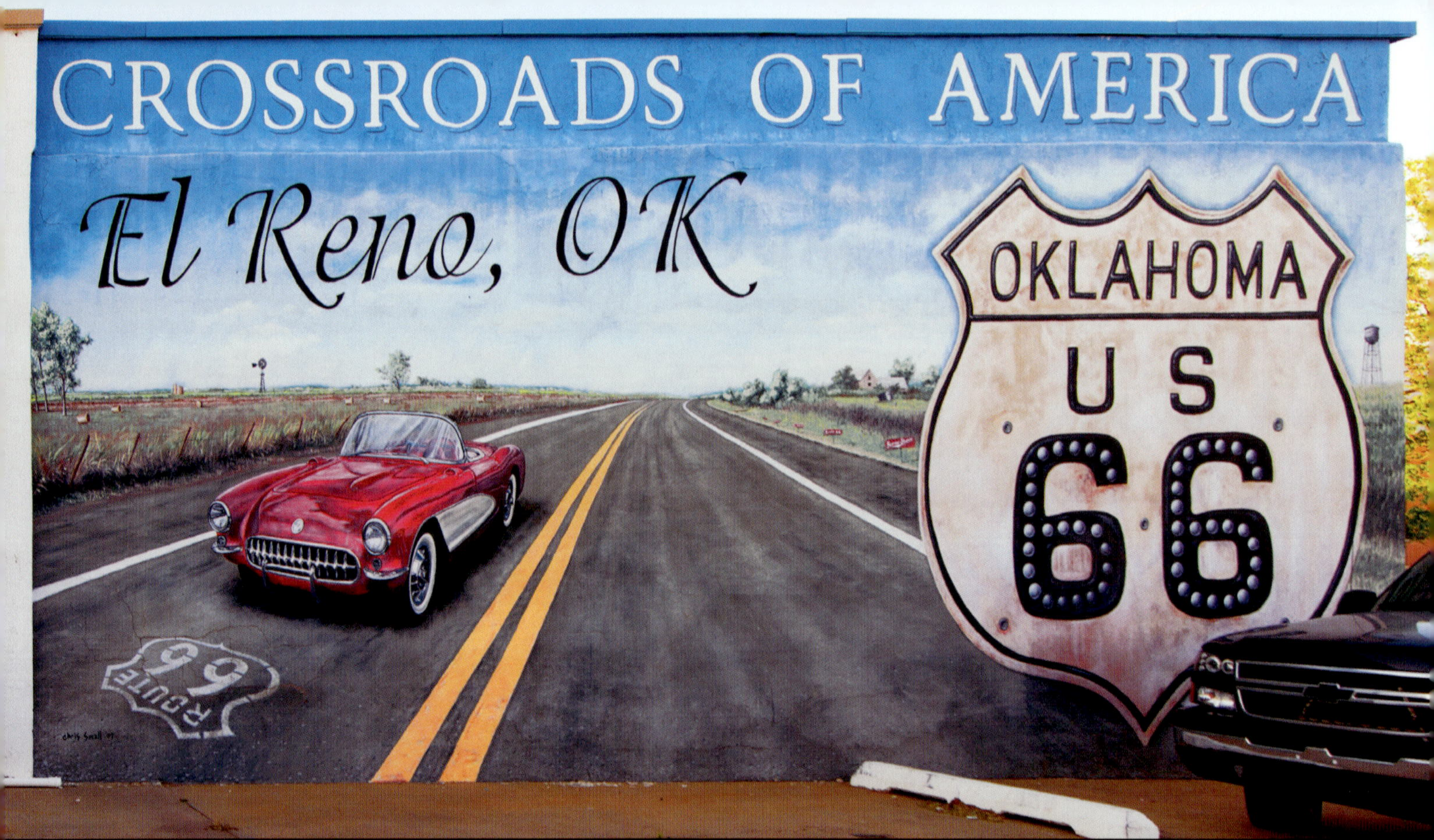

Above: The *Crossroads of America* mural (by Chris Small) in El Reno, OK, at the intersection of two historic highways, the Old Chisholm Trail (US81) and Route 66. Note the parked vehicle, which led to a little perspective manipulation in Photoshop.

Opposite: The *Arizona 66* mural (by Sandy Rusinko) in Kingman, AZ. In this case, a parked car made a straight-on view impossible.

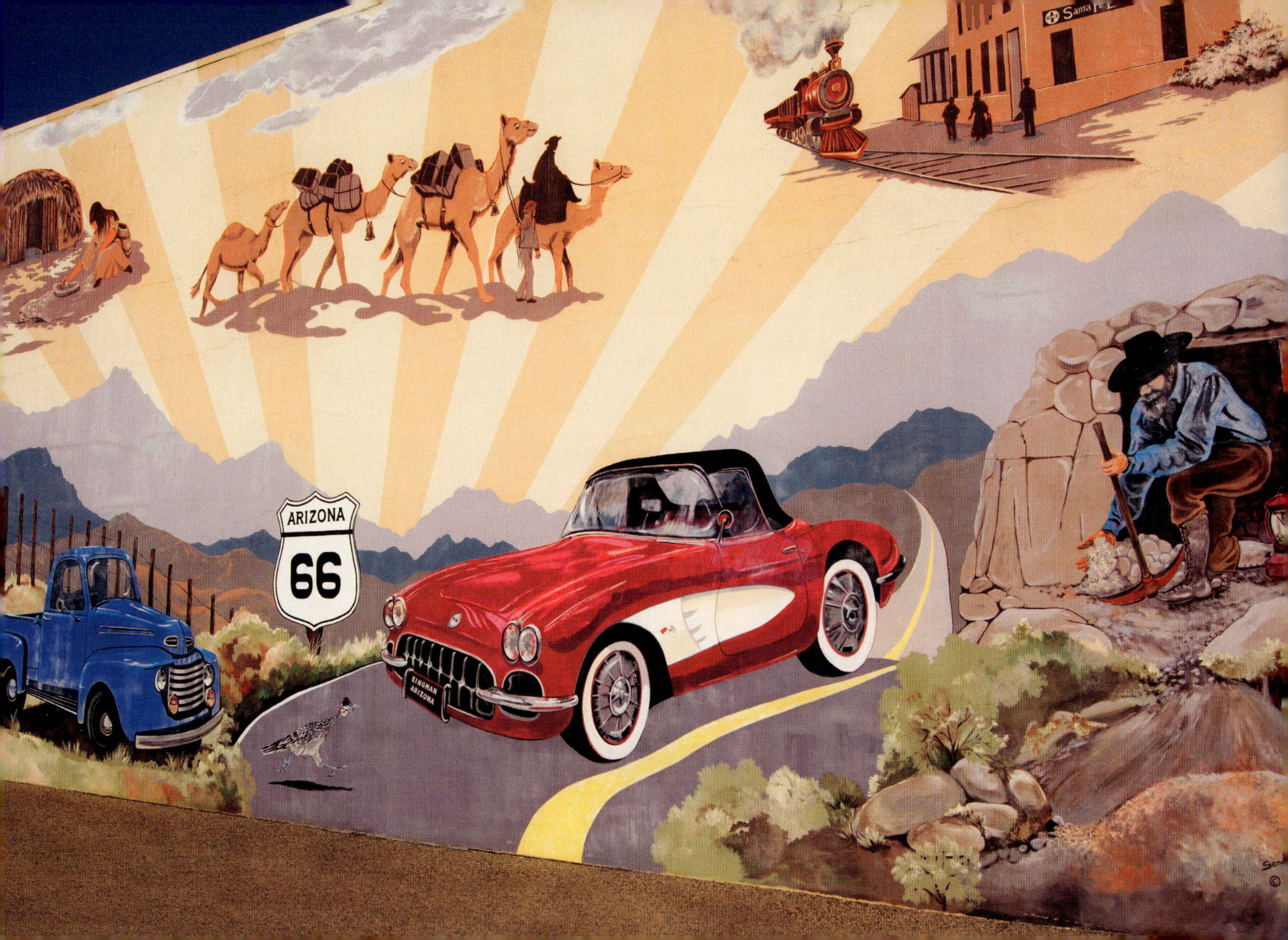
Santa Fe
ARIZONA
66
KINGMAN
ARIZONA

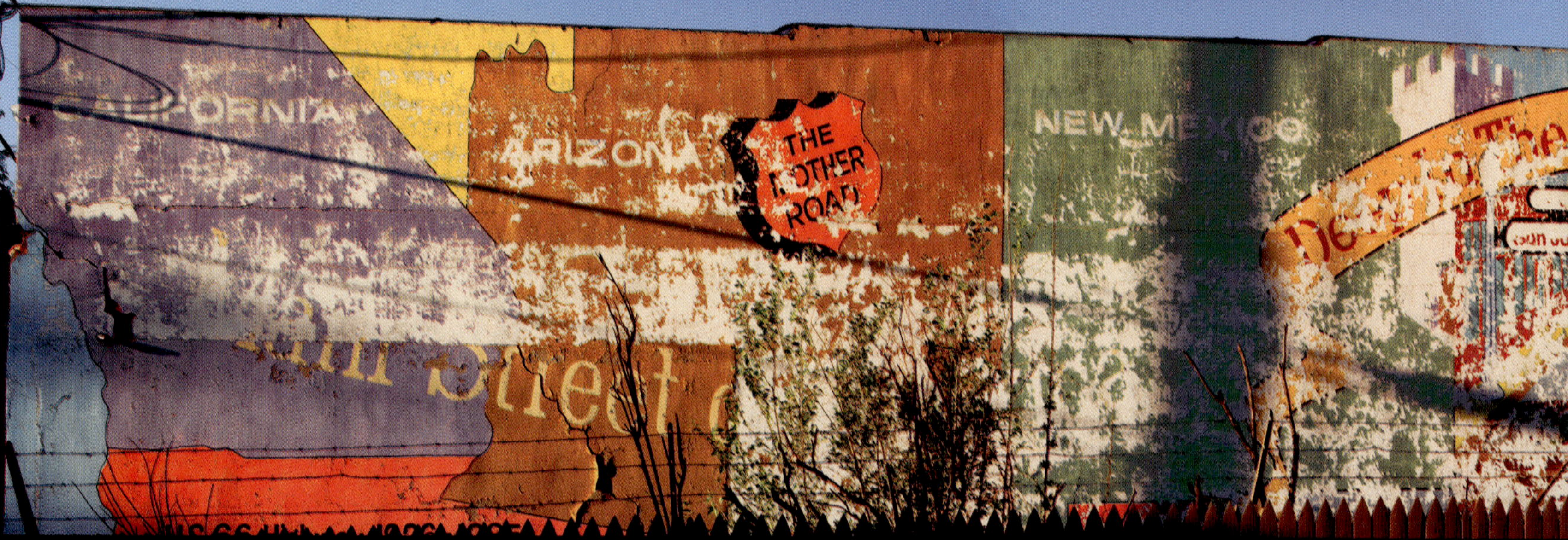
NEW MEXICO

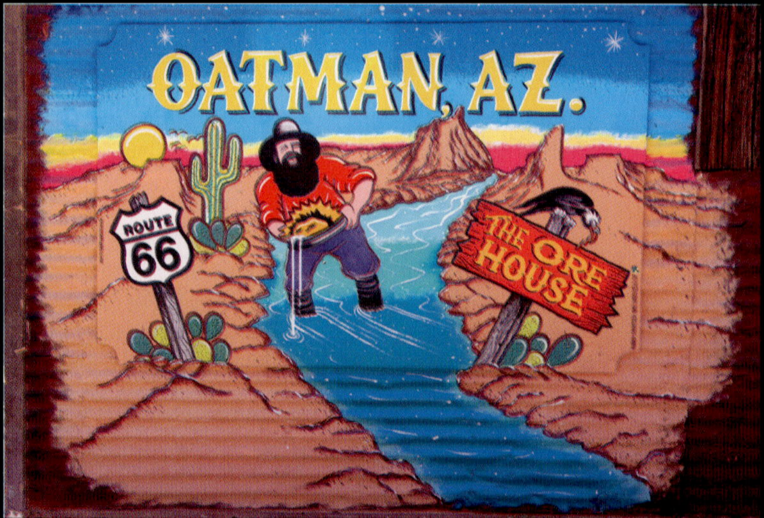
OATMAN, AZ.
ROUTE 66
THE ORE HOUSE

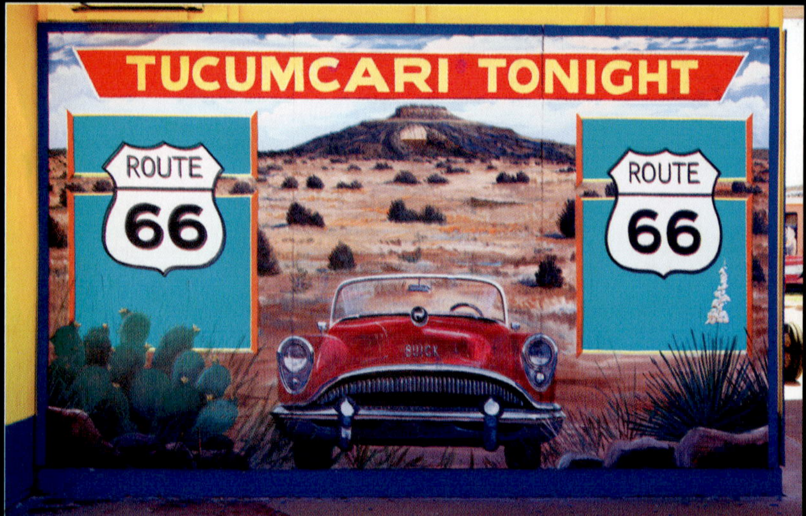
TUCUMCARI TONIGHT
ROUTE 66
ROUTE 66

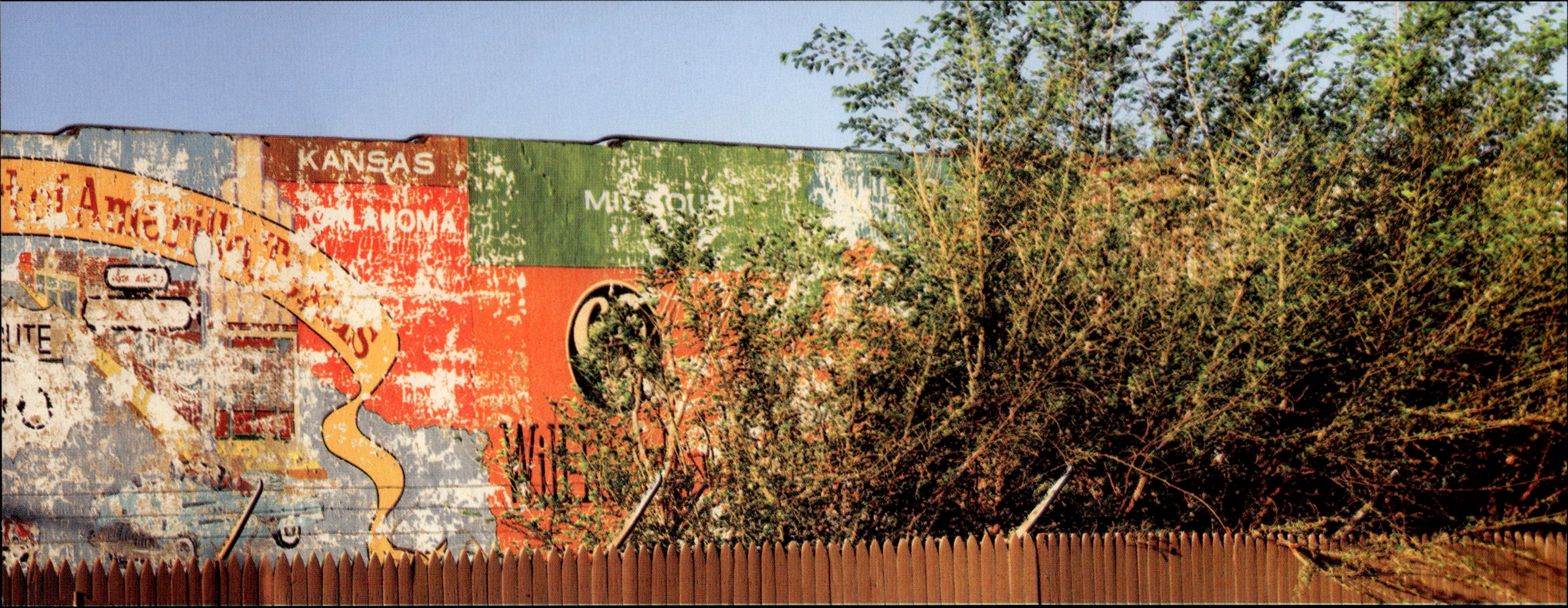

Above: A lucky last view of the *Deep in the Heart of Amarillo Texas* mural (by Jonas & Co., 1994), which depicted the course of Route 66 across the eight states. This ghost mural (on SW 6th Avenue, west of S Alabama Street, Amarillo, TX) has since become completely hidden by trees.

Opposite below left and right: Murals advertising towns on Route 66: Oatman, AZ, and Tucumcari, NM.

Right: A mural on a fence advertising the Desert Hills Motel in Tulsa, OK – not necessarily forever!

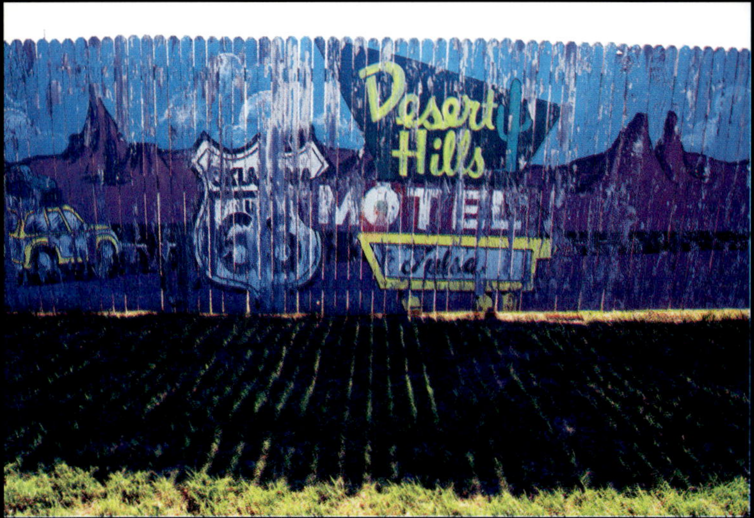

Chapter 9
CULTURE

This book is centred on the premise that Route 66 is an American icon and the observation that the 'Route 66 brand' has become embedded in American culture.

The road's connection with John Steinbeck's 1939 Pulitzer Prize-winning novel *The Grapes of Wrath* has already been covered and, although its brief mention of 'the mother road' was appropriated much later by Route 66 aficionados, it is one of the earliest elements of Route 66 culture. Of course, Cyrus Avery and the other originators of the Route had no idea, in 1926, that parts of the road would become a major migration route during the Dust Bowl crisis of the 1930s, and Steinbeck was simply reporting on the fact, but that hasn't stopped 66ers from adopting *The Grapes of Wrath* as part of its heritage. The 1940 film of the same name, directed by John Ford and starring Henry Fonda as Tom Joad, simply adds to the cultural background and several museums feature an ancient Hudson truck dressed up as the Joad's converted Super-Six sedan [p. 111].

Another cultural adoption from the 1930s involved the nefarious antics of outlaws Bonnie and Clyde, who had an apartment in Joplin, Missouri, and were even photographed in front of a Missouri US 66 highway shield. A hot-rod in Springfield, Missouri, for example, uses a likeness of Bonnie and Clyde to advertise a garage [p. 113].

After the Second World War and the increase in car ownership, tourist traffic on Route 66 increased to the point where a song celebrating the journey did not seem unreasonable. 'Get Your Kicks on Route 66', written by Bobby Troup and recorded by Nat King Cole in 1946, begins 'If you ever plan to motor west / travel my way, take the highway that's the best'. It was later covered by many other artists from Bing Crosby to the Rolling Stones, which further enhanced the road's standing in American culture. To be honest, the lyrics are a bit light on narrative, but do include a lot of place names, which worked well in terms of local marketing, with phrases such as 'Don't forget Winona' entering the 66 vernacular.

Like Steinbeck's *Grapes*, Jack Kerouac's 1957 novel *On the Road* has become linked to Route 66. Again, the highway is barely mentioned in the book and it seems likely that this is another example of cultural appropriation for marketing the Route 66 brand.

Then, between 1960 and 1964, CBS aired a TV drama series called *route 66* (complete with 'hip' lower-case r) which, though not entirely restricted to travels on that road, became a part of the culture and even spawned a Route 66 travel game. Most significantly, in terms of iconography, the series featured two adventurers who cruised the highway in a Chevrolet Corvette sports car; interestingly, though, it wasn't a red Chevy because other, less vibrant colours registered better on black-and-white TV. Apparently, Kerouac considered suing over the similarities with his book, but as a biographer pointed out, you can't copyright 'two guys in a car'!

Arguably, the 1969 film *Easy Rider* had more in common with *On the Road*, because of its drugs and counter-culture themes, but it too has little to do with Route 66 (apart from a scene that shows the riders in Flagstaff, Arizona, passing the lumberjack statue mentioned in Chapter 6). Despite the loose associations of these movies, their role in the legend of Route 66 is clear: they epitomise the ethos of the 'open road' that has become a standard of Route 66 culture.

Other movies with connections to Route 66 include *The Blues Brothers* (1980), filmed in Chicago and a prison in Joliet, Illinois, and the road-trip-inspired *Bagdad Café* (1987), filmed not in Bagdad, California, but in Newberry Springs, at the Sidewinder Café (later renamed for marketing reasons!).

A more recent film, which is clearly influenced by Route 66, is the 2006 Pixar movie *Cars*, which features various types of motor vehicles as its characters. The story of how the US interstates bypassed small towns and businesses is well-portrayed in the film by the decline of the small, forgotten town of Radiator Springs, which mirrors the real-world of abandoned Route 66 settlements. Indeed, Ramone's Bodyshop is obviously a cartoon version of the art deco Conoco gas station in Shamrock, Texas, while a mountain range mimics the upturned Caddies of Cadillac Ranch. Elsewhere, the Cozy Cone Motel is clearly based on the Wigwam Motels in Holbrook and San Bernadino. Apparently, the film's working title was 'Route 66' but was changed to avoid confusion with the 1960s TV series.

Interestingly, some of the characters from *Cars* are now icons on Route 66, so the cultural influence has turned full circle! The fact that they do not seem out of place speaks volumes about the quirky sense of humour that personifies the Route. This can be seen to effect in towns like Seligman, where tailor's dummies are posed on building facades and with classic vehicles (sometimes even under them!). And who else but a 66er would think of fitting a digger bucket and a backhoe to a yellow Ford Edsel and posing it in a parking lot [p. 114]? I'm not sure this type of humour would work outside America, and critics could view it as twee and unsophisticated, but when you're there, embedded in the culture of Route 66, it seems acceptable. It's simply a way of celebrating this endearing highway.

Beyond books and films, the culture of Route 66 is an eclectic mix spanning art deco architecture and Harley-Davidson motorcycles. The former is an interesting diversion, but the latter is more obvious on the road. Although much of the Route, today, is more of a ghost road than a busy highway, the peace is sometimes broken by the idiosyncratic burble of the large motorcycle engine. Although they may be channelling *Easy Rider*, riders usually wear the uniform of black leathers, blue jeans and helmets, but you can still see the odd bandana and 'hell-raiser' tattoos on show. Personally, I have a preference for four wheels and air-conditioning, but on Route 66 a feeling of envy seeps in as I watch a Harley burble by, knowing I'm just not cool enough to carry it off.

Whether or not you like the Blue Whales, Edsel diggers and humorous signage, it is hard to deny that Route 66 typifies the term Americana. It may suffer an almost institutionalised cultural branding – from Steinbeck's 'mother road' to Bobby Troup's 'Get Your Kicks' – but there's more to it than taglines. Route 66 may be over 2,000 miles in length, but there's a feeling of camaraderie, togetherness and even love that ties it together.

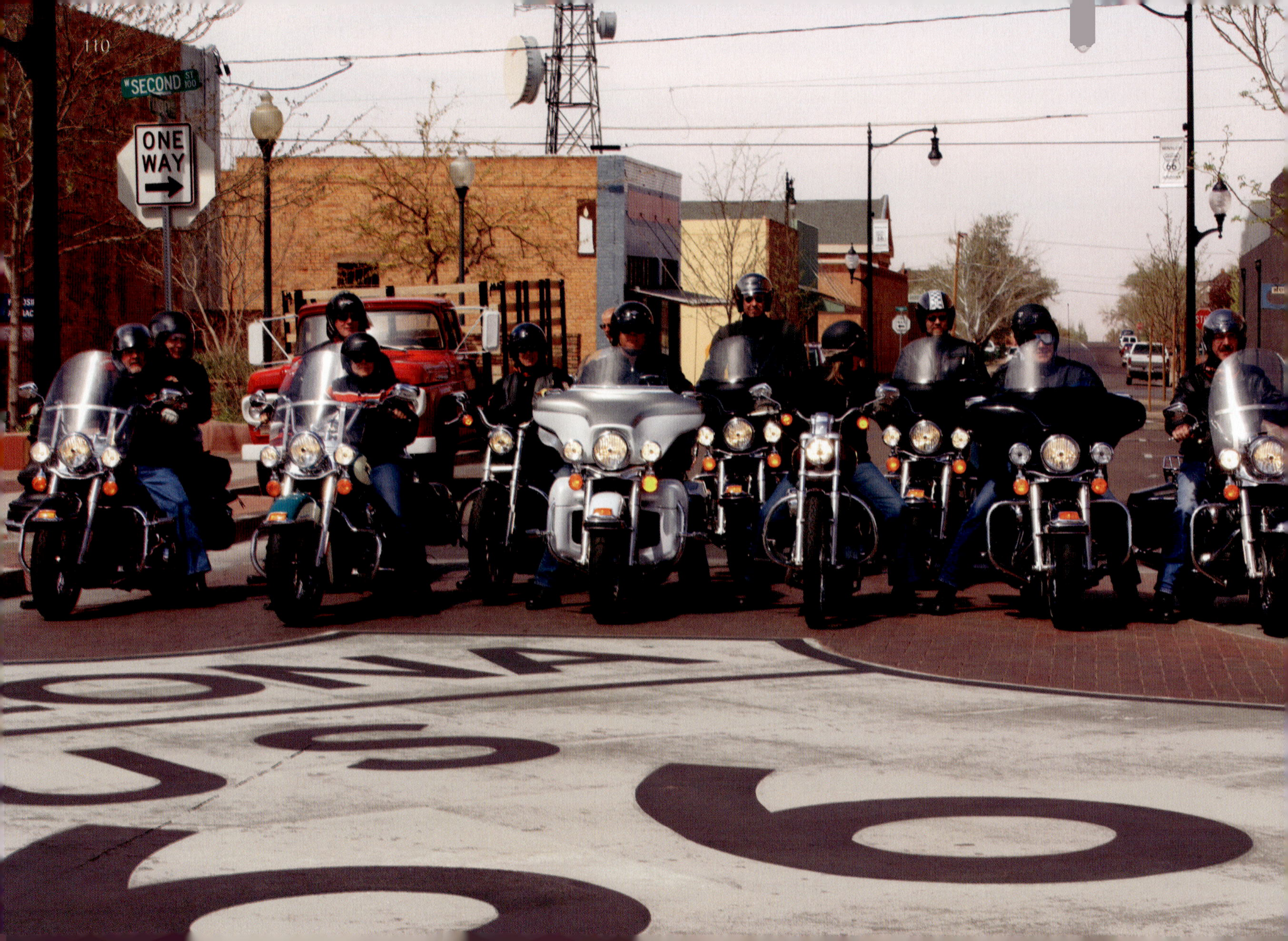
W SECOND ST 100
ONE WAY

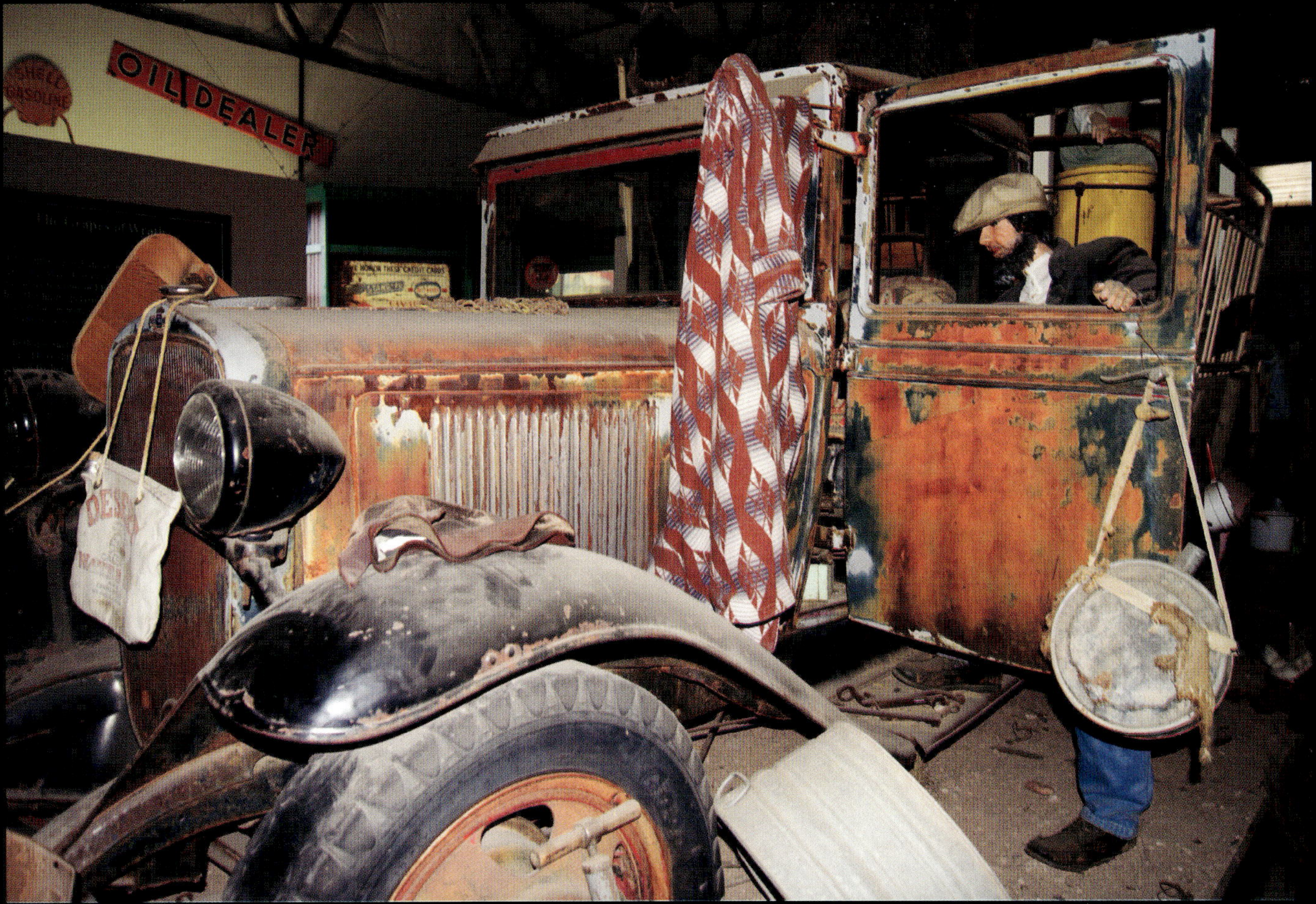

Above: A *Grapes of Wrath* display at the Arizona Route 66 (Powerhouse) Museum in Kingman, AZ (note the water bag on the radiator and the canteen on the door handle).

Opposite: A group of bikers pose for photographers behind a massive Route 66 shield at Standin' on the Corner junction in Winslow, AZ. Note: they weren't posing for me but I hijacked the shot anyway!

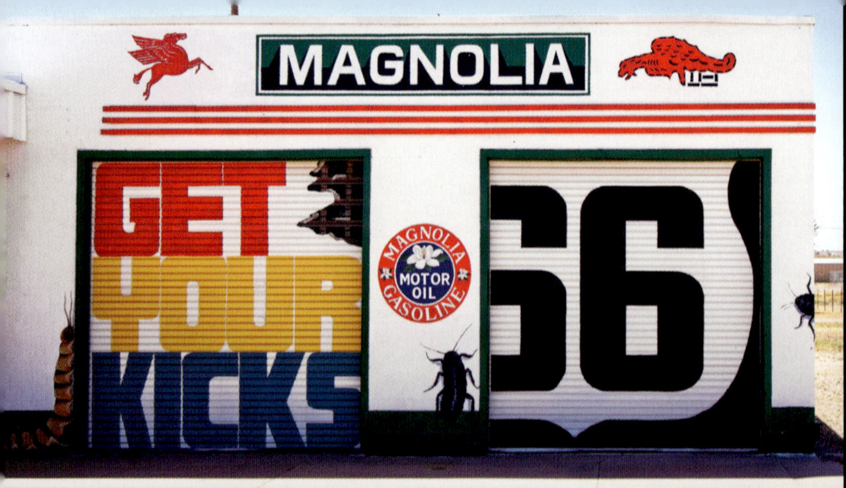

Above: A bug-ridden 'Get Your Kicks' artwork on a Magnolia station in Tucumcari, NM.

Below: A modern hoarding in Adrian, TX, advertising Tucumcari as a place to stay.

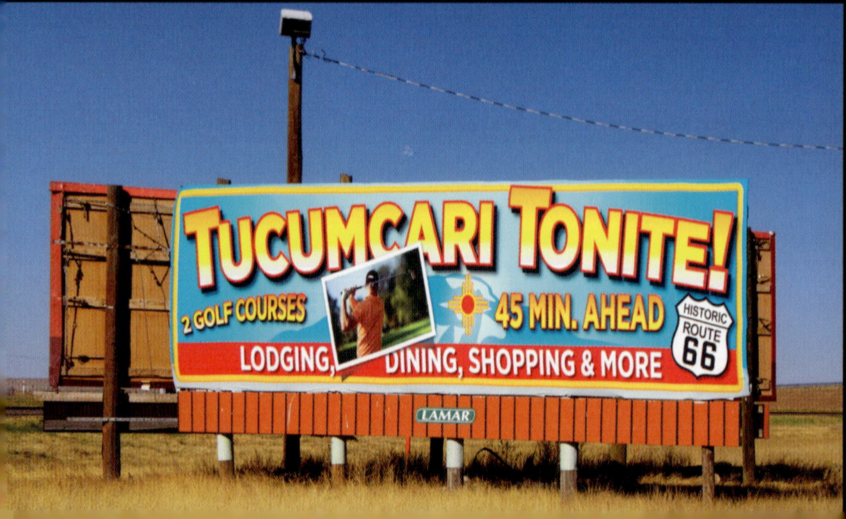

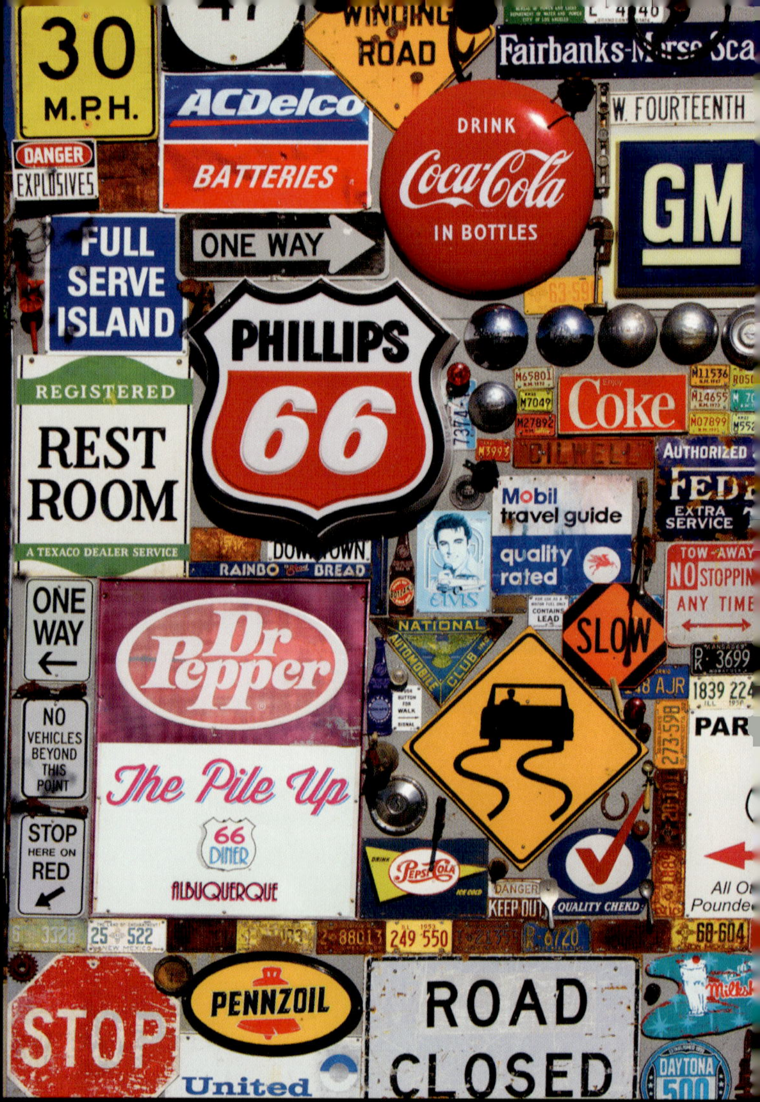

Above and opposite left: A magnificent display of historic signage outside the 66 Diner in Albuquerque, NM.

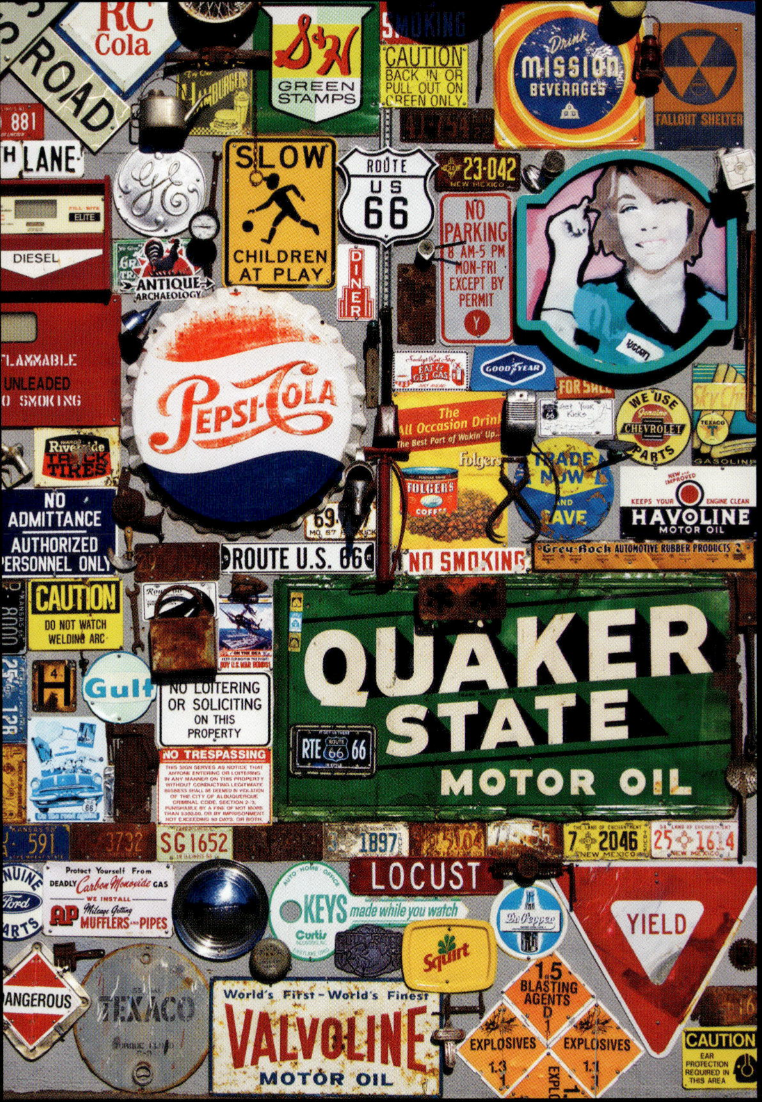

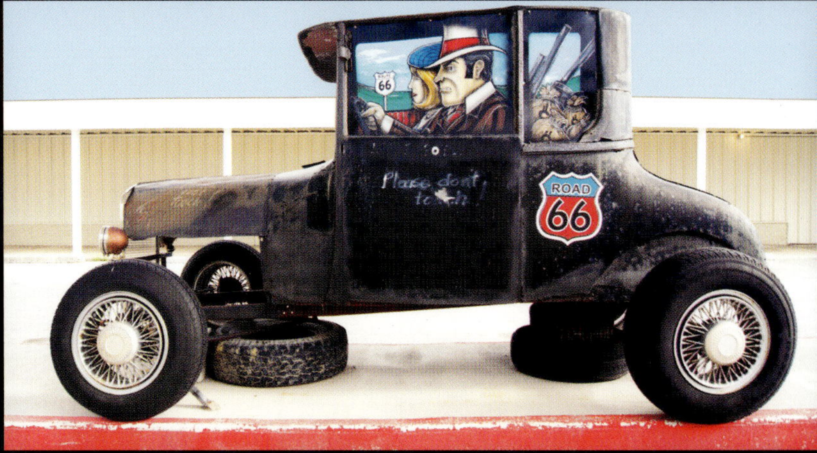

Above: A hot-rod 'accommodating' outlaws Bonnie and Clyde at Bud's Tire and Wheel, Springfield, MO.

Below: A display of historic licence plates outside an old gas station at Davenport, OK.

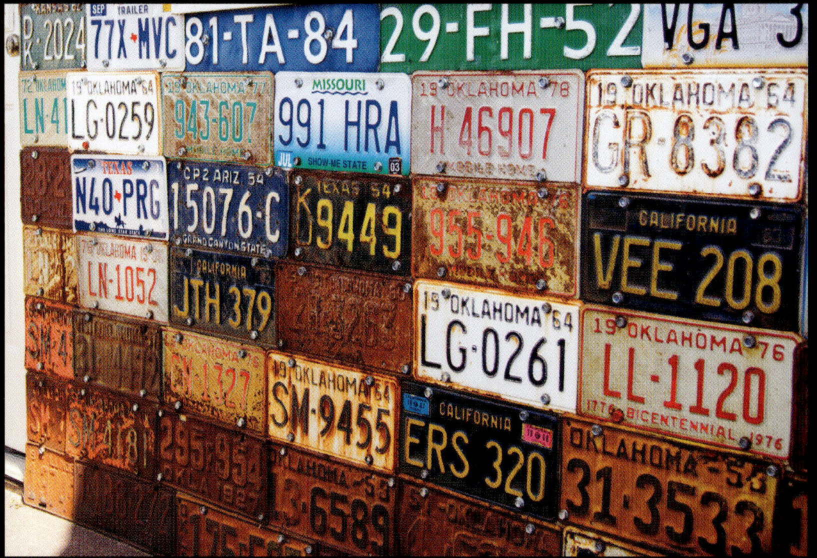

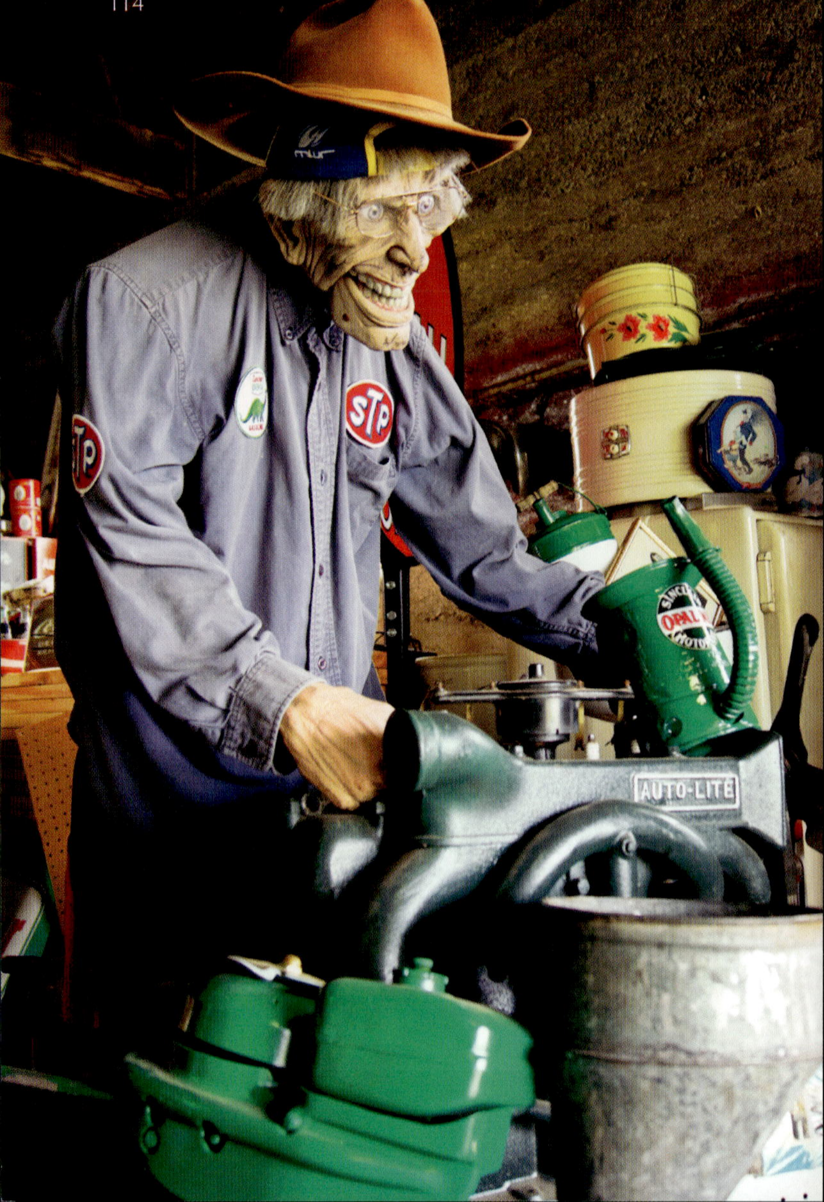

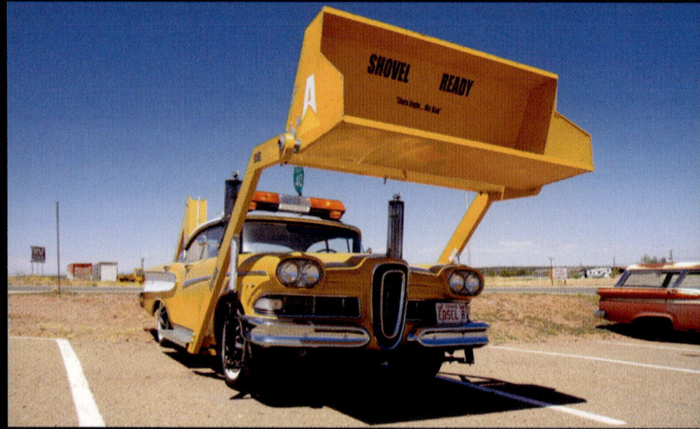

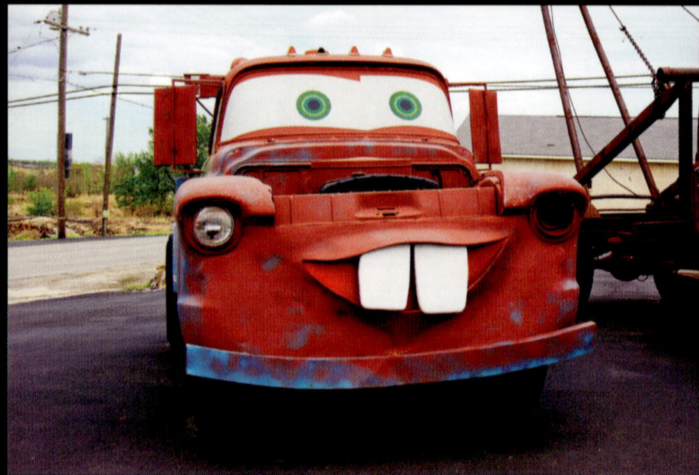

This spread: Route 66 humour: one of the 'older hands' at Gay Parita station, Paris Springs Junction, MO; a digger bucket and backhoe mated to a Ford Edsel at the Route 66 Auto Museum, Santa Rosa, NM; a tow-truck made up to resemble the Tow Mater character from the *Cars* movie at Cars on the Route, Galena, KS; Elvis and friend on the front bumper of a pink Cadillac in Seligman, AZ; a 1949 Mercury at Gay Parita station dressed as the Sheriff character from *Cars*; a Harley warning sign at Elbow Inn, Devil's Elbow, MO (seen and noted!).

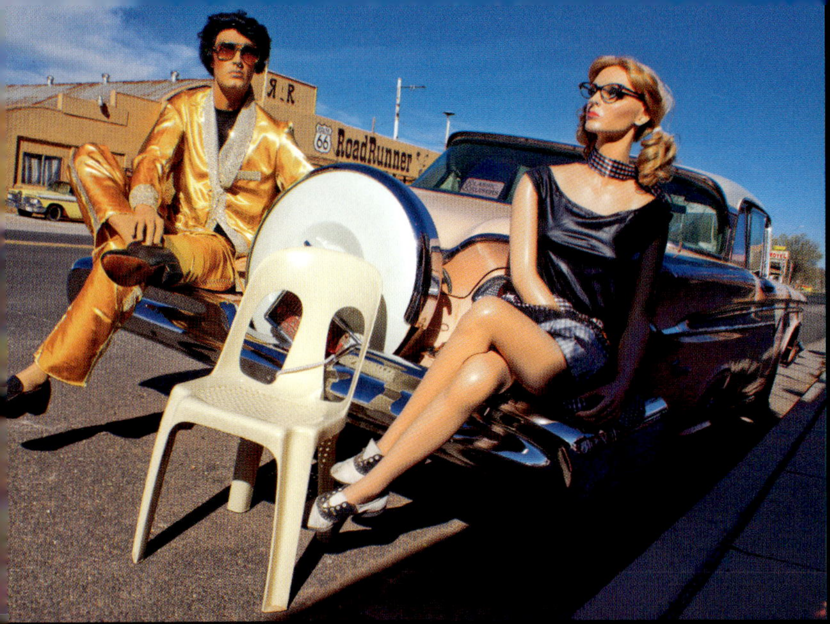
RoadRunner

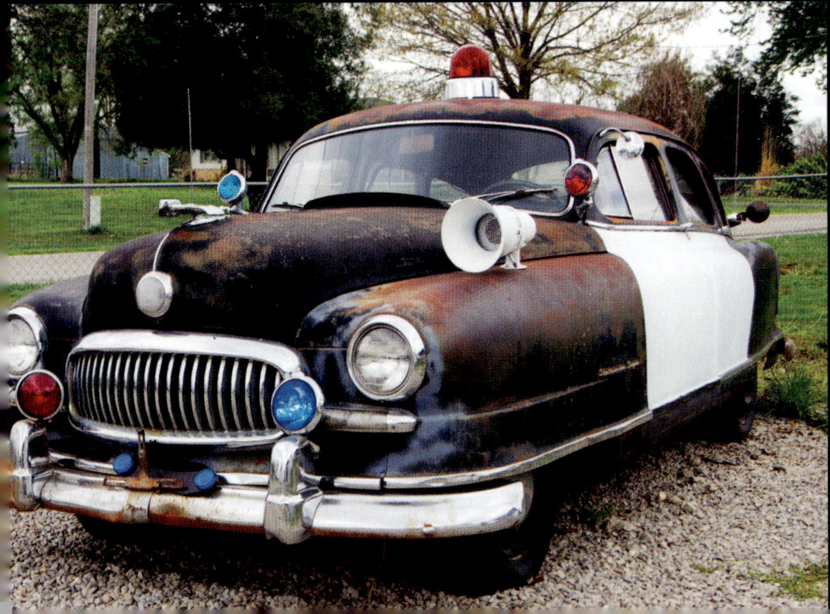

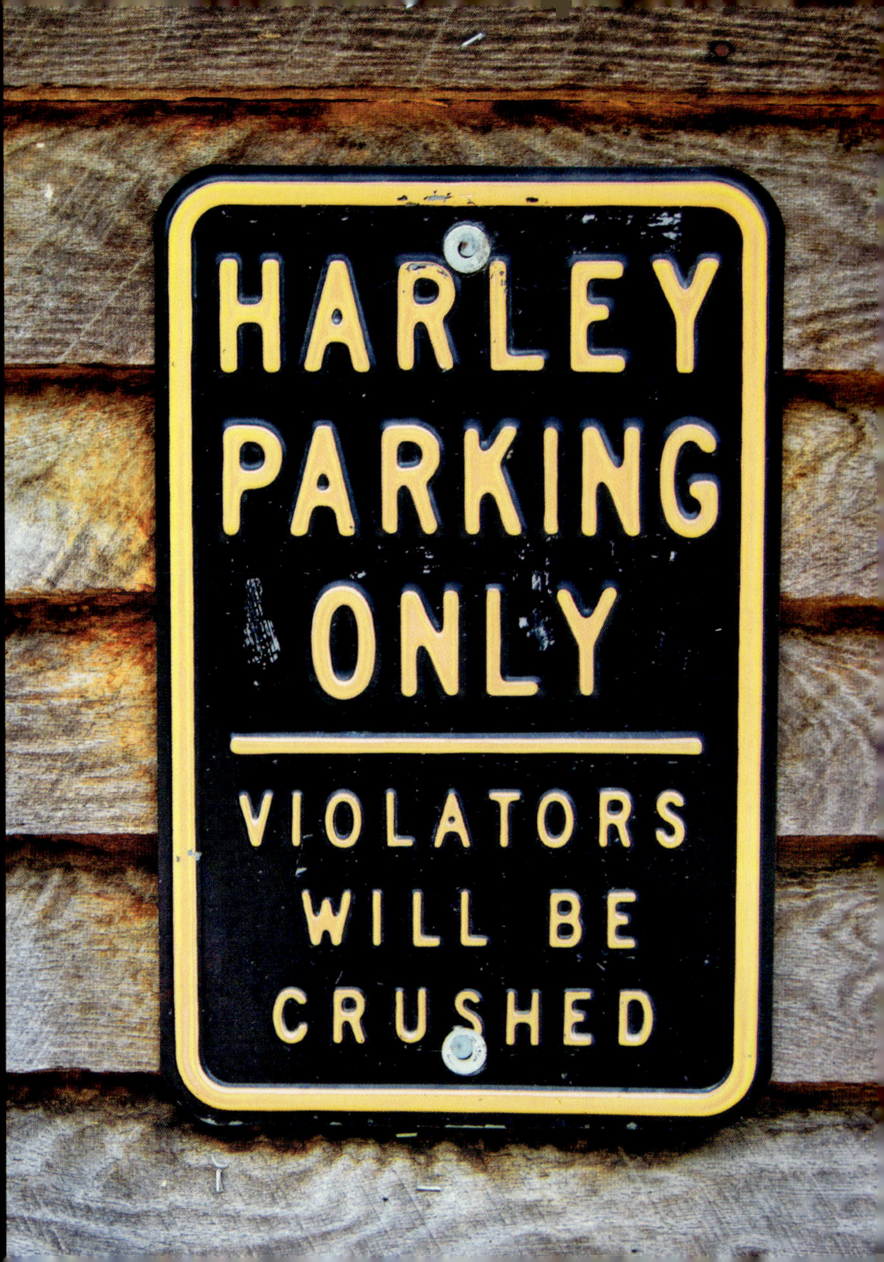
HARLEY
PARKING
ONLY
VIOLATORS
WILL BE
CRUSHED

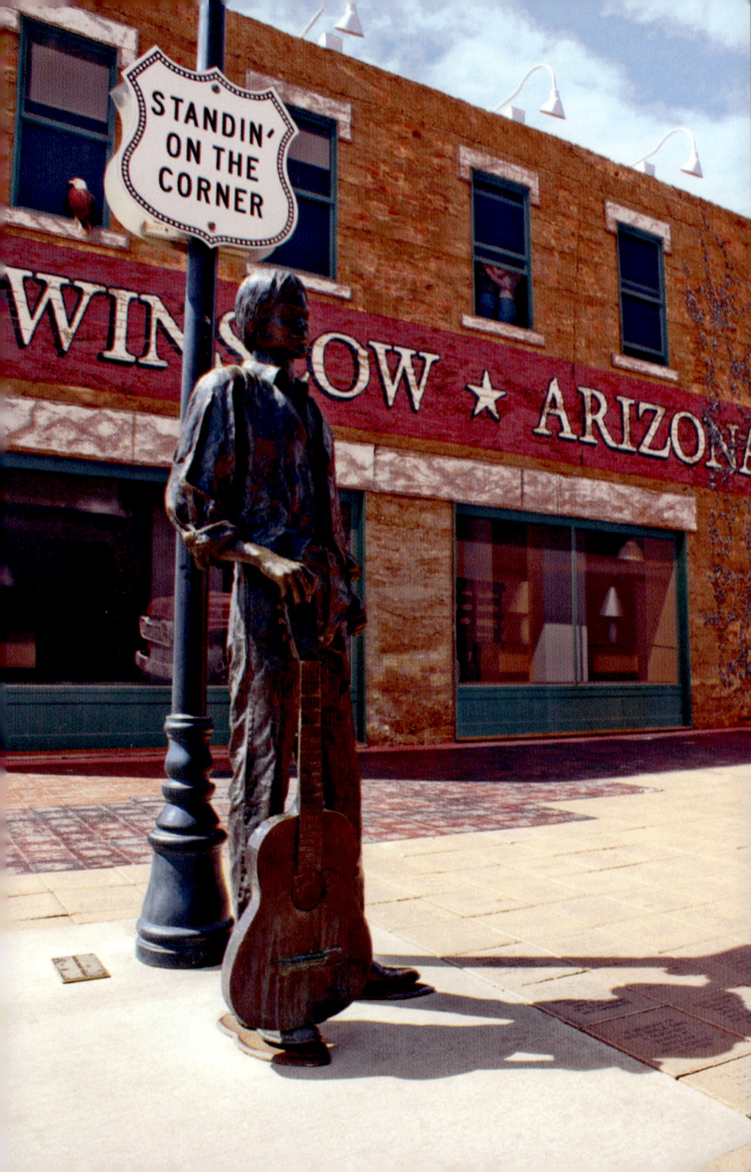

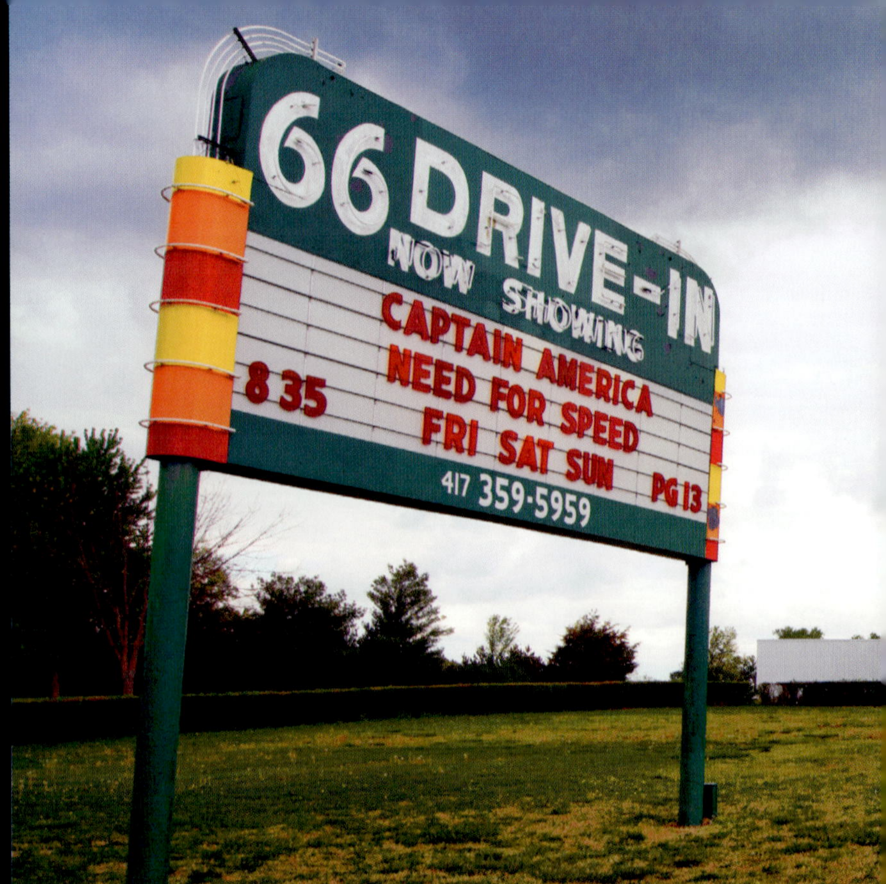

Above: The 66 Drive-in Theatre in Carthage, MO, which opened in 1949 (the concept of the drive-in cinema was patented by Richard Hollingshead in 1932 and the first opened in Camden, New Jersey, in 1933).

Left: The 1999 *Standin' on the Corner* art installation in Winslow, AZ, by sculptor Ron Adamson and muralist John Pugh, which references the 1972 Eagles song 'Take it Easy'.

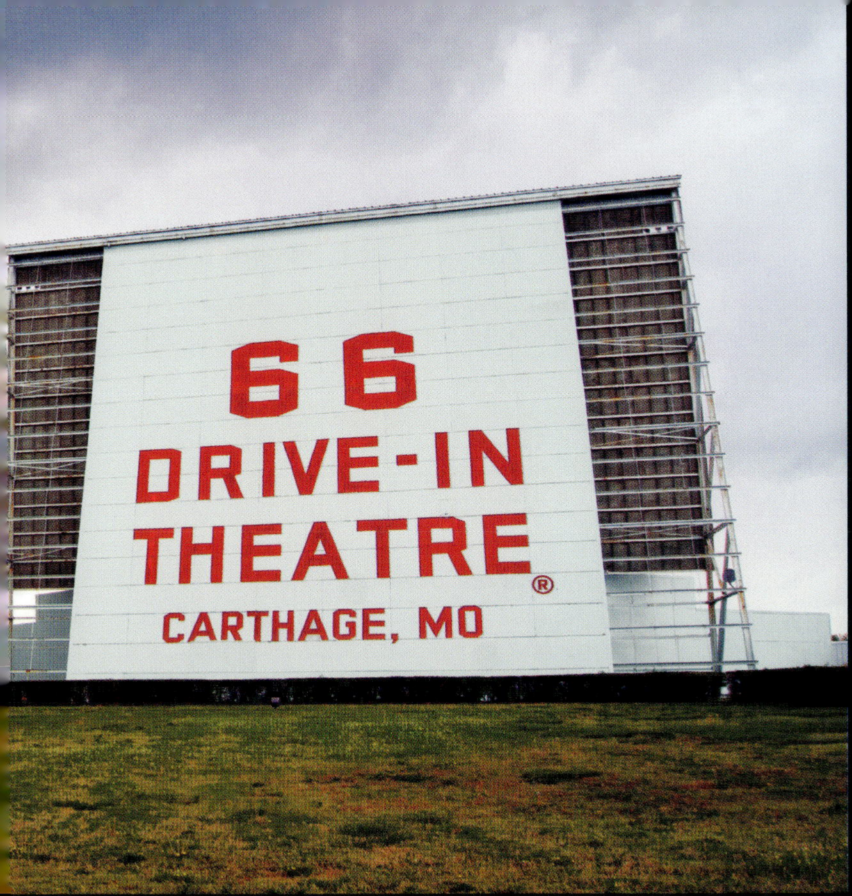

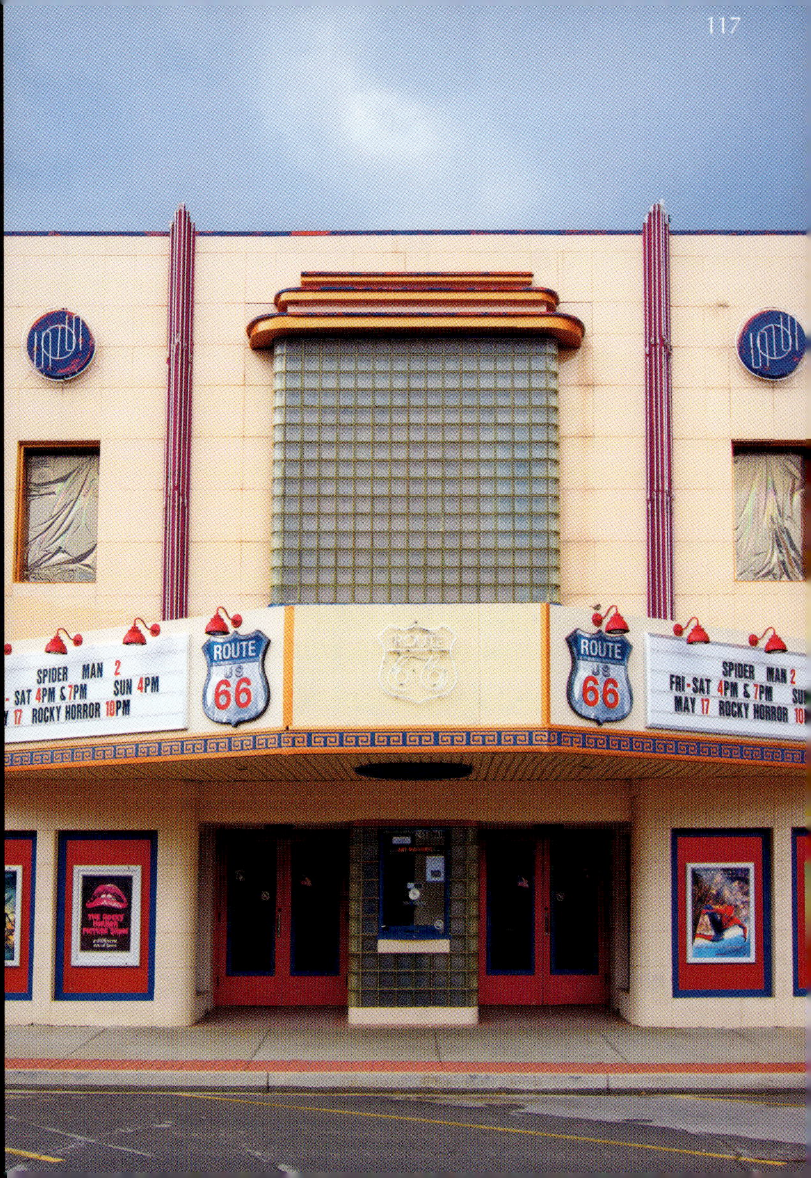

Right: The art deco Route 66 Theater in Webb City, MO.

Chapter 10
LEGACY

To the uninitiated, Route 66 is a collection of run-down motels, abandoned diners, rusting gas pumps and 'memorabilia-stops' established by business owners keen to make a fast buck from gullible tourists. However, as America in general has begun to recognise its heritage, organised groups and individuals have emerged to save some of the crumbling infrastructure by buying and renovating places to safeguard them for the future. They are helping to preserve the legacy of Route 66.

In an academic sense, the story of Route 66 is a commentary on the ramifications of the development of road transport infrastructure and the wider built environment. The frontage roads, business loops and ghost roads show that America's highways and byways have been in a continual state of evolution since the Conestoga wagons made their way along the Oregon Trail. Clearly, however, the rate of that evolution has been greatest since the birth of the interstate system.

Unfortunately, the USA seems particularly prone to the detrimental effects of what would otherwise be seen as improvements. Perhaps because of the huge amount of undeveloped land available, it seems common for US communities to die as their inhabitants move to virgin territory. Near the interstates it produces ghost towns, while in cities, it leaves large tracts of uninhabited or derelict land, as new developments move further towards the outskirts. The result is cities that are increasingly dependent on motor vehicles and new roads (which is where we came in).

Route 66 typifies the bypass phenomenon, but it has occurred in many parts of the USA. One example is Tucson's 'Miracle Mile', the northern gateway to the Arizonan city for much of the mid-twentieth century and part of the Old Spanish Trail Highway. According to a local study, the 1970s oil crisis reduced the desire for road trips, which led to the area's downfall; and, by the end of the twentieth century, the motels, gas stations and other facilities had fallen into disrepair and disrepute as a haven for drug addicts and prostitutes. Now, however, the buildings are being bought up and redeveloped as galleries, art studios and low-income housing developments; and thanks to local road improvements the development is only a matter of minutes from the interstate. Could this offer a model for the city-based stretches of old Route 66?

Route 66 is also a product of what has been dubbed 'the American Century'. Despite the Great Depression of the 1930s, the Second World War and the Cold War period, America continued to prosper during the twentieth century … and Route 66 continued to represent the American Dream. This was recognised by the 101st US Congress in the Route 66 Study Act of 1990, which concluded that Route 66 had 'played a significant role in the 20th century history of our

Nation [and] has become a symbol of the American people's heritage of travel and their legacy of seeking a better life'. It also recognised that the Route had become 'enshrined in American popular culture' and thus mandated the National Park Service to consider plans to preserve the road.

This led, eventually, to the designation of Route 66 as a National Scenic Byway, which is officially defined as a road recognised by the US Department of Transportation for one or more of six 'intrinsic qualities': archaeological, cultural, historic, natural, recreational and scenic. For Arizona, Illinois, New Mexico and Oklahoma, the designation was made in June 2000; California and Missouri were added in February 2021.

A budding photographer might ask why it could ever be worth capturing images of Route 66 when so many million images exist in books and online photo libraries. The simple answer is that there is always something new to photograph on Route 66. The Route is not a fixed and immutable concept; it is in a constant state of flux. Just as it was under continual development and realignment during its operational lifetime, it continues to evolve in its life as a tourist attraction.

The photographs included in this book do not represent the Route 66 of today. They record Route 66, but they are not a definitive documentary. Since these images were captured, some of the subjects will have deteriorated while others will have been restored. A diner here will have closed, but a gas station there will have been bought and transformed into an attraction. Indeed, it is not unrealistic to suggest that you can drive from one end of Route 66 to the other, documenting as you go, and find that something has changed before you review your pictures. Route 66 is far from dead … it remains a living entity.

Sometimes places survive an initial decline and are renovated only to fail again, perhaps due to a fire or when the owner 'runs out of gas'. We have to face the fact that people get old, or die, leaving no one with the desire to make a business out of their hobby or passion.

So, what will help to keep the spirit of Route 66 alive for future generations? The answer, as with many other aspects of society, is the younger generations; without their support and innovation, Route 66 will eventually suffer another decline. It has already made a successful transition from critical infrastructure to tourist attraction, but its future will depend on its advocates and the continuing recognition of Route 66 as an American icon.

Perhaps the key is to recognise Route 66 as an 'idea': it was an idea in the minds of politicians and business leaders for a decade prior to 1926, then a real road for sixty-odd years, and now it's an idea again. The image of Route 66 formed by modern-day 66ers is, to a large extent, influenced by authors, museum curators and a rapidly decreasing population of 'survivors' who experienced it in its heyday. Thus Route 66 is a collective concept of a bygone past, a notion of nostalgia for those halcyon days. Although most realise that it's a rose-tinted idea of history they are trying to preserve, the need for an identifiable national heritage remains strong. As the 101st US Congress recognised, the legacy of Route 66 symbolises the ideas of confidence, self-improvement and personal development that permeate American culture.

In the final analysis, the good news is that, although Route 66 was officially removed from the US Highway System in 1985, its spirit never died. It remains alive in the collective imagination as well as on the road itself.

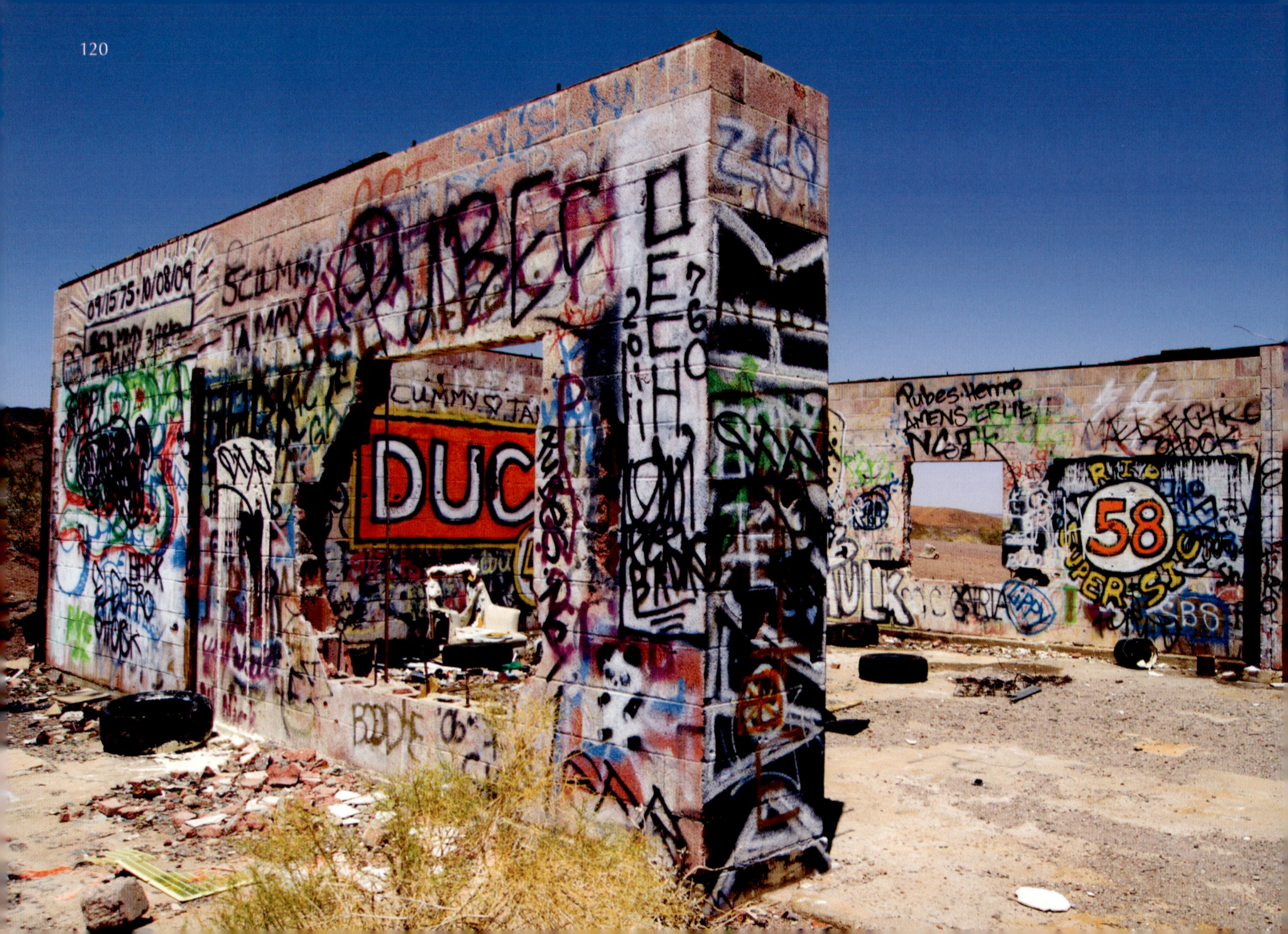
DUC
58

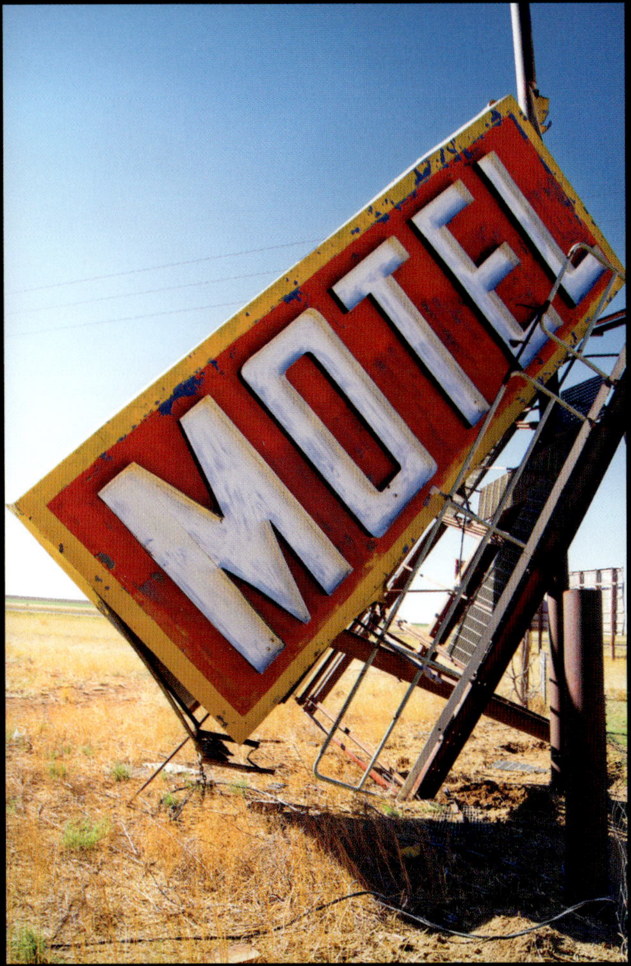

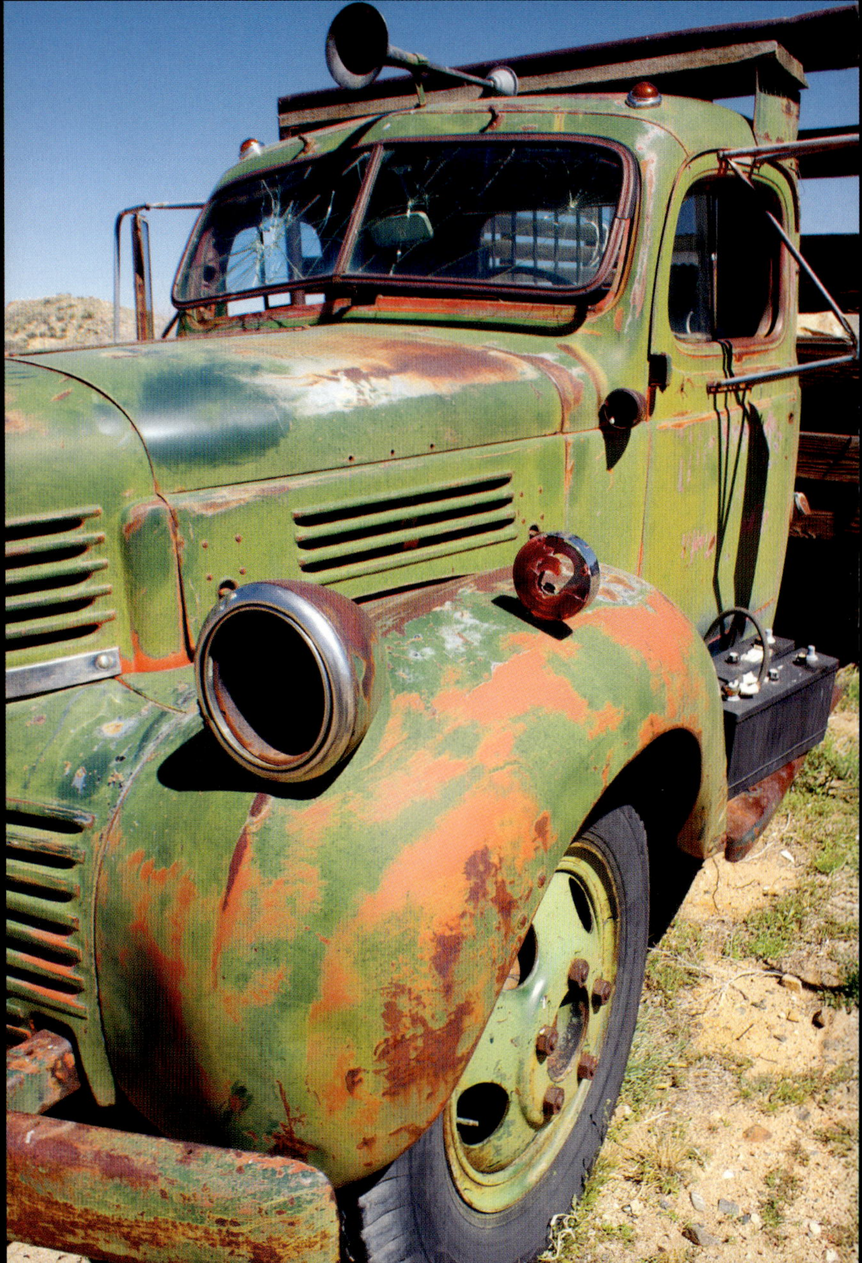

Above: A fallen motel sign behind the Fabulous 40 Motel in Adrian, TX.

Right: An abandoned truck at Hackberry General Store, AZ.

Opposite: The heavily graffitied ruins of a garage building at Cadiz Summit in the mountains just east of Chambless, CA.

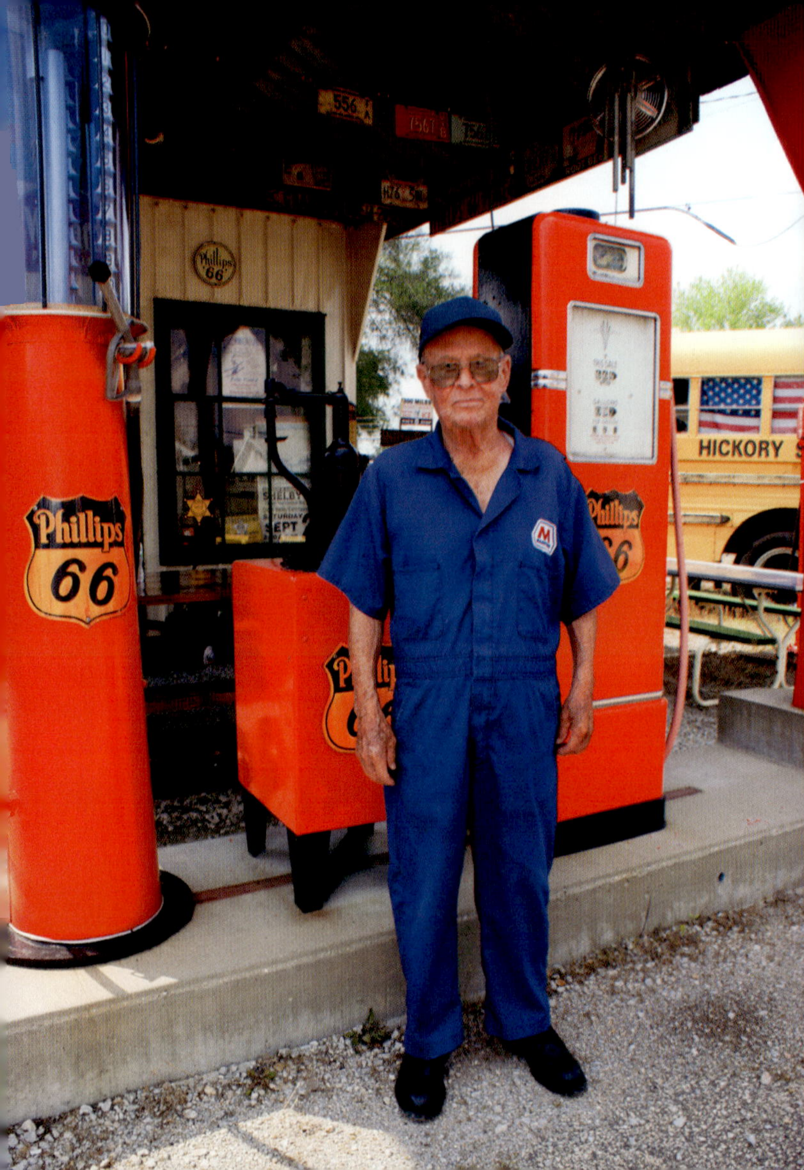

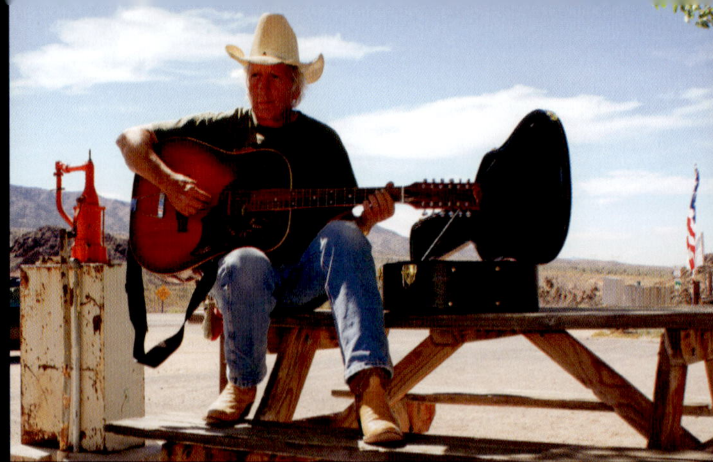

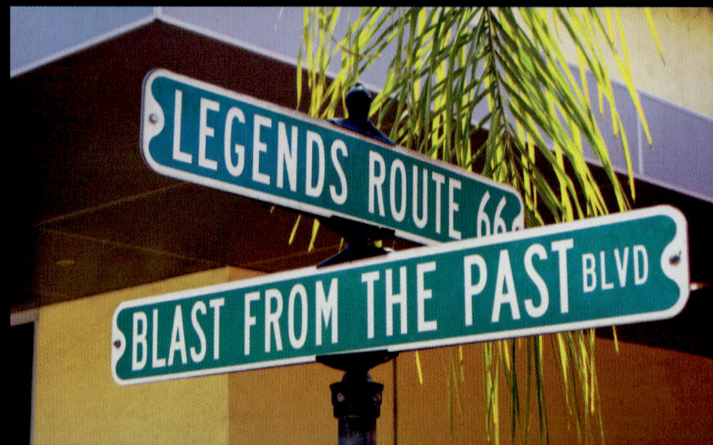

This spread: Route 66 personality Bill Shea at his gas station in Springfield, IL (now partly dismantled); an anonymous but tuneful guitarist outside Hackberry General Store, AZ; signs outside a diner near Asuza, CA; Ramona Lehman, former owner of the 1946 Munger Moss Motel in Lebanon, MO; an appropriately decorated bench outside Angel & Vilma Delgadillo's store in Seligman, AZ; Gary Turner at his reconstructed gas station at Paris Springs Junction, MO.

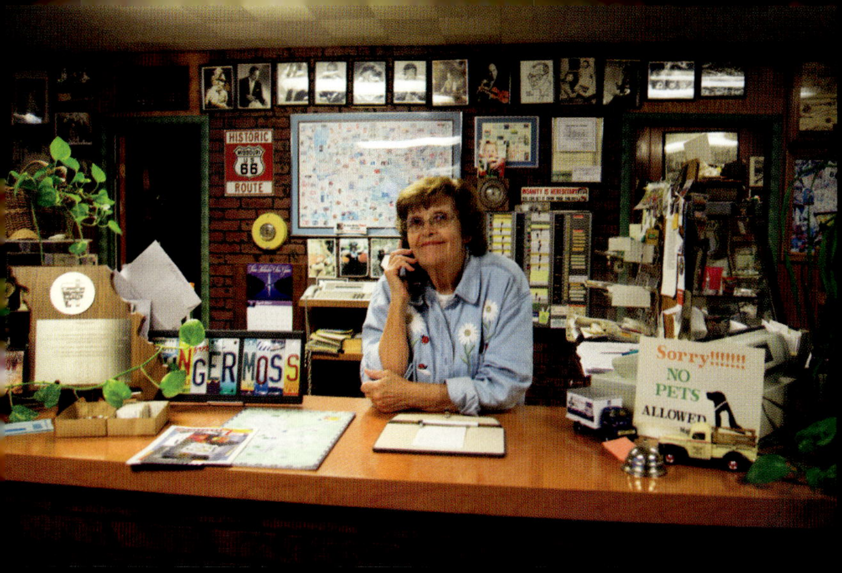
HISTORIC
66
ROUTE
Sorry!!!!!!
NO
PETS
ALLOWED

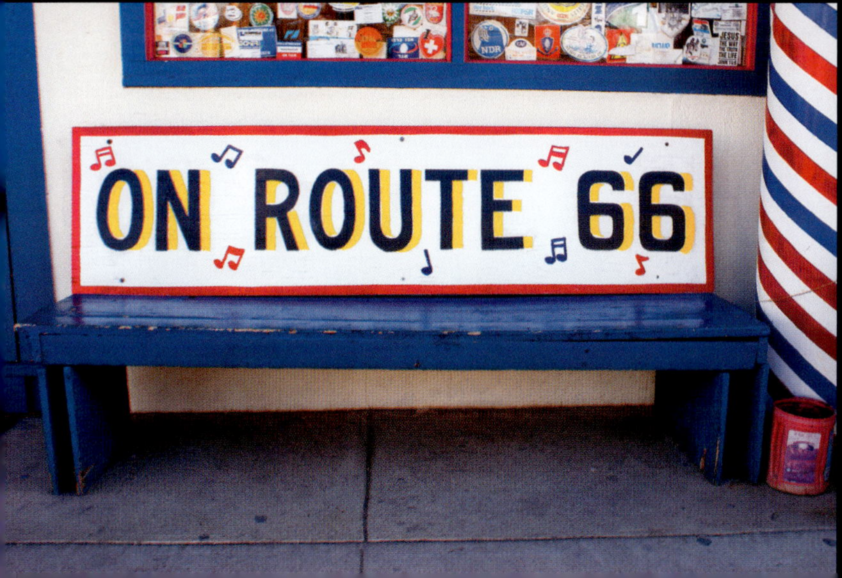
ON ROUTE 66

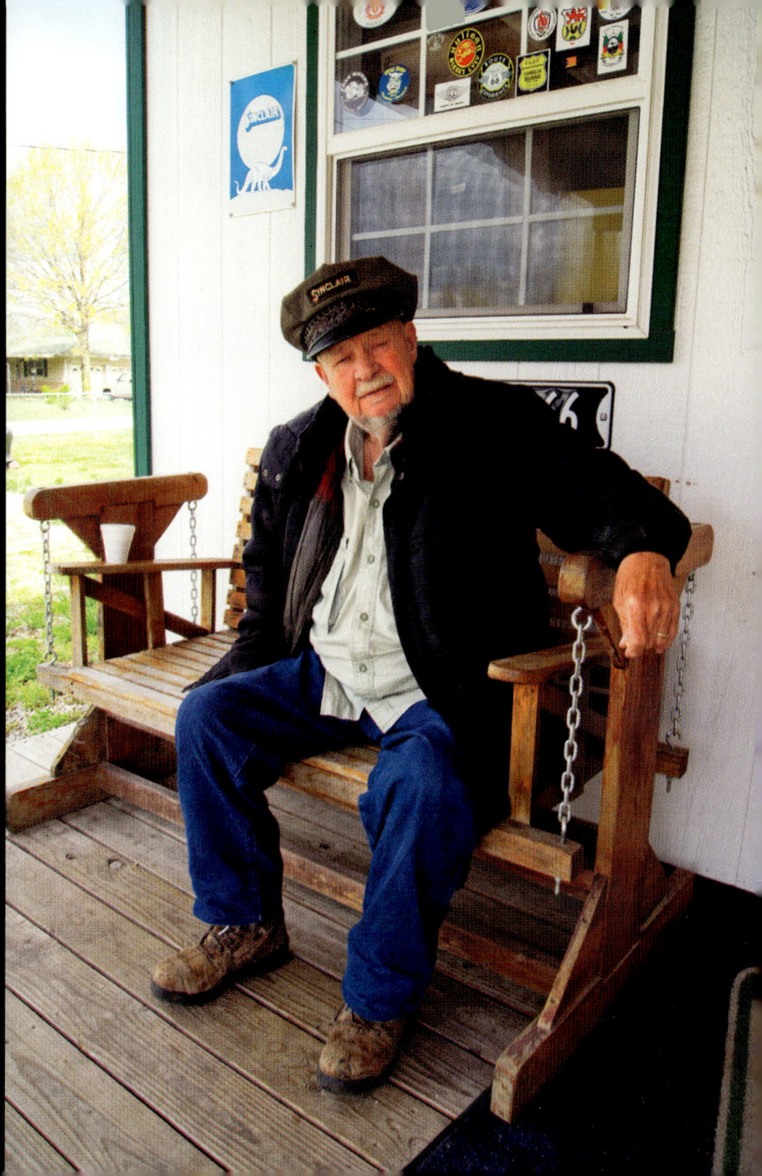
SINCLAIR

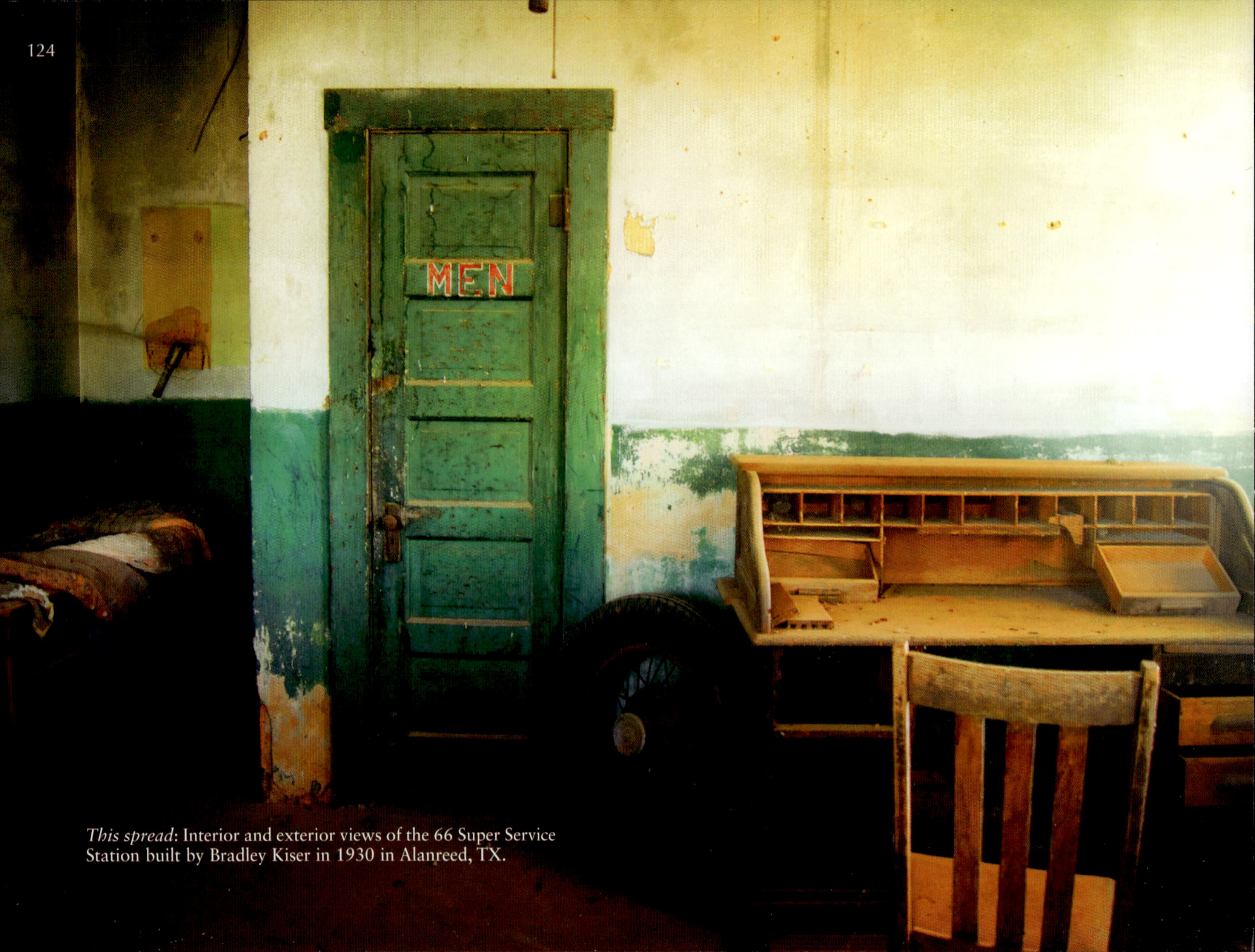

This spread: Interior and exterior views of the 66 Super Service Station built by Bradley Kiser in 1930 in Alanreed, TX.

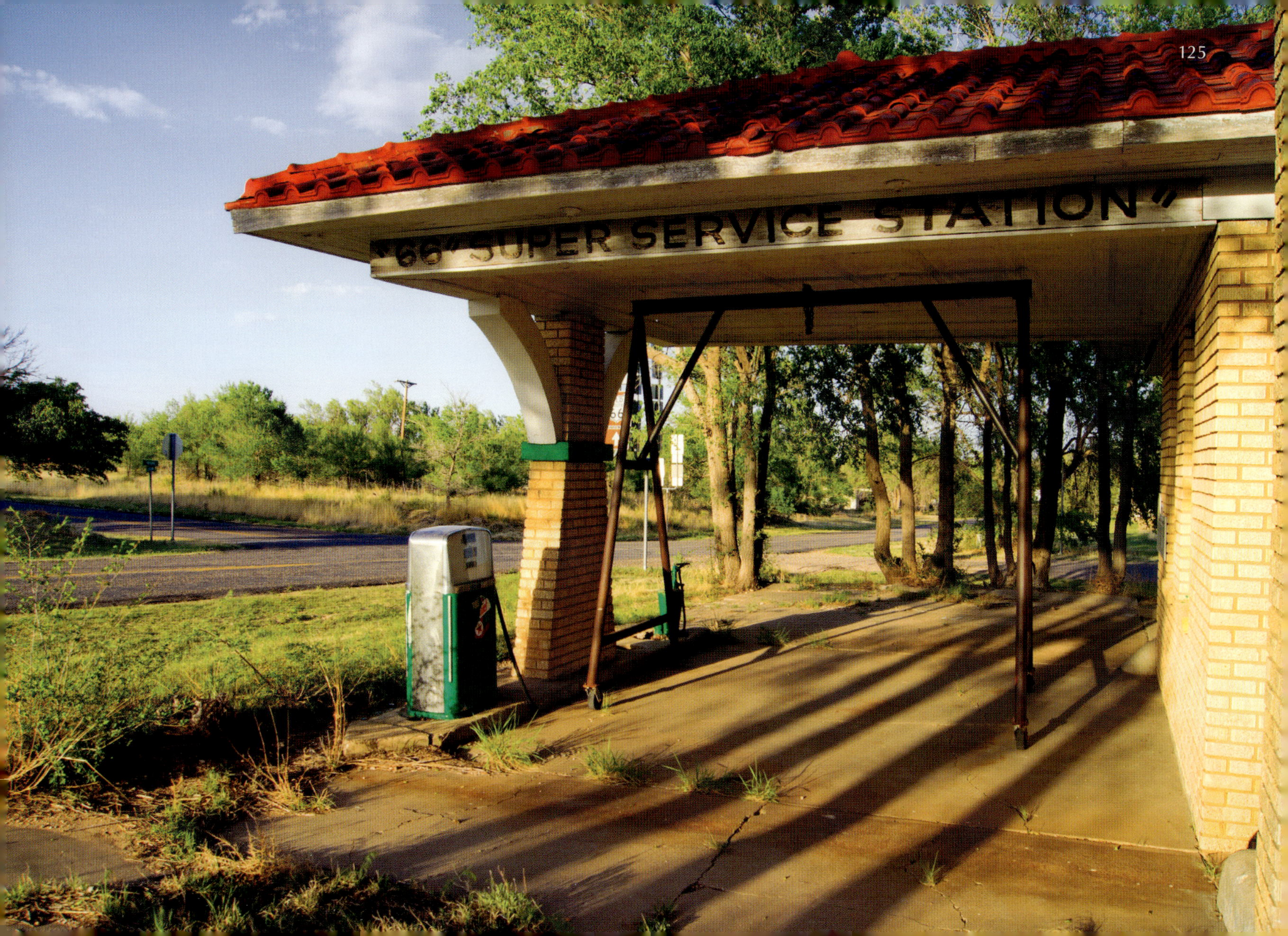
"66" SUPER SERVICE STATION"

GLOSSARY

A guide to some of the most important Route 66 terminology.

adobe an architectural style used for some motels on the western stretches of Route 66; structures tend to be single storey (in contrast with **pueblo** style)

alignment a specific path taken by Route 66 at a particular time; there is no definitive alignment of Route 66, which was re-routed continually throughout its operational history

America's Main Street an epithet for Route 66 coined by **Cyrus Avery** as 'The Main Street of America'

art deco an architectural style, popular in the 1920s and 1930s, used for some motels and diners on Route 66

Avery, Cyrus a businessman and highways commissioner from Tulsa, Oklahoma, known as the 'Father of Route 66' (1871–1963)

blacktop a dark bituminous substance used to surface roads, known outside America as **tarmac** (short for tarmacadam)

business loop a loop-road extension of a designated road, along which businesses are located (abbreviated 'Bus'); through traffic remains on the main road

Chicago the location of the recognised starting point of Route 66, when considered an east–west route

divided highway a category of road in which traffic directions are separated by a central reservation, known outside America as a dual carriageway

expressway an alternative name for a **divided highway** or **freeway**, sometimes with tolls

Federal Aid Highway Act US legislation of 1921 that funded a system of paved two-lane interstate highways (which, from 1926, included Route 66)

freeway a **highway** without tolls and free of encroaching properties and access roads, a term coined by US lawyer Edward Bassett; sometimes called an **expressway**

frontage road a road adjacent to, and usually parallel with, a **divided highway** or **freeway**; many parts of Route 66 comprise a frontage road adjacent to a major highway or interstate

ghost sign signage painted on a building or other surface, usually for advertising purposes, which has faded with the passage of time

ghost town a town of reduced or zero population, often the result of being bypassed by the Interstate Highway System (e.g. Glenrio, Texas, Two Guns, Arizona and Amboy, California)

highway any major road connecting population centres; see also **expressway, freeway, parkway**

Interstate Highway System the network of highways (commonly known as 'interstates') that form major routes across and between the US states

Main Street of America	an epithet for Route 66 coined by **Cyrus Avery**
Midpoint	a name adopted by the town of Adrian, Texas, to describe its position on Route 66, midway between Chicago and Santa Monica
Mother Road	an epithet for Route 66 coined by John Steinbeck in his 1939 novel *The Grapes of Wrath*
Muffler Men	fibreglass figures holding car exhausts (known in the USA as mufflers), originally used to advertise local garages and later repurposed for other roadside businesses
Ozark Trail	a historic **highway** network which was superseded in some states by Route 66
Parker truss	a common type of bridge on Route 66, formed from a truss of triangular metal elements (designed by Charles H. Parker and patented in 1870)
parkway	a **highway** designed primarily for recreational use, a term coined by US lawyer Edward Bassett
pavement	a general term in North America for a paved (concrete or **tarmac**) road surface, as opposed to an unconsolidated surface
pueblo	an architectural style used for some motels on the western stretches of Route 66; structures tend to be double storey, often terraced (in contrast with **adobe** style)
Ribbon Road	a descriptive name for a 15-mile, single-track section of Route 66 between Miami (pron. My-am-ah) and Afton, OK, also known locally as the Sidewalk Highway
Rittenhouse, Jack	the author of the 1946 Route 66 classic *A Guide Book to Highway 66* (1912–91)
Route 66	a historic interstate highway that linked Chicago, Illinois, with Santa Monica, California, between 1926 (when its numerical designation was assigned) and 1985 (when it was decommissioned)
Santa Monica	the location of the recognised endpoint of Route 66, when considered an east–west route
Sidewalk Highway	see **Ribbon Road**
superslab	a descriptive name for the Interstate that references its concrete slab construction
tarmac	a dark bituminous substance used to surface roads, known in America as **blacktop**
toll road	a road on which a charge is made for its use
turnpike	a **highway** on which a charge is made, otherwise known as a **toll road**
washboard road	a corrugated road surface formed by the passage of traffic over unconsolidated particulate materials (named after the grooved board for scrubbing clothes)
Will Rogers Highway	an epithet for Route 66 named after the American actor and humorist, Will Rogers, an early advocate of the Route

INDEX

Bold figures refer to image pages.